THE PRIVATE RENTED HOUSING MARKET

This book is dedicated to the memory of Prof. Bengt Turner (1946–2007) who was a founder member and Chairman of the European Network of Housing Research

The Private Rented Housing Market
Regulation or Deregulation?

Edited by

DAVID HUGHES
De Montfort University, UK

and

STUART LOWE
University of York, UK

LONDON AND NEW YORK

First published 2007 by Ashgate Publishing

Reissued 2018 by Routledge
2 Park Square, Milton Park, Abingdon, Oxon OX14 4RN
605 Third Avenue, New York, NY 10017

First issued in paperback 2021

Routledge is an imprint of the Taylor & Francis Group, an informa business

A Library of Congress record exists under LC control number: 2007018838

ISBN 13: 978-0-8153-9812-7 (hbk)
ISBN 13: 978-1-3511-4564-0 (ebk)
ISBN 13: 978-1-138-35816-4 (pbk)

DOI: 10.4324/9781351145640

Contents

List of Figures

List of Tables

List of Contributors

Peter Bibby is Lecturer in Town and Regional Planning at the University of Sheffield.

Max Craglia is a senior researcher at the Institute for Environment and Sustainability of the Joint Research Centre of the European Commission, Ispra, Italy.

ADH (Tony) Crook is Pro Vice Chancellor and Professor of Housing Studies, University of Sheffield.

Martin Davis is Principal Lecturer, School of Law, De Montfort University, Leicester.

Rachael Houghton is part-time Lecturer, School of Law, De Montfort University, Leicester.

David Hughes is Professor of Housing and Planning Law, De Montfort University, Leicester.

Diane Lister is Associate Professor in the Centre for Peace Studies, University of Tromsø, Norway.

Stuart Lowe is Senior Lecturer in Social Policy at the University of York.

David Ormandy is Professor and Principal Research Fellow at the Safe and Healthy Housing Unit, School of Law, University of Warwick.

David Rhodes is Research Fellow in the Centre for Housing Policy, University of York.

Steven Rowley is Lecturer at the Business School at Curtin University of Technology, Australia.

Julie Rugg is Senior Research Fellow in the Centre for Housing Policy, University of York.

Preface

This collection follows on from our previous publication *The Private Rented Sector in a New Century: Revival or False Dawn?*[1] Nearly five years on the question in the title of that volume has been decisively answered with the unpredicted, rapid expansion of buy to let investment injecting new capital into the British PRS after nearly a century of decline. At last a new generation of investors, many with no previous experience in property investment and untainted by the ghost of Rachman and 'slum landlordism' of deeper history, have ridden to the rescue. So recent and so rapid has been the revival of this market that questions still remain about its sustainability in the long-term, for there is evidence of considerable turnover both in properties and investors. Adding to this sense of fragility there is also a package of potential constraints arising from the government's attempts to improve the management of the PRS, new Health and Safety standards for rental housing (all of which has already found legislative form in the Housing Act 2004) and European Commission directives on fair trading. This new package involves at the 'hard' end of the regulatory spectrum mandatory licensing of landlords and, at the softer end, voluntary accreditation schemes. All this adds up to a new agenda for the PRS and this volume, as with its predecessor, has brought together the latest research from policy analysts and legal experts to answer the new questions facing the PRS. Buy to let was an industry-led initiative that has snowballed. How attempts at state regulation will play in this precocious market is the subject of this collection.

With the imminent retirement of Prof Hughes this volume is the last in a modest canon of works and collections written and edited by David Hughes and Stuart Lowe, which date back to 1991.[2] Such professional collaboration could not be sustained without mutual respect and shared interests. Of particular significance has been the cross over between law and social policy, the one a core discipline the other a more inter-disciplinary field but with a strong political science foundation. We hope to have contributed to understanding British housing policy and issues of housing need by utilising our combined intellectual resources. If nothing else our collaboration has enabled each of us to see more clearly the real world outside our disciplinary traditions. Perhaps because of this meeting of minds there has never been a cross word said or thought, many lighter moments and time to inquire about the health and well-being of our families.

Finally, we would like to thank all the contributors to this volume who without exception have produced the goods in the context of already over-busy lives. Thanks are due also to Claire O'Kell who proof-read the draft chapters and to our publisher,

---

1 Lowe, S. and Hughes, D. (eds), *The Private Rented Sector in a New Century: Revival or False Dawn?* (Bristol, The Policy Press, 2002).

2 Hughes, D. and Lowe, S., *A New Century of Social Housing* (Leicester, Leicester University Press, 1991).

especially Ashgate's commissioning editor Caroline Wintersgill for being quietly supportive and unflustered.

David Hughes and Stuart Lowe,
Leicester and York.

Chapter 1

The New Private Rented Sector – Regulation in a Deregulated Market

Stuart Lowe

Introduction

The purpose of this collection is to consider the related questions of what kind of market the private rented sector (PRS) has become in the early years of the twenty-first century, and how it might respond to, and be affected by, the new regulatory framework, imposed particularly through the licensing of certain types of landlord and new health and safety regulations arising from the Housing Act 2004. The wider question, touched on by all the contributors in one way or another, is how the performance of a new and thriving market might respond to attempts at its regulation. This form of governance is typical of the 'new' Labour agenda, attempting both to loosen the delivery of public policy – in this case by endorsing the earlier deregulation of the PRS – and at the same time to steer from the centre, imagining that a socially responsive, more efficient and better-managed market can be created by centrally directed policy.

The idea that the government increasingly 'steers' rather than 'rows' as it responds to the pressures of globalization,[1] becoming in the process more 'hollowed out', is intriguingly tested in the case of the attempt to reform the modern PRS, a market that has 'grown like Topsy' in recent years and is showing no signs of slowing. 'Hollowing out' refers to the idea that modern governance is increasingly less about the old central–local relationship, based on a hierarchy of power from the top down ('command and control'), and is more about a variety of agencies, quasi-governmental bodies, private companies and the voluntary sector that together have taken on the main role in delivery and implementation of public policy, and have become increasingly influential in shaping it.[2] While it is not the intention here to examine this issue in any detail, it is perhaps worth remembering that the PRS is not alone in being part of the new 'regulatory governance', in which there is a tension between market and state. A related example of this is the creation of the Housing

1 Osborne, D. and Gaebler, T., *Reinventing Government*, (Reading, MA., Addison-Wesley Publ. Co.,1992).

2 Rhodes, R.A.W., The New Governance: Governing without Government. *Political Studies* 44 (1996) pp. 652–67;

Rhodes, R.A.W., *Understanding Governance: Policy Networks, Governance, Reflexivity and Accountability* (Buckingham, Open University Press, 1996).

Market Renewal Fund, the latest policy designed to tackle urban regeneration. Previous regeneration policy was centrally managed, but this time, with the aim of integrating housing, planning and economic development, there is a much looser – but complex – governance structure built around a network that involves regional development agencies (RDAs), local authorities, local housing forums (representing businesses, builders and voluntary groups as well as local authorities) and a Housing Board, under the umbrella of the government regional offices. These bodies work as an autonomous network with much less central direction, although implementation is monitored by the Audit Commission.

What then is the practical evidence of what is happening in the PRS, and what kind of market has it become since it was deregulated in the late 1980s and 1990s? Who are the new landlords, tens of thousands of whom have invested in property for the first time? Above all is the question of how such a loose market, which is characterized by a rapid turnover of both properties and tenants, will respond to the new-style regulatory framework that is descending on it. The possibility of over-regulation is very real, as the new regulatory framework encompasses, at least in theory, a very large part of the market. Of most immediate significance is the Housing Act 2004, with three varieties of landlord licensing, a tenants' deposit scheme and a new health and safety rating system. Waiting in the wings is the EU competition directive, intent on compelling companies, including most probably landlords, to trade fairly – in addition to existing 'fair trade' regulation of landlords (see Chapter Seven) and the Law Commission's proposals to define tenancy conditions more transparently. The danger, of course, is that in attempting to regulate the PRS, the government may kill the golden goose – if indeed it is golden.

This chapter provides an introduction and context for the rest of the collection, beginning with a brief historical overview of the traditional PRS and its rebirth in a different form in the late 1980s and 1990s. While this is primarily meant to be 'context', it provides evidence of the nature of the PRS in Britain, and so adds to our understanding of what might happen in the future. The chapter then briefly introduces the key features of the 'new PRS', and explains how and why it differs from what went before, particularly in terms of the rise of the buy to let market and the problems that have arisen in areas where housing demand is very low – giving rise to a limited form of licensing of landlords, which replaces the criminally-based sanctions previously applicable to Houses in Multiple Occupation (HMOs) with a new style of regulatory control.

Private Renting – A Brief History

Private renting was a housing tenure in terminal decline through most of the twentieth century. In the 1920s, powerful and subsidized competitors, owner occupation and council housing began to eat into the historic position of private renting as the normal housing tenure of nineteenth-century industrial society. Ninety per cent of the population, rich and poor alike, rented their housing from private landlords up to the early 1920s. The detailed histories have been written, and there is no need here to revisit this well-trodden path,[3] except to sketch issues relevant to this book.

The origins of the long decline

Some scholars[4] argued that it was the introduction of rent controls during World War I that set in motion the decline of the sector, but the evidence suggests that it was already severely stressed by then, and declining sharply to such an extent that had the war not happened, there would still have been a major crisis with similar outcomes. The war, however, did happen, and rent control was imposed by the government in 1915, capping rents for working-class housing (and also mortgage payments) at pre-war levels. The origin of the crisis is rather more deeply embedded in the character of nineteenth-century landlordism causing problems, then as now.

The critical factor is that private renting in the nineteenth century was largely the domain of small-scale landlords owning only one or a few properties, more or less as an income supplement and 'pension' fund. Then as now, private renting was a cottage industry run by amateurs. The *petit bourgeois* character of private landlordism is one of the main reasons for the onset of its decline. In the first place, it was never an easy task to collect rents – often on a weekly basis – and manage the investment. When easier alternatives came along, many landlords took the opportunity to get out of such a troublesome market and invest in more easily available financial stocks and equities.

It should particularly be remembered that because private landlords were a disparate group of people, they were not represented by either of the major political parties, so that when it came to the debate about what to do about the provision of working-class housing before and during World War I, theirs was not an organized voice, unlike landlords on the wider European continent, where private renting took a very different path.[5]

Because of the huge scale of shortages after World War I and the inflated costs of building, rent control was continued, indeed expanded to include middle-class housing. Put simply, the perception was that private landlords could not be trusted with a national reconstruction programme, and it was on the one hand state-subsidized 'council housing', and on the other state-subsidized (and unsubsidized) owner occupation, that provided the new supply of housing in the inter-war period. Only in the late 1930s, when building costs were cheap and interest rates low, were houses again built for private renting, but then not for people at the bottom end of

3 Harloe, M., *Private Rented Housing in the United States and Europe* (Beckenham, Croom Helm, 1985).

Holmans, A.E., *Housing Policy in Britain* (London, Croom Helm, 1987).

Kemp, P.A., *Private Renting in Transition* (Coventry, Chartered Institute of Housing, 2004).

4 Damer, S. (1980), 'State, Class and Housing: Glasgow 1885–1919' in Melling, J. (ed.) *Housing, Social Policy and the State* (London, Croom Helm, 1980) pp. 73–112.

5 Daunton, M.J., *Housing the Workers* (Leicester, Leicester University Press, 1990).

Lowe, S., *Housing Policy Analysis: British Housing in Cultural and Comparative Context*, (Houndmills, Palgrave/Macmillan, 2004).

the market. Rent and mortgage controls were again imposed during World War II, and it was not until the 1957 Rent Act that an attempt was made to deregulate large parts of the PRS. This was decades too late. At the bottom end of the market, yields from rental income were too low to produce a corresponding investment surge. Rent control had made rental housing much more affordable to millions of households in controlled tenancies, but there was virtually no new supply at such low rents. It was this gap that subsidized council housing continued to fill. Higher up the market, the costs of renting and buying a property with a mortgage were equivalent, so that home ownership continued its inexorable growth. Once landlords found it easier to gain vacant possession of properties, and as house prices began to accelerate, they took the opportunity to sell. Nearly 40 per cent of the growth of owner occupation during the twentieth century was accounted for by sales by private landlords (often to the sitting tenant) quitting an uneconomic market. Slum clearance in the 1950s and 1960s also accounted for the demolition of well over a million privately rented houses (usually replaced by council houses), a significant number in a total stock in 1950 of about 12 million dwellings.

Because it was an uneconomic investment, especially in the rent-controlled sectors of the market, the PRS declined by the mid-1980s to only 8.5 per cent of households. Early attempts at a renaissance of the sector in the 1980 Housing Act, particularly through the introduction of assured tenancies (which allowed approved landlords to charge a market rent outside the prevailing fair rent system), had only limited success. There was a growing consensus, however, that there was a role for a PRS suited to a younger, more mobile market, including an increasing demand arising from the expansion of higher education. The notion of an easy-access tenure able to facilitate employment mobility was the immediate motivation for a major rethink of law and policy.

The Consequences of Deregulation

The full-scale deregulation of the PRS began in the 1988 Housing Act, through the provision of assured shorthold tenancies. The 1996 Housing Act made assured shortholds the standard tenancy: these can provide agreements for as little as six months, with assured tenancies generally applying only to tenants of 'registered social landlords'. The new regime completely changed the logic of the relationship between landlord and tenant, providing landlords with much easier access to their properties in the event of rent arrears, and enhanced powers to gain possession.

The speed with which the 'traditional' regulated PRS was reconfigured into a mainly unregulated market was astonishing. In 1988, nearly 60 per cent of tenancies were regulated (under previous legislation); a decade later, the figure had fallen to just 8 per cent, a decrease from 1.1 million tenancies to only 190,000. Currently, rather fewer than 5 per cent of tenancies fall into this group, and the figure is still falling. Most remaining regulated tenancies fall under the system of 'fair rents' of the Rent Act 1977. As Table 1.1 shows, there are a few other sources of lettings, most of which are not publicly available – accommodation that is 'tied' to a particular job or status (health authorities, landowners, police authorities and university and college halls of residence). Together, these 'closed' arrangements accounted for 20 per cent of lettings in 1994/5; by 2004/5, this had fallen to 14 per cent.

The latest data suggests that this is basically the established pattern of the 'new' PRS: about three-quarters in the mainstream assured sector, with a small number of residual regulated tenancies, plus accommodation that is tied to a particular purpose and some resident landlord properties. The data suggests that in 2004/5 the PRS had achieved a 'steady state' after 15 years of rapid transition.

Table 1.1 Tenure structure of the PRS

	1994/5 %	*1999/2000* %	*2004/5* %
Assured	56.6	65.8	72.8
Regulated	14.2	6.7	5.0
Other publicly available	9.6	8.3	8.0
Not publicly available	19.6	19.2	14.2
Total	100.0	100.0	100.0

Although the relative size of the PRS seems to be established at nearly 12 per cent of households (11 per cent of housing stock), with the major part of the market being assured shortholds, there are important nuances in this pattern that are critical to issues of regulation in the sector. Most significant here is the very rapid turnover of properties in the market. The scale of mobility is astonishing: more than a third of properties move in or out of the PRS over a five-year period,[6] with most of the flows accounted for by movements in and out of the owner-occupied market. The size of the PRS is thus very sensitive to what happens in the wider housing market. For example, during the house price slump in the early 1990s, the PRS grew sharply because builders opted not to sell until prices recovered, and households obliged to move often rented properties in their new locations and let their existing homes.

The evidence also suggests that a buoyant market with increasing rents does not lead to increasing flows of investment from existing landlords. This price insensitivity means that the size of the PRS is mainly determined by new investors and flows of stock to and from owner occupation.[7] The main financial vehicle for the new wave of investors was the introduction of buy to let mortgages, which have grown at a phenomenal rate, accounting for over 11 per cent of housing market transactions in 2006, very nearly a 50 per cent increase over 2005.[8]

6 ODPM, *English Housing Conditions Survey 2001, Building the Picture* (London, Office of the Deputy Prime Minister, 2003).

7 Bramley, G., Satsangi, M. and Pryce, G., *The Supply Responsiveness of the Private Rented Sector: An International Comparison* (London, Department of the Environment, Transport and the Regions, 1999).

8 CML, *Statistics, Table MM6*, (London, Council of Mortgage Lenders, 2007).

Buy to Let

Buy to let was introduced through the initiative of the Association of Residential Letting Agents (ARLA) in September 1996. The scheme offered mortgages at rates closer to those available to conventional owner occupiers, rather than the much more expensive loans offered to investment-orientated landlords. This was an initiative developed in the industry with the aim of enabling the further expansion of the deregulated PRS market, especially as house prices were recovering after the slump in the early 1990s, and builders who had 'parked' property in the PRS were beginning to sell on their stocks. Preferential interest rates were offered to investors who agreed to the properties being managed by ARLA members, giving lenders the assurance that they would be professionally managed. Lenders subsequently realized that they need not be so cautious, and similar 'buy to let' mortgages began to be offered outside the terms of the ARLA scheme.

The unprecedented speed with which buy to let caught on was dramatic. Three years after the ARLA scheme started, £3.6 billion of loans had been approved, but by 2003, 334,800 loans worth £31.2 billion in total had been agreed, and there was growing evidence that new private investors were being attracted into the market.[9] As Kemp pointed out, there were a number of reasons for this interest: poor trading conditions on the stock market and historically low interest rates, enabling the recovery of the owner-occupied market, and at the same time making lending to investment landlords cheap, whereas money on deposit was poorly remunerated.[10] These financial conditions also coincided with the expansion of student numbers: parents and investment landlords alike took advantage of this growing new market. The number of outstanding buy to let mortgages continued to grow rapidly, and at the beginning of 2007 (latest available statistics) there were over 850,000 mortgages, worth £94.8 billion. Buy to let has grown in the space of five years to a position in which it represents nearly one in ten of all mortgage balances.[11] Several of the subsequent chapters show that these bald figures must be read in context. The huge expansion of buy to let was never fully anticipated, and having taken the market by storm, will buy to let landlords stay in it for the long term? Many entrants are new investors in rental property, and in Chapter Three David Rhodes reports on his findings of interviews with buy to let landlords, especially concerning their motivation in entering this new market.

A Rapid Turnover Tenure

One of the key features of the new PRS is not only the rapid turnover of the stock of properties, but also the people within it. The two are not, of course, necessarily congruent. The flow of tenants in and out of the tenure is very revealing of the role that it plays in the overall housing system, providing a ladder for people moving up

9 Pannell, B. and Heron J.,'Goodbye to Buy-to-Let?' *Housing Finance*, No. 52 (2001) pp. 18–25.

10 Kemp, p. 72.

11 CML, Press Release 14/02/07 (London, Council of Mortgage Lenders, 2007).

or down. It became apparent in the decade from the mid-1980s to the mid-1990s that the turnover of tenants was increasing. The proportion of tenants who had been at their current address for less than one year increased from 25 per cent to about 40 per cent in that period, and has stabilized near that figure. It is noticeable, however, that in the under-30 age groups the figure was 65 per cent. If measured by those who had been at their present address for three years or less, the figure increased to well over 90 per cent. That indications of mobility were present *before* deregulation is indicative of the increasingly youthful character of the sector. Its main contemporary function is as the provider of flexible accommodation for a restless, mobile population of younger people. Kemp and Keoghan's interrogation of the Survey of English Housing confirmed that there was a large amount of 'churning' in the PRS, and that there were almost as many leavers as there were entrants. Of the entrants, most were young, leaving the parental home for the first time and moving into furnished accommodation, often sharing (20 per cent were students).[12]

There is also evidence that large numbers of social housing tenants moved into the PRS out of choice, hoping to find a better neighbourhood or better housing.[13] Largely because of new investors and the inflow of formerly owner-occupied housing, the social perception of the PRS began to improve. The chance of a better way of life away from rundown housing estates became more attractive. Provided that rent was below the local rent ceiling, and depending on household income, housing benefit (HB) was available to private tenants to cover most if not all rental costs. This trend originated during the early years of deregulation, when virtually the whole of the growth of the PRS could be attributed to the rapidly rising numbers of households supported by HB. An easy-access deregulated market coincided with an unreformed HB system, inducing a large-scale migration of tenants out of social housing. Wilcox calculated that there was an 80 per cent increase in the number of HB claimants in the PRS between 1988 and 1995, after which the amount of rent eligible for HB was limited with the introduction of local reference rents and 'single room rent', which staunched the in-flow.[14] These changes to HB regulation did not, however, reverse the growth of the PRS or the enthusiasm of new buy to let investors. One of the new roles now played by the PRS is as a way out of rundown social housing, especially from the worst estates, for families as well as young people leaving home for the first time.

The Stock of Dwellings

The context against which the Housing Health and Safety Rating System (HHSRS) is being implemented is the long history of generally inadequate standards in the PRS. This is partly a reflection of the fact that a great deal more of this sector of housing is old when compared to the housing stock as a whole. Private renting was

12 Kemp, P.A. and Keoghan, M.,'Movement Into and Out of the Private Rented Sector in England' *Housing Studies*, Vol. 16, No. 1 (2001) pp. 21–7.

13 Wilcox, S., 'Housing benefit and social security' in Lowe, S. and Hughes, D. (eds), *The Private Rented Sector in a New Century: Revival or False Dawn?* (Bristol, The Policy Press, 2002).

14 Wilcox, p. 36.

the historic tenure of nineteenth-century industrialization, and there is a residual effect of this in the current housing stock. Six out of ten privately rented properties are at least half a century old, compared to four out of ten owner-occupied dwellings. Forty per cent of the PRS stock was built before World War I.[15] Given the likelihood that older properties have higher maintenance needs than newer dwellings, and the problems landlords have traditionally had in funding repairs from rental income, it is not surprising that the PRS contains the highest proportion of dwellings in poor condition, although the situation has improved significantly in recent years. This improvement has been due to the rate of turnover of property entering and leaving the sector, with newer property (particularly through buy to let investors) causing the overall standard to rise. The proportion of dwellings in the PRS built in the last 25 years has increased considerably. This is the main reason for the overall improvement in standards. Improving standards are the product of the rate of turnover of property bringing in newer and improved stock, not the result of existing landlords investing more as a result of being able to charge market rents.[16]

The types of dwelling that predominate in the PRS also reflect this ageing profile. This too is an important aspect of the legal and policy background to the sector. For example, more than one sixth of PRS dwellings are converted flats, almost always in older terraced housing that has been horizontally divided. This figure compares to less then one twentieth in the housing stock as a whole. Ninety per cent of pre-conversion houses were originally built before World War I. This situation is graphically illustrated in the case of London, where the 2001 census revealed that much of the population growth of the capital had been absorbed by the division of houses into flats, the vast majority being conversions of nineteenth- and early twentieth-century terraces. Some of these conversions will have contributed to the pattern of improvement, as full-scale conversion must comply with current building regulations, but some take place on a 'change of use' basis with little or no structural alteration and little effective local oversight by either planning control or building regulation. Partly for this reason, it would appear that the stock of PRS accommodation in London, already disproportionately high (about a fifth of all PRS stock, although only an eighth of the national stock of dwellings), is increasing.

Poor conditions in houses in multiple occupancy

Although the situation is improving, it remains the case that the worst conditions in the PRS are found in HMOs. There are three main types: bedsits, shared flats/houses and households with lodgers. In total, there are estimated to be about 450,000 HMOs in the PRS in England, accommodating nearly one million people (counting lodgers only in that category). Traditionally, bedsits were in the worst condition, and this remains the case. Normally these are found in pre-1919 houses

15 ODPM, *English Housing Conditions Survey 2001, Building the Picture* (London, Office of the Deputy Prime Minister, 2003).

16 Crook, A.D.H., 'Housing conditions in the private rented sector within a market framework' in Lowe, S. and Hughes, D. (eds), *The Private Rented Sector in a New Century: Revival or False Dawn?* (Bristol, The Policy Press, 2002).

that have been sub-divided, providing high yields to landlords willing to operate at the bottom end of the market. Bedsits suffer from poor condition due to their failure to provide satisfactory fire escapes, washing and wc facilities and adequate cooking arrangements. The most recent study of HMOs found that two-thirds of bedsits were unfit because they met neither required standards for all dwellings nor the special facilities required in HMOs.[17] A previous study[18] conducted in the mid-1980s found that four out of five HMOs were in poor condition, which suggests that conditions have improved.

The shared housing market is by far the largest part of the HMO market in terms of the number of people who live in such accommodation in England: well over half a million, with an average of three people per dwelling. In 1999, there were just over 200,000 households with a lodger (almost always only one person).[19] The lodger market is the most unsettled and transient type of HMO: tenants move on frequently, and landlords regularly move in and out of this sub-market.

The Fitness Standard

An important context for a number of chapters in this book concerns the changing definitions of unfitness, reflecting the overall advances that have been made over the last half century, and new measures of housing standards (see Chapter Six). The 1996 English House Conditions Survey, for example, introduced the idea of 'poor housing', which extended the traditional indicators of fitness (inside wc, hot running water, wash-hand basin and so on) to include estimates of general unfitness and disrepair. By this measure, nearly 20 per cent of tenants in the PRS lived in poor housing, often the elderly, unemployed and younger people.[20] This reflects, of course, the ageing character of this stock and the fact that much of it was built without the basic amenities.

Until the Housing Act 2004, the statutory minimum standard for housing was the Fitness Standard specified in the Local Government and Housing Act 1989, which laid down nine requirements including freedom from damp, adequate heating and lighting, structural stability and freedom from specified repair problems. Nearly a quarter of properties in the PRS failed to meet this standard in 1991 (compared to 5.4 per cent of owner-occupied dwellings), but the picture was much improved by the time of the 2001 English House Conditions Survey, when the figure for unfitness was down to 10 per cent (compared to owner-occupied dwellings at 2.9 per cent).[21]

---

17 DETR, *Houses in Multiple Occupation in the Private Rented Sector* (London, Department of the Environment, Transport and the Regions, 1999).

18 Thomas, A.D. with Hedges, B., *The 1985 Physical and Social Survey of HMOs in England and Wales* (London, HMSO, 1987).

19 DETR, *Houses in Multiple Occupation in the Private Rented Sector*.

20 DETR, *English House Conditions Survey 1996* (London, The Stationery Office, 1998).

21 ODPM, *English Housing Conditions Survey 2001, Building the Picture* (London, Office of the Deputy Prime Minister, 2003).

New Labour further advanced housing standard indicators in the 2001 English House Conditions Survey[22] with the concept of 'decent homes', signifying housing that satisfied four criteria:

1. the statutory minimum facilities;
2. being in a reasonable state of repair;
3. provision of reasonably modern facilities and services;
4. provision of a reasonable degree of thermal comfort.

On the basis of this new set of indicators, it was found that half the stock of dwellings in the PRS were not decent, compared to only a third in the housing stock as a whole. This was, however, a marked improvement compared to the survey five years previously, when the figure was 63 per cent. Nevertheless, the stock in 2000 contained large numbers of properties that failed the 'decent homes' standard, including 10 per cent that failed on all four counts, and 40 per cent that failed to meet the thermal comfort standard.

The worst housing conditions in the PRS are found in shared dwellings in cities. These properties are often occupied by tenants on low incomes and in receipt of HB. Most of this stock is owned by long-term investment-orientated landlords, whose interest in the PRS market is primarily one of commercial gain. The advent of market rents appears to have done nothing in itself to cause this type of landlord to spend more on improvement. Because rental yields are higher at the bottom end of the market, especially among the HMOs, there is very little short-term incentive for landlords in this sector to improve their properties. As Crook suggests, 'the market is not providing rational investors with sufficient incentive to undertake the work that is needed on the worst properties'.[23] It also has to be said that in the contemporary PRS, it is not necessarily an irrational decision by tenants to want accommodation that is fitted out with white goods, televisions and internet access but is not in good structural repair. It does not really concern them until problems begin to appear, and when this happens it is usually quite easy to move on.

Housing Act 2004

The issue of housing conditions and how they are defined is radically addressed by the Housing Health and Safety Rating System (HHSRS) in Part I of the Housing Act 2004. This is an evidence-based system that replaces the Fitness Standard with an emphasis on risks to the health and safety of tenants, rather than the condition of the property. Inspectors now have to classify faults in the dwelling into one of ten bands, with recommendations of what should be done in the event of problems being identified. Hazards identified come under four main headings (although there are many sub-divisions of these): physiological requirements, psychological requirements, protection against infection and protection against accidents. A key

22 ODPM, *English Housing Conditions Survey 2001, Building the Picture*.

23 Crook, p. 172.

issue here is the effect that the new regulatory regime might have on profit-motivated landlords. The background to the new framework and its wider implications are discussed by Ormandy and Davis in Chapter Six.

When New Labour came to power in 1997, they very largely accepted the Conservative Party's view on housing, and especially the importance of the PRS. Their Green Paper, eventually published in 2000,[24] argued that the PRS was under-performing with regard to new investment, and also because of continuing evidence that it contained a disproportionately large amount of poor condition housing, and a significant minority of landlords intent on making money through the exploitation of tenants. Poor management practice was identified as in need of reform, including landlords who failed to deal with anti-social tenants. Their aim was '… to secure a larger, better quality, better managed private rented sector'.[25] One of the central intentions of the 2004 Housing Act was to put in place a licensing system outlined in the housing Green Paper. There are three different forms of licence:

- mandatory;
- discretionary;
- selective.

Mandatory licensing is targeted at the largest HMOs (those with three or more storeys and two or more households). These contain the worst housing conditions and often the poorest and most socially marginalized tenants, notwithstanding that students commonly inhabit this sort of property. The Act also includes a discretionary power for local authorities to issue licences to eligible landlords of other types of HMO. This process involves evidence that voluntary schemes of improved management, such as those under accreditation schemes discussed by Hughes and Houghton in their chapter (Chapter Eight), have failed to improve conditions, and must also include opportunities for representations from landlords and/or tenants. Licences will be issued to 'fit and proper landlords', and will specify the number of tenants in the HMO. Licences may also indicate areas for improvement in the condition of the property or in management practices, with time limits set for these changes to be implemented. Operating without a licence is a criminal offence. Mandatory licensing of landlords is not, however, extended to the entire rental sector.

To this panoply of regulatory measures (and not part of the 2004 legislation) should be added a fourth category, under the heading 'voluntary accreditation'. Here, pioneering schemes from the early 1990s aimed to confer on good landlords a 'kitemark' for good practice, such that they might gain a competitive edge in the marketplace. As Hughes and Houghton argue in Chapter Eight, which outlines the logic behind the accreditation idea with case study evidence, the 'stick' element is the potential for its withdrawal, or those who apply may simply fail to meet the required

24 Department of the Environment, Transport and the Regions, *Quality and Choice: A Decent Home for All. The Housing Green Paper* (London, HMSO, 2000).

25 Department of the Environment, Transport and the Regions, *Quality and Choice: A Decent Home for All. The Housing Green Paper*, pp. 44–5.

standard. The issue here is a further addition to the market-regulation spectrum, and raises questions about self regulation and voluntary conduct in a competitive market.

Selective Licensing in Areas of Low Demand

Many of the worst problems in the PRS are found in areas of low demand, where normal housing market conditions have come under severe strain. Extensive pockets of low demand for housing of all types are found mainly in the cities and ex-mining communities of the north of England and the Scottish industrial heartland, which lost their traditional manufacturing base during the 1980s and 1990s. The scale of the loss of full-time male jobs began to be felt with the onset of 'difficult-to-let' council housing estates in the 1980s, but by the 1990s areas of low demand began to appear in all the old industrial cities. Communities stripped of their basic economic viability became places oversupplied with rental housing and collapsing house prices, as people who could do so moved away.[26]

One paradox within areas of low demand is that tenants can move round from one landlord to another, whether public or private, very easily. Evidence of serial moving behaviour, with people moving three or four times a year, was first discovered in Newcastle's West End. Single parents fleeing debt, people with more than one address and more than one partner, and families escaping from drug-abusing neighbours and related vandalism and theft destroyed the stability of community life. Many of the social customs and mores that were the glue of traditional neighbourhood came unstuck.[27] As communities spiralled downwards, services and facilities withdrew. Economically active residents moved to areas of new employment (often in the suburbs), and housing was abandoned.

In such areas, private landlords were caught in housing markets that lacked viability, in which house prices and rental values collapsed and vacancies were widespread. Unable either to sell or let properties, some unscrupulous landlords resorted to fraud, using ghost tenancies to claim HB. This combination of quite widespread abuse, declining values and increasingly dysfunctional communities is the context in which areas of low demand have become subject to 'selective licensing' schemes.

In areas selected by local authorities, landlords and managing agents are required to obtain a licence, and as with the other types of licence no rent is chargeable on unlicensed property. Conditions may be outlined concerning the management of the property and/or its upkeep and maintenance. Licences will only be granted if evidence can be produced of the safety of gas and electrical appliances and furniture,

---

26 Lowe, S., Keenan, P. and Spencer, S., 'Housing Abandonment in Inner Cities: The Politics of Low Demand for Housing' in *Housing Studies*, Vol. 14, No. 5 (1999) pp. 703–16.

27 Keenan, P. (1998), 'Residential mobility and low demand: A case history from Newcastle' in Lowe, S., Keenan, P. and Spencer, S. (eds), *Housing Abandonment in Britain: Studies in the causes and effects of low demand housing* (York, Centre for Housing Policy, University of York, 1998);

Mumford, K. and Power, A., *The Slow Death of Great Cities: Urban abandonment or urban renaissance?* (York, York Publishing Services, 1999).

and of the provision of smoke alarms, written tenancy agreements and references for tenants. These requirements have not been replicated in respect of HMO licences. As Kemp argues, this means that the purpose of selective licensing is '… not about improving unfit housing but rather about criminal justice, including anti-social behaviour'.[28] Areas of low demand have suffered rapid and spiralling economic collapse. Whether the licensing of landlords within what is implicitly a criminal justice framework will address the problems these communities face is debatable. Selective licensing is at any rate considerably out of line with the 'housing' focus of the rest of the 2004 Housing Act.

Conclusion

The key theme linking all the subsequent chapters in this book is the connection between the new regulatory framework and the real world of the open market. Could it be that this is not a symbiotic relationship but one that may be harmful to the wider interest of the sector? Or could it be that concern about all this is irrelevant, because it is almost a law of political science that policy implementation is messy and unpredictable? One of the most famous and best-documented cases of policy failure arising from the inability of policy makers to read the circumstances of the day or understand the consequences of their actions was the 1957 Rent Act. Designed to 'revive' the PRS through removing wartime restrictions on rents and security of tenure, in practice deregulation of the 'traditional' PRS was by then decades too late, and the Act caused an even more rapid demise of the sector. Policy failure on this scale is not common, but is a salutary lesson nevertheless in the context of a book about rental markets.

It is clear that in recent years the open rental market and its attendant creation of a loose, rapid-turnover housing sector has attracted tens of thousands of new investors. This new supply is built upon new types of demand, especially from young people, including large numbers of students, and the role of the PRS as an 'exit' option from social housing's 'worst estates'. As a result of these new landlords, the PRS dwelling stock has for the first time in almost a century improved, and the image of the sector has become considerably more upbeat compared to its historic legacy as an unprofitable and difficult investment. One particular aspect of the 'new' PRS is the large-scale commercial provision of new-build accommodation for students by specialized commercial providers. Such new property will meet planning requirements and building regulations, even though still technically comprising HMOs. Its management, and not its condition, is likely to be its most controversial feature – a matter examined by Hughes and Houghton in their consideration of accreditation schemes.

The dangers of over-regulation vie with the need to improve the behaviour of a minority of landlords, particularly in the HMO sub-sectors. This story involves not only the law in the guise of the Housing Act 2004; as Davis and Houghton show, even small-scale amateur landlords, who are the bread and butter of the UK's PRS,

28 Kemp, p. 68.

may be caught in the grip of EU directives on fair trading. This is a symptom of the new and more complex policy context typical of modern governance resulting from globalization. Deregulation of the PRS in the UK is part of the process of wider economic deregulation, which has accompanied the response that Britain – with a heritage as a trading nation – has been compelled to make. At the same time, the nation state has reconfigured itself for this new role as a spearhead for the economy, and this includes attempts by central government to control social progress by innovative means, acknowledging that it has to 'loosen' policy delivery. 'New' regulation and deregulation are part and parcel of the new governance agenda.

This leads to the second 'leitmotif' of this collection: what happens at the point of delivery, the critical moment of policy implementation when 'street level bureaucrats'[29] remake policy? Buy to let landlords, 'traditional' landlords and their agents, tenants, commercial providers of student accommodation, local authority inspectors, local officials of banks and building societies, solicitors, surveyors, the notorious faceless EU bureaucrat and not least judges – all will shape and reshape what happens in practice to the UK's PRS. It will be unsurprising when the new licensing system and the HHSRS settle down to find that the market has not responded according to the intentions of the policy makers. Taken together, however, these chapters provide some very useful clues about what might happen.

---

29 Lipsky, M., 'Street-level bureaucracy and the analysis of urban reform', *Urban Affairs Quarterly*, 6 (1971) pp. 391–409.

Chapter 2

A GIS Analysis of Rent Formation in the Private Rented Housing Sector in England

Peter Bibby, Max Craglia, ADH (Tony) Crook, and Steven Rowley

Introduction

This chapter uses over 530,000 rental observations to develop a model for estimation of private rental values for any property type at small-area level across England. These data represent market evidence drawn from estate and letting agents across the country. These data were organized into hectare cells on the basis of their unit postcodes and represented within a Geographical Information System (GIS), facilitating estimation of the impact of census and other socio-economic variables within a hedonic rent estimation framework. The chapter considers the analytic techniques employed and key results.

Literature Review

While there is a substantial literature on the hedonic analysis of house prices, there has been limited research on the related topic on rent formation. Nevertheless, it will be useful to examine the literature on market rent formation, focussing in particular on the very limited literature relating to the UK, to identify key influences on market rents.

The contrast between the dearth of literature relating to the UK private rented sector, and the far more substantial North American literature is explained partly by the limited data available in the UK, and partly by the nature of policy in North America. North American policy initiatives (such as the introduction of housing vouchers) have more frequently stimulated the development of models to predict market responses. Within the UK, despite more than a decade of rent deregulation and despite the growth of the market sector, previous work has been limited. Much of this has been conducted by members of this project's research team, using data from the English House Condition Surveys of 1991 and 1996 and from special purpose surveys. (Some of this latter work was originally undertaken for the Department of the Environment and also for its successor government departments, focussing on identification of the impact of physical conditions on market and regulated rents.)

Rent Formation Models

The hedonic equation takes the simplest form of: R = f (S,N,L,C,T)
Where

R = rent
S = Structural characteristics
N = Neighbourhood characteristics
L = location within the market
C = Contract conditions or characteristics such as whether utilities are included in rent
T = Time of rent observation

Theory says little about the actual specification of the hedonic model[1] and it is up to the researcher to justify the adoption of a specific functional form, including whether additive or multiplicative models are appropriate.[2]

It is the structural, neighbourhood, locational and other characteristics which form the independent variables in the hedonic equation that this literature review attempts to identify. The literature in the US and Europe since the 1970s utilises different independent variables in an attempt to isolate the impact of such variables to inform a theoretical assumption, for example how the condition of a property impacts upon the rent payable.[3]

The majority of the hedonic literature concentrates on house prices due to the wider availability of such data. The US has also led the way in the use of this technique for the same reason. However, there have been a number of studies which have analysed the impact of housing characteristics on rental values.[4]

---

1 Malpezzi, S., 'Hedonic pricing models: A selective and applied review', in O'Sullivan, T. and Gibb, K., *Housing Economics and Public Policy* (2003).

2 Sheppard, S., 'Hedonic analysis of housing markets', in Cheshire, P.C. and Mills, E.S., *Handbook of Regional and Urban Economic* (1999) vol. 3.

3 Crook, A.D.H., Henneberry, J. M. and Hughes, J.E.T., *Repairs and Improvements to Privately Rented Dwellings in the 1990s* (London, Department of the Environment, Transport and the Regions, 1998);

Crook, A.D.H., Henneberry, J.M., Hughes, J.E.T. and Kemp P.A., *Repair and Maintenance by Private Landlords* (London, Department of the Environment, Transport and the Regions, 2000).

4 Buchel, S. and Hoesli, M., 'A hedonic analysis of rent and rental revenue in the subsidised and unsubsidised housing sectors in Geneva', *Urban Studies*, 32/7 (1995) pp. 1199–1213;

Awan, K., Odling-Smee, J. and Whitehead, C.M.E., 'Household attributes and the demand for rental housing', *Economica*, 49 (1982) pp. 183–200;

Crook A.D.H., Henneberry, J. M. and Hughes, J.E.T., *Repairs and Improvements to Privately Rented Dwellings in the 1990s*;

Rhodes, D. and Kemp, P.A., *The Joseph Rowntree Index of Private Rents and Yields: Technical Specification* (York, Centre for Housing Policy, University of York, 1996);

Rhodes, D. and Kemp, P.A., 'Rents and returns in the residential lettings market', in Lowe, S. and Hughes, D. (eds), *The Private Rented Sector in a New Century: Revival or False Dawn?* (Bristol, The Policy Press, 2002);

One of the main problems to overcome with analysis of rent formation is the analysis of additional variables unique to the tenure. Variations in lease terms, various lease incentives and key money payments[5] all require analysis if the data are not standardized. To some extent this can be handled by disaggregation of the available data.

Key Determinants of Rent

All the UK literature reviewed highlighted the same key variables as having the most significant influence on rent. These were:

- Measures of location;
- Property type, floor area, property size, number of bedrooms (these variables have been shown to be strongly correlated).

In addition to these key variables the studies have added additional variables to improve the explanatory power of the model(s). Such variables include:

- Condition;
- Number of bathrooms;
- Furnished or unfurnished tenancy;
- New or renewed tenancy;
- Distance to public transport;
- Presence of a garage.

This review of existing research confirms the absence of a comprehensive study analysing the impact of a wide range of socio-economic variables, including the character of neighbourhoods, on market rent formation.

Measures of Location

In the UK, data are typically collected and organised by region and then by town or city. Where data are collected for levels below the town or city level, researchers will often use pre-defined neighbourhoods or construct such definitions and organize the data into these distinct groupings. Postcodes are often used to define neighbourhoods, either at the postcode sector level (e.g. S10 2) or, as with this research, the unit (or full) postcode (e.g. S10 2TN).

Hoesli, M., Thion, B. and Watkins, C., 'A hedonic investigation of the rental value of apartments in central Bordeaux', *Journal of Property Research*, 14/1 (1997) pp. 15–26;

Phillips, R.S., 'Unravelling the rent–value puzzle: An empirical investigation', *Urban Studies*, 25 (1998) pp. 487–96.

5 Malpezzi, S.,'Welfare analysis of rent control with side payments: A natural experiment in Cairo, Egypt', *Regional Science and Urban Economics*, 28/6 (1998) pp. 773–96.

Such recent studies of market rent formation in the UK as have been undertaken confirm that location is the key determinant of rental value.[6] Studies examining national data in the UK have found that the region has the greatest impact on rental values, with sharp differentials separating rents in Greater London and the South East, from those elsewhere. Indeed, this impact is so strong that it often masks the influence of other key variables. Rhodes and Kemp[7] (1996, 2002) argued that it was necessary to construct separate models for individual regions or groups of similar regions while others have used dummy variables to control regional effects.[8]

Definition of sub-markets has been used to attempt to minimize the effects of wider location. Sub-markets attempt to capture collections of dwellings in a city or region which might be considered close substitutes (i.e. having attributes regarded as closely equivalent by consumers e.g. Adair *et al.* 2000, Bourassa *et al.* 1999[9]). Within such sub-markets, each unit is considered substitutable in terms of its general location and it is only the property characteristics and more subtle location attributes, such as distance to public transport, which influence rental value. Examples of studies defining and using various sub-markets areas include Maclennan and Tu, Adair *et al.*, Hoesli *et al.* and Din *et al.*[10]

---

6 Crook, A.D.H., Henneberry, J.A., Hughes, J.E.T. and Kemp P.A., *Repair and Maintenance by Private Landlords*;

Kemp, P.A., Crook, A.D.H. and Hughes, J.E.T., *Private Renting at the Cross-roads* (London, Coopers and Lybrand, 1995);

Green, H., Deacon, K. and Down, D., 'Factors which affect rent', in *Housing in England 1996/97* (London, Department of the Environment, Transport and the Regions, 1998);

Rhodes, D. and Kemp, P.A., *The Joseph Rowntree Index of Private Rents and Yields: Technical Specification*;

Rhodes and Kemp, 'Rents and returns in the residential lettings market';

Crook, A.D.H. and Hughes, J.E.T. 'Market signals and disrepair in privately rented housing' *Journal of Property Research*, 18(1) (2001) pp. 21–50.

7 Rhodes and Kemp, *The Joseph Rowntree Index of Private Rents and Yields: Technical Specification*;

Rhodes and Kemp, 'Rents and returns in the residential lettings market'.

8 Crook and Hughes, 'Market signals and disrepair in privately rented housing'.

9 Adair, A.S., McGreal, W.S., Smyth, A., Cooper, J. and Ryley, T., 'House prices and accessibility: the testing of relationships within the Belfast urban area', *Housing Studies*, 15/5 (2000) pp. 699–716;

Bourassa, S.C., Hamelink, F., Hoesli, M. and MacGregor, B.D., 'Defining housing sub-markets', *Journal of Housing Economics*, 8 (1999) pp. 160–83.

10 Maclennan, D. and Tu, Y., 'Economic perspectives on the structure of local housing markets', *Housing Studies*, 11 (1996) pp. 387–406;

Adair, A.S., McGreal, W.S., Smyth, A., Cooper, J. and Ryley, T., 'House prices and accessibility: the testing of relationships within the Belfast urban area';

Hoesli, M., Thion, B. and Watkins, C., 'A hedonic investigation of the rental value of apartments in central Bordeaux';

Din, A., Hoesli, M. and Bender, A., 'Environmental values and real estate prices', *Urban Studies*, 38/100 (2001) pp. 1989–2000.

Within defined sub-markets, alternative measures of location are adopted which attempt to identify the influences of any neighbourhood attributes. There have also been attempts to quantify neighbourhood quality through the use of rating systems and ordinal measures based on subjective quality assessments.[11]

When analysing data at the sub market level, the quality of the neighbourhood may be a factor which affects value. For example Crook and Hughes[12] used neighbourhood appearance, Adair *et al.*[13] used the availability of shopping and distance to transport nodes and Din *et al.*[14] measured quality of schools and the 'social standing' of the area. These are incorporated as dummy variables into the hedonic equation. Distance to the city centre either by public transport or by foot is also a common measure of the quality of a location within a sub-market. However, distance to city centre has been found to have no impact on rental values.[15] The 'quietness' of a neighbourhood has also been used as a measure of its quality.[16]

The use of GIS techniques to define location and to structure data spatially might be considered to be the next step forward in the use of the hedonic technique.[17] Several studies have already used GIS systems to allow varying specification and valuation of location.[18] This is the approach adopted in this analysis.

Property Characteristics

Hedonic analysis requires the collection of details of all the main physical characteristics of individual properties. These include both physical and contractual features. The literature identifies the following features as having an influence on rents:

- *Property size.* The size of the property is strongly positively correlated to its rental value.[19] If details of the floor area of the property are not available then the number of bedrooms or living rooms are a substitute;

---

11 Din, A., Hoesli, M. and Bender, A., 'Environmental values and real estate prices'; Hoesli, M., Thion, B. and Watkins, C., 'A hedonic investigation of the rental value of apartments in central Bordeaux'.

12 Crook and Hughes, 'Market signals and disrepair in privately rented housing'.

13 Adair, A.S., McGreal, W.S., Smyth, A., Cooper, J. and Ryley, T., 'House prices and accessibility: the testing of relationships within the Belfast urban area'.

14 Din, A., Hoesli, M. and Bender, A., 'Environmental values and real estate prices'.

15 Hoesli, M., Thion, B. and Watkins, C., 'A hedonic investigation of the rental value of apartments in central Bordeaux'.

16 Din, A., Hoesli, M. and Bender, A., 'Environmental values and real estate prices'.

17 Malpezzi, 'Hedonic pricing models: A selective and applied review'.

18 Gillen, K., Thibodeau, T. and Wachter, S., 'Anisotropic autocorrelation in house prices', *Journal of Real Estate Finance and Economics*, 23/1 (2001) pp. 5–30.

19 Kemp, P.A., Crook, A.D.H. and Hughes, J.E.T., *Private Renting at the Cross-roads*; Adair, A.S., McGreal, W.S., Smyth, A., Cooper, J. and Ryley, T., 'House prices and accessibility: the testing of relationships within the Belfast urban area'.

- *Property type*. The classification of the property type (terraced, detached, semi-detached, flat etc) has a strong influence on rent.[20] This variable is strongly correlated with property size and the number of bedrooms and bathrooms;

- *Number of bedrooms*. This variable is positively related to rent and has a strong impact on rental values.[21] This variable is strongly correlated with property size and property type;

- *Number of bathrooms*. This can be used as an indicator of the age and comfort of a dwelling.[22] Again this variable has a positive impact on rents and is strongly correlated to property type and size;

- *Furnished or unfurnished*. Whether the property is furnished or unfurnished can have an impact on the rent of the property.[23] The extent of this impact is dependent upon region;[24]

- *Tenancy details*. Details such as whether the tenancy is new or a renewal and its commencement date have been shown to have an impact on rental levels;[25]

- *Property condition*. The condition of the property has only a weak influence on rental levels.[26] Condition is measured using either the tenant's opinion of condition or by the value of outstanding repairs.[27]

---

20 Kemp, P.A., Crook, A.D.H. and Hughes, J.E.T., *Private Renting at the Cross-roads*.

21 Rhodes, D. and Kemp, P.A., 'Rents and returns in the residential lettings market'.

22 Hoesli, M., Thion, B. and Watkins, C., 'A hedonic investigation of the rental value of apartments in central Bordeaux'.

23 Kemp, P.A., Crook, A.D.H. and Hughes, J.E.T., *Private Renting at the Cross-roads*.

24 Rhodes, D. and Kemp, P. A., 'Rents and returns in the residential lettings market'.

25 Hoesli, M., Thion, B. and Watkins, C. 'A hedonic investigation of the rental value of apartments in central Bordeaux';

Kemp, P.A., Crook, A.D.H. and Hughes, J.E.T., *Private Renting at the Cross-roads*;

Rhodes, D. and Kemp, P.A., *The Joseph Rowntree Index of Private Rents and Yields: Technical Specification.*

26 Crook, A.D.H., Henneberry, J.M., Hughes, J.E.T. and Kemp P.A., *Repair and Maintenance by Private Landlords*;

Crook, A.D.H. and Hughes, J.E.T., 'Market signals and disrepair in privately rented housing', *Journal of Property Research*;

Adair, A.S., McGreal, W.S., Smyth, A., Cooper, J. and Ryley, T., 'House prices and accessibility: the testing of relationships within the Belfast urban area'.

27 Crook, A.D.H., Henneberry, J.M. and Hughes, J.E.T., *Repairs and Improvements to Privately Rented Dwellings in the 1990s*.

Socio-Economic Variables

Socio-economic variables such as income, inflation, tax rate and unemployment for example are variables used to measure the demand side of the rental market and are more relevant at a national level for forecasting future trends. Employment levels, percentage of professionals, education and crime, for example, are variables that can be used to measure neighbourhood quality. Low levels of crime and high levels of education might indicate a high quality neighbourhood. Such socio-economic data would need to be measured across a number of sub markets in order to identify their impact on rents. No literature was found that attempted to quantify the impact of these variables on rents, probably due to a lack of available data in an appropriate form at the appropriate spatial level.

Studies have attempted to include racial, ethnic and religious variables as influences on house prices and rental values. These include the number of Catholic households in Belfast neighbourhoods[28] and the distribution of racial groups in transitional neighbourhoods.[29]

Data

The data was provided by The Rent Service (TRS) an executive agency of central government whose task is to collect data on market rents. It uses this information to assess rents for Housing Benefit purposes. It collects and records two different types of data used for this analysis. The first, Market Evidence Data (MED) are collected from estate and letting agents and are direct observations of private rental transactions. TRS record the rent and the property variables within their database. These rental observations are used as evidence in setting rent for Housing Benefit (HB) purposes. When a rent is assessed for HB, this rent is also recorded (along with the property characteristics). Over 60,000 MED records were made available by TRS for this analysis. The original intention was to develop a model based solely on MED. The spatial coverage of the data and the actual number of observations proved insufficient to develop a model at the required geographic scale. As a result, a sample of Housing Benefit rental determinations were also used in modelling work after an initial analysis of the MED. This resulted in a database of 537,000 rental observations on which to base the model. The data was drawn from records for the year 2002–03.

The data were organized using a GIS framework based on a regular grid. England was recursively divided into quarters, sixteenths and so on, so that after 13 divisions the resulting analytic units were hectare cells (i.e. areas 100m × 100m). Each hectare cell is uniquely identified. At this spatial level, cells can inherit the characteristics of individual dwellings as well as the characteristics of broader areas such as census tracts. Using such a grid representation allows the effect of

28 Adair, A.S., McGreal, W.S., Smyth, A., Cooper, J. and Ryley, T., 'House prices and accessibility: the testing of relationships within the Belfast urban area'.

29 Chambers, D., 'The racial housing price differential and racially transitional neighbourhoods', *Journal of Urban Economics*, 32/2 (1992) pp. 214–32.

location to be examined at 12 hierarchical levels and avoids the statistical problems associated with administrative areas of different sizes and shapes.

Each of the 537,000 records used carries a unit (i.e. full) postcode, a unique property type identifier (see below), an identifier to distinguish between HB or MED data, a property rent and a vector of property characteristics. As each postcode is tied to a 100m grid reference, it links directly to a particular hectare cell, which in turn allows it to be associated with small area census data (for output areas). The property type identifier assigns each unit to a broad type identified from the available data (summarizing more than 600 categorical combinations). Thirteen types cover over 80 per cent of all observations and reflect common property forms (terraced, semi-detached, flat etc) and sizes (1 bedroom, 2 bedroom etc). Other contextual variables are attached to the grid, including over 100 socio-economic variables from the 2001 census, a flag indicating a MOSAIC neighbourhood grouping, house price data from HM Land Registry, and other derived variables.

Data Analysis

Initial analysis of rent variations

The first stage of the analysis establishes the geographic scale of rent variation within the MED data using the grid. At the first spatial division (referred to as Level 1) with England divided simply into quarters, location only accounts for 10 per cent of variation of monthly rent. After seven divisions, however, location accounts for between 45 to 75 per cent of the variance of monthly rent, depending upon the property type (see Figure 2.1). This spatial scale is referred to as Level 7, or the 6.4km scale (this being half the length of the side of grid cells at this level).

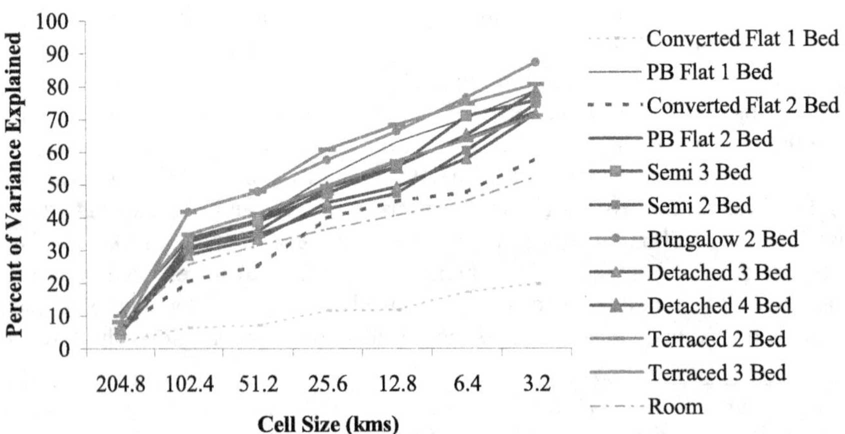

Figure 2.1 Percentage of variance explained by location at different scales

Location rent: The market echo

The distinction between HB assessments and MED accounted for only 3 per cent of rental variation indicating that the HB closely reflected market evidence. Given the close association, HB data were added to the MED at this stage to increase the number of rental observations for the next step in the analysis.

HB and MED observations were used together to analyse rental variations with a view solely to estimating a pure location rent. This was achieved using the general linear model to estimate the notional rent for a dwelling of unspecified type with no bedrooms. The justification for using HB determinations alongside pure market evidence is that in the context of estimating a location rent, HB data are likely to represent an 'echo' of market outcomes. Figure 2.2 shows the pattern of imputed location rents. It is clear from this figure that location rents in London and the South East are far higher than the rest of the country.

The location rent focuses just on the influence of location. Having estimated location rent, the rack rent is then modelled (i.e. the gap between the observed rent and the modelled location rent). The number of bedrooms and the neighbourhood characteristics are included to explain the variation between observed rents and the location rent. The number of bedrooms adds 35 per cent to the explanatory power of the model.

Geodemographic classifications such as MOSAIC use cluster analysis techniques to identify families of areas whose social and demographic characteristics are broadly similar (having regard to census data and other variables). The MOSAIC classification used here, based on the 1991 Census, and updated annually with a wide range of additional socio-economic, administrative (e.g. electoral register), and market variables, divides unit postcodes into 12 main groups and 52 sub-types. Each cluster has a descriptor intended to epitomize its character: for example one cluster is labelled 'stylish singles' and another is labelled 'Victorian low status'.

The neighbourhood groupings were attached to the data by reference to the unit postcode to assess their relationship to rent. Given the strong influence of broad location on rent, it is not surprising that variation between MOSAIC groups was dwarfed by variation within them and so the groups represent poor predictors of rental value *on their own* (R^2 of 0.109). Adding the MOSAIC classifications to modelled location rent adds 8 per cent to the proportion of the overall variability of rent accounted for (see Table 2.1).

Having considered the value of a composite indicator of neighbourhood character (MOSAIC), it may be instructive to consider the individual and combined contributions of a range of socio-economic variables in accounting for the gap between location rent and observed rent. The 106 census variables studied reflect the following dimensions:

- Ethnicity;
- Economic activity;
- Occupation;
- Qualifications;

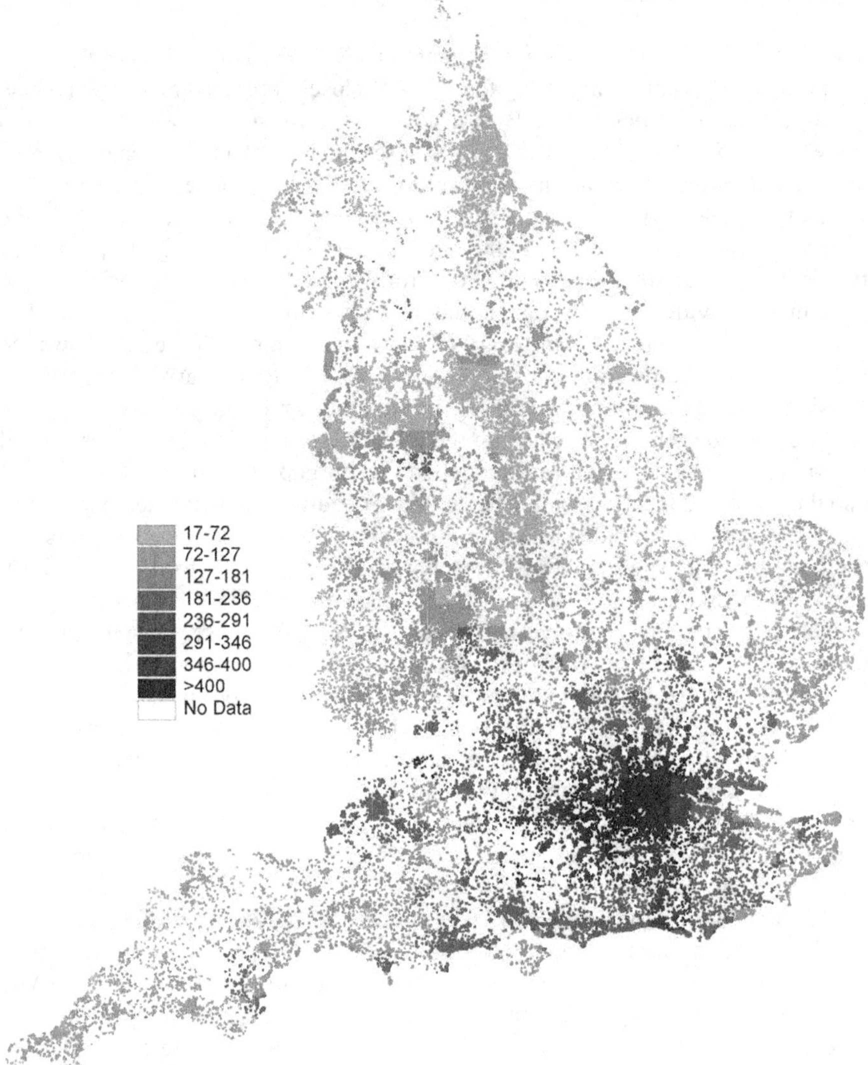

Figure 2.2 Location rent variation at 6.4 km grid square

- Social class;
- Type of accommodation;
- Tenure;
- Car ownership;
- Household composition.

The percentage of workers in professional occupations had the most substantial effect (accounting for 10 per cent of the variance of observed rents).

Table 2.1 Explaining the gap between location and property rent: number of bedrooms and MOSAIC

Source	Type III Sum of Squares	df	Mean Square	F	Sig.	Partial Eta Squared
Corrected Model	782275901[a]	13	60175069.29	3461.686	.000	.417
Intercept	1173565.957	1	1173565.957	67.512	.000	.001
BEDS	595697962	1	595697961.5	34268.663	.000	.353
MOSAGRP	93604793.6	12	7800399.466	448.733	.000	.079
Error	1091784706	62807	17383.169			
Total	7217447597	62821				
Corrected Total	1874060607	62820				

a. R Squared = .417 (Adjusted R Squared = .417)

Refining the Model

In order to move towards a predictive model of rents at hectare cell level, a pragmatic regression model was developed using all available rent estimates (HB and MED) with rents converted to a log scale.

Table 2.2 Initial model

Dependent Variable	*Observed Market Rent*
Independent variables	Log Location Rent (43%, Cumulative variance of the dependent variable accounted for)
	Log number of bedrooms (60%)
	Log professional Qualifications (67%)
	Other Census Variables (71%)

Using moving geographic averages to 'smooth' the residuals over a 200m radius allows the identification of consistent over- or underestimation of rents in particular localities.

House Price Multiplier

Expressing house prices (averaged using an 800m moving window) relative to modelled location rent might provide an indicator of confidence in a locality, possibly influencing rent. This measure is termed here the 'house price multiplier.' (High location rent responds to pressures at a much broader geographic scale than the neighbourhood – see above.) Where house prices are high relative to location rent, there is evidence of commitment to improve or develop at the neighbourhood scale; where house prices are low relative to location rent there is evidence that potential value of location is for some reason not being realized. There is a general relationship between the house price multiplier and the degree of under- or over- prediction for a location and helps explain some of the rental variations not explained in the previous model. The house price multiplier may contribute to explaining some of the rental variations not accounted for in the model outlined in Table 2.2.

Education

A range of additional variables were included to explore their potential contribution to rent determination. The effect of variation in school performance was estimated by producing a composite indicator for each primary school of attainment in English, Maths and Science at Key Stage 2 (age 11). Estimation of geographic averages of these scores at the 2km scale provided a measure of potential attainment at hectare cell level (this, however, accounted for only an additional 0.6 per cent of variation in rent, variation in social composition having already been accounted for).

Table 2.3 Contribution of KS2 results to variations in rent

Model	*R*	*R square*	*Std. error of the estimate*
Predictors: (Constant), LNBASE	.712	.507	.28781
Predictors: (Constant), LNBASE, LNBEDS	.783	.613	.25495
Predictors: (Constant), LNBASE, LNBEDS, KS22KC	.787	.619	.25315
Predictors: (Constant), LNBASE, LNBEDS, KS22KC, KS21KC	.787	.619	.25295

Crime

Given concern about the potential impact of crime on variation in housing rent, a series of standardized measures of crime rates were examined. Measures of robbery, thefts from vehicles, thefts of motor vehicles, violence against the person, sexual offences and burglary had statistically significant, but infinitesimal effects. The most powerful indicator, robbery, adds 0.3 per cent to the variability explained by location rent and number of bedrooms, while adding a further five crime variables adds only a further 0.2 per cent to the percentage of the variance of rents explained. These results do not indicate that crime is unimportant, but that the scale at which crime data is made publicly available is not appropriate to account for localized variations in rent levels.

Occupancy

A measure reflecting variation in vacancy was derived by expressing the number of households at unit postcode level recorded in the 2001 census relative to the number of domestic postal delivery points in each unit postcode at the same time (as recorded by Royal Mail). This allowed an analysis of occupancy rates at hectare cell level. Using geographic moving averages to smooth this measure over an 800m radius highlights meaningful variations in levels of vacancy. High occupancy rates might be assumed to track high demand (relative to supply), with low occupancy indicating the reverse. Although these measures highlight problem areas within cities (and the incidence of second homes elsewhere), the measure adds less than 0.5 per cent to the variance of housing rent explained.

Proximity to London Underground

A further concern was to test anecdotal evidence concerning the influence of proximity to London Underground stations on rent levels in the capital. For this purpose, a (single contiguous) area was defined within 3.5km of any tube station (shown in pale grey in Figure 2.3). Within this area, concentric rings were defined within 100, 200, 300, 400, 500, 600, 700, 800, etc. up to 1,200m of a tube station. Areas between 1200m and 3.5km away were treated as being distant from the tube, and places beyond 3.5 km being excluded from the analysis.

Overall, location by distance band accounts for 2.4 per cent of the variance of rent. The explanatory power of proximity to the tube is highest for one-bedroom flats. In the case of one-bedroom converted flats, location relative to Underground stations accounts for 4.5 per cent of the variability of rents (Table 2.4), (while if distance from a tube station is treated as a continuous variable, it accounts for 4.1 per cent of the variance of the rent of such property).

The conclusions to be drawn from this analysis are that there are significant, though small, effects associated with the London Underground. They tend to occur in the 400m to 1km horizon and are associated with particular property types.

The Indicative Model

The final output of the work is a model derived using step-wise regression intended to indicate the potential and limitations of adopting a hedonic approach to estimating private sector housing rents in England (referred to as the Indicative Model). It admits 85 predictor variables, though 14 of these provide 99.8 per cent of the explanatory effect (see Tables 2.5 and 2.6). (The additional 71 variables are not shown in the table because together they add only an additional 0.2 per cent of observed variance.) The strongest effect (consistent with the literature review) is due to modelled location rent at the 6.4km scale (LNBASE). This is followed by the number of bedrooms (LNBEDS), and the average house price of all properties within 800m of each property (HPRICE8), acting as a proxy for neighbourhood 'quality'.

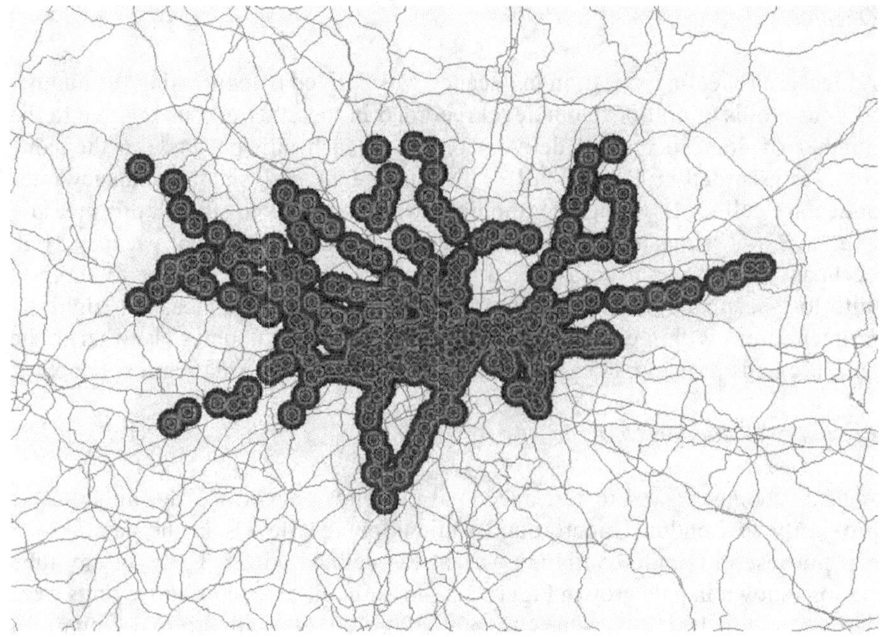

Figure 2.3 Buffer zones around London tube stations

Table 2.4 Distance from London Underground stations: Monthly rents for one-bed converted flats

Distance	*Mean*	*Std. deviation*	*N*
>1200m	548.2475	121.76699	3263
>1100m	558.7481	147.00829	306
>1000m	589.9265	169.68140	318
>900m	607.4263	155.76272	463
>800m	607.1705	165.30314	459
>700m	626.0898	164.62691	482
>600m	630.3965	172.18780	433
>500m	679.7794	246.42716	611
>400m	690.8502	233.32987	811
>300m	724.5729	266.87378	595
>200m	721.9104	266.56872	559
>100m	709.6762	213.41869	329
<= 100m	720.7732	216.93263	183
Overall	619.3656	196.94970	8812

Table 2.5 Model variables

LNBASE	The natural log of the location rent at the 6km scale
LNBEDS	The number of bedrooms
HPRICE8	The 800m moving average house price
RP20K	The 20,000m moving average of residential density
PNOQUAL	The percentage of relevant persons without any educational qualifications for the output area associated with the hectare cell
DETACHED	The percentage of detached property within the output area associated with the hectare cell
PPHIMANA	The percentage of persons in higher managerial occupations in the output area associated with the hectare cell
PWHITEO	The percentage persons from ethnic groups classified as white other within the output area associated with the hectare cell
PPRRENT	The percentage of households renting from a private landlord within the output area associated with the hectare cell
PHARENT	The percentage of households renting from a housing association within the output area associated with the hectare cell
LNHPM	The natural log of the house price multiplier (the ratio of HPRICE8 as defined above to the base rent as defined above)
PCHHNOKI	The percentage of households without children within the output area (OA) associated with the hectare cell
PHHSPBF	The percentage of household spaces within the output area associated with the hectare cells which take the form of flats
POOCMORT	The percentage of households owning dwellings, with a mortgage within the output area associated with the hectare cell

Table 2.6 The Indicative Model

Model	*R*	*R square*	*Std. error*
LNBASE	.713	.509	.28755
LNBASE, LNBEDS	.784	.615	.25458
LNBASE, LNBEDS, HPRICE8	.806	.649	.24310
LNBASE, LNBEDS, HPRICE8, RP20K	.812	.660	.23930
LNBASE, LNBEDS, HPRICE8, RP20K, PNOQUAL	.818	.668	.23627
LNBASE, LNBEDS, HPRICE8, RP20K, PNOQUAL, DETACHED	.820	.672	.23487
LNBASE, LNBEDS, HPRICE8, RP20K, PNOQUAL, DETACHED, PPHIMANA	.821	.674	.23442
LNBASE, LNBEDS, HPRICE8, RP20K, PNOQUAL, DETACHED, PPHIMANA, PWHITEO	.821	.674	.23409
LNBASE, LNBEDS, HPRICE8, RP20K, PNOQUAL, DETACHED, PPHIMANA, PWHITEO, PPRRENT	.822	.676	.23350
LNBASE, LNBEDS, HPRICE8, RP20K, PNOQUAL, DETACHED, PPHIMANA, PWHITEO, PPRRENT, PHARENT	.823	.677	.23317
LNBASE, LNBEDS, HPRICE8, RP20K, PNOQUAL, DETACHED, PPHIMANA, PWHITEO, PPRRENT, PHARENT, LNHPM	.823	.678	.23291
LNBASE, LNBEDS, HPRICE8, RP20K, PNOQUAL, DETACHED, PPHIMANA, PWHITEO, PPRRENT, PHARENT, LNHPM, PCHHNOKI	.824	.678	.23270
LNBASE, LNBEDS, HPRICE8, RP20K, PNOQUAL, DETACHED, PPHIMANA, PWHITEO, PPRRENT, PHARENT, LNHPM, PCHHNOKI, PHHSPBF	.824	.679	.23251
LNBASE, LNBEDS, HPRICE8, RP20K, PNOQUAL, DETACHED, PPHIMANA, PWHITEO, PPRRENT, PHARENT, LNHPM, PCHHNOKI, PHHSPBF, POOCMORT	.824	.679	.23235

Table 2.7 The final model

LNRENTS = 3.665 + 0.332*LNBASE + 0.281*LNBEDS + 5.880E - 7*HPRICE8 + 8.124E - 5*RP20K - 0.002*PNOQUAL + 0.189*DETACHED + 0.004*PPHIMANA + 0.006*PWHITEO - 0.001*PPRRENT - 0.001*PHARENT + 0.042 LNHPM + 0.001*PCHHNOKI + 0.0001*PHHSPBF + 0.001*POOCMORT

The Indicative Model accounts for 68.1 per cent of the variation in observed rents at the hectare cell level. In order to ensure that small areas were not consistently over- or under-estimated, clusters of residuals were sought, though very few areas of systematic clustering were found. Thus, it was concluded there was very little value in attempting to identify further variables that could add to the model and account for the geographically very confined exceptions.

The Model as a Predictive Device

While it is possible to account statistically for a large proportion of the variability of rent, it does not follow that the modelled rents are sufficiently close to market rents to be of practical value. A substantial part of the residual error reflects variation at the individual property level. It is clear that even within unit postcodes (i.e. the same part of the same street), rents may vary markedly between properties where the property type and number of bedrooms is the same.

As an example, variations in rents are described in Table 2.8 for a two-bedroomed terraced house in a particular part of a particular street in a market town in South East England.

Table 2.8 Variation in rents for a two-bedroomed terraced house in a particular unit postcode area of a market town in South East England

Postcode	*Type*	*Observed rent*	*Modelled rent*	*Error*	*Pct error*
XXX XXX	terrace 2 bed	750	679	71	-9
XXX XXX	terrace 2 bed	407	679	-272	67
XXX XXX	terrace 2 bed	750	679	71	-9.5
XXX XXX	terrace 2 bed	600	679	-79	13

In one case shown in the table, the prediction of the Indicative Model is more than £270 per month greater than that recorded in the database. It is immediately clear, however, that the recorded rent varies dramatically from those of neighbouring properties of apparently identical size and type. Such differences may arise from the particular character of the individual property, from clerical error, or the simple fact that unless consumers have perfect information, different rents may be achieved on identical properties. Associated prediction error is irreducible, whichever may be the case.

Output areas are the smallest units for which socio-economic data are released from the Census. They vary broadly in geographic extent, but typically include 130 households (300 persons), and are designed to be relatively socially homogenous. It must be recognized that variation between the rents achieved for the same type of property, with the same number of bedrooms in the same output area accounts for 20.9 per cent of all the variability in rents between properties. If presence in the same output area were treated as implying identical location, then one fifth of the variability of rent would be attributable to variation between properties of identical size and type and at identical locations. This provides some indication of variability of rents of apparently similar property across very small areas, and sets an upper limit on the possible predictive power of any statistical model.

Comparison of Recorded and Modelled Rents: Some Examples

Table 2.9 compares observed rents with predictions from the Indicative Model (aggregated to local authority district level), average absolute error and percentage error.

Table 2.9 Examples of predicted results for four property types

Property type/ location	*Average rent (£ per month)*	*Average modelled rent (£ per month)*	*Average error (£ per month)*	*Percentage error*
Purpose built flat: 2 bedrooms				
Metropolitan district in North East	293	312	-19	7
Metropolitan district in Yorks	446	377	69	-15
District council in North West	373	362	11	-3
District council in South West	448	424	23	-5
District council in South East	641	567	74	-12
District council in East	410	385	25	-6
Outer London Borough	735	687	48	-7
Inner London Borough	874	832	41	-5

Terraced: 2 bedrooms				
Metropolitan district in North East	317	307	10	-3
Metropolitan district in Yorks	320	305	14	-5
District council in North West	400	365	35	-9
District council in South West	463	439	24	-5
District council in South East	654	556	98	-15
District council in East	394	399	-6	1
Outer London Borough	753	669	85	-11
Inner London Borough	1157	846	310	-27
Semi-detached: 3 bedrooms				
Metropolitan district in North East	373	351	22	-6
Metropolitan district in Yorks	384	356	28	-7
District council in North West	449	425	23	-5
District council in South West	515	487	28	-6
District council in South East	772	628	144	-19
District council in East	457	459	-1	0
Outer London Borough	864	763	102	-12
Inner London Borough	1213	921	292	-24
Detached: 4 bedrooms				
Metropolitan district in North East	599	541	58	-10
Metropolitan district in Yorks	708	537	171	-24
District council in North West	1512	561	951	-63
District council in South West	728	618	111	-15
District council in South East	1047	800	247	-24
District council in East	777	584	192	-25
Outer London Borough	1345	1022	324	-24

The results show a much greater margin of error for the detached four-bedroom house type when compared to the smaller and generally more homogenous flats and two-bedroom terraced properties. There were larger variations in the district in the South East and the inner London Borough than other areas. The model performed particularly well in the North East, Yorkshire, North West and South West districts where errors were under 10 per cent for all rent estimates (with the exception of four-bedroom detached houses and, in the Yorkshire district, two-bed flats). When results are aggregated to local authority district level, average rents are underestimated in almost all the examples as the modelling fails to capture anomalous high rents (this effect is intensified by the logarithmic form of the equation). Antilogs must be taken to derive the estimates of rent and this may amplify the gap between observed and predicted rents. In any application of the model, it would be desirable to apply post-hoc adjustments at local authority district level to mitigate this effect.

The model might be successfully employed as an aid to property valuation when applied to relatively homogenous property types. The variability in rents amongst large properties – even within the same output area – is too significant to model successfully, however.

Summary and Conclusions

The examples above illustrate that even though the indicative model uses only a single equation for the whole of England and for all property types, it performs reasonably well in tracking variability in housing rents at small area level. Most of the remaining unexplained variation relates to the particular characteristics of individual properties rather than the areas in which they are located.

The weakness of the Indicative Model is that it effectively censors rents that are extremely low – or more importantly extremely high – relative to property characteristics. To the extent that the loss of extreme values might be a problem, the focus of concern should be on the loss of higher rental values for those property types which themselves tend to be highly heterogeneous, such as four-bedroom detached houses.

The Indicative Model used in this chapter provides estimates of rents for properties which have been compared to rent estimates coming from both MED and HB sources. While there might be seen to be advantage in comparing model results with pure market evidence (MED) alone, the coverage of the data available for the project was too thin to allow the sorts of comparison illustrated above.

In summary, the chapter examines a problem not previously considered at this scale in the UK. It presents an indicative model accounting for over 68 per cent of the variance in rents at hectare cell level across the whole of England. The model, unsurprisingly, is more successful with the more homogenous property types such as two-bedroom terraced houses predicting rents to within 10 per cent of observed rents in many of the areas where performance has been examined in detail.

Acknowledgement

The work reported in this chapter was commissioned by The Rent Service, at the time of the commission an executive agency of the Office of the Deputy Prime Minister (now an agency of the Department of Work and Pensions). The authors are very grateful for all the help received by the staff of TRS but are solely responsible for the analysis and results reported here which do not necessarily reflect the views of TRS or of its sponsoring department.

Chapter 3

Buy to Let Landlords

David Rhodes

Introduction

This chapter explores the characteristics, attitudes and experiences of a group of private landlords that were interviewed as part of a research project on the 'buy to let' initiative. The chapter sets out the key findings from the research to illuminate this dimension of the modern private rented sector, and considers some of the possible longer-term implications of buy to let for the future of private renting.

What is Buy to Let?

Buy to let was launched in September 1996 by the Association of Residential Letting Agents (ARLA) and a panel of four mortgage lenders, comprising Halifax Mortgage Services Ltd, Mortgage Express, Paragon Mortgages, and the Woolwich building society. 'Buy to let' initially referred to a relationship between people who had received advice from an ARLA member being able to apply for a mortgage from one of the panel's lenders. This relationship was seen as being mutually beneficial, in that it helped generate business for the agents whilst providing 'high quality' referrals to the mortgage lenders. However, buy to let quickly became a generic tag for mortgages that are now widely available for the purchase (or re-mortgage) of residential property to let from one of the numerous lenders that rapidly entered this new market. Thus the effect of buy to let was to make available for the first time in a systematic way mortgage-style loans specifically for the purchase of residential property to let, and in this sense the initiative was intended to principally appeal to the small-scale, individual investor. This new form of finance for the private rented sector contrasts with the situation prior to buy to let in which it would often have been necessary to use commercial business loans (as many, particularly larger-scale, landlords often continue to do); or mortgages that were not specifically designed for such a use, and which were therefore more difficult to obtain, and usually on relatively unfavourable terms.

It would appear that buy to let mortgages have begun to account for a substantial amount of funding within the modern private rented sector. Estimates produced by the Council of Mortgage Lenders (CML), indicate that by the end of the first half of 2006 there was a total number of 767,000 outstanding buy to let mortgages in the

UK, which were collectively worth a total value of £83.9 billion.[1] These figures, however, do not represent net additions to the private rented stock because they include re-mortgages, and will also include some mortgages for properties that were already within the privately rented sector but under different ownership. Other private rented properties will also have been leaving the sector over the same period through switches in tenure, demolitions, and changes of use.

The Research

The research on the buy to let initiative was funded by the Joseph Rowntree Foundation, and is reported in full elsewhere.[2] The research was largely qualitative in nature, involving depth, semi-structured interviews with three groups of people and organisations involved with buy to let. The first of these comprised a series of contextual interviews with 11 key stakeholders in ten different organizations with differing forms of involvement with buy to let. These interviews were completed during the spring of 2002, and collected details on the development, structure and operation of the buy to let initiative. A second stage of the research included an interview with an established letting agent involved with buy to let within each of the case study areas included in the research. These interviews were also completed during the spring of 2002, and collected contextual market information on the nature and operation of the local buy to let market, and whether there were any specific issues that had a bearing on the operation of the local private rented market.

The third and main stage of the research was a series of interviews with buy to let landlords. The landlords were contacted via three leading buy to let lenders that agreed to help with the research: Birmingham Midshires, Mortgage Express, and Paragon. Customers of these lenders who had a buy to let mortgage on a property in one of the six case study locations were invited to participate in the research. Interviews were subsequently completed with 47 buy to let landlords in the six areas between the summer of 2002 and the spring of 2003. Due to the method used to obtain these interviews, the buy to let landlords included in this research cannot be assumed to be fully representative in a statistical sense of buy to let landlords as a whole. Within this inevitable constraint, the intention of the research was to collect information that would help illuminate some of the main issues, experiences and concerns surrounding the buy to let initiative.

The six case study areas included in the research were chosen to reflect a range of differing market contexts and geographical locations, so that possible impacts of local variations in market conditions could be considered. Selection of the areas was partly informed by the contextual interviews, and partly through an analysis of the buy to let lenders administrative data, which had been made available to the research for analysis. The six case study areas selected for inclusion in the research were the cities of Canterbury, Edinburgh, Leicester, and Manchester; and within

1 CML press release, Buy-to-let sets new records, www.cmlorg.uk (16 August 2006).

2 Rhodes, D. and Bevan, M., *Private Landlords and Buy to Let* (York, Centre for Housing Policy, University of York, 2003).

London the two areas of the Isle of Dogs (E14 postal district) and Wandsworth (SW18 postal district).

The Growth of Buy to Let

From the contextual interviews it emerged that there were generally thought to be four key ingredients in the development of the buy to let initiative. The first of these was widely held to be the provisions contained within the Housing Act 1988, which was seen as laying the foundation for buy to let, or any revitalisation of the PRS subsequent to the Act, to be successful. Following the continued decline in the PRS over the twentieth century, the sector did in fact reach its smallest size in 1988, since when it has expanded in all regions of the UK.[3] It was thought by the contextual interviewees that a general consequence of the Act had been that it had signalled the importance of the private rented sector within the modern housing system.

More specifically, the deregulation of rents by the 1988 Act allowing landlords to charge a market rent was thought to have been of importance, although some research indicates that prior to the Act many regulated tenancies already had rents that were privately agreed between landlord and tenant, rather than 'fair rents' as introduced by The Rent Act 1965.[4,5] Of more importance than deregulation of rents, was seen to be the introduction of the new style assured tenancy by the Housing Act 1988, as subsequently modified by the Housing Act 1996, that allowed landlords to gain repossession after a period of six months. Whilst this new ability to guarantee repossession was originally intended to be an incentive for private landlords themselves, it was also an important form of reassurance for lenders in the development of buy to let mortgages:

> Before 1988 a lender could never get possession to realise its security if it needed to. Now they can. Effectively nowadays the mortgage lender can look at a tenanted property in the same light as an owner occupied property. [Contextual interview]

A second component in the development of buy to let was viewed as being the downturn on the owner occupied housing market during the early 1990s. As many as around one in ten private lettings could have been owned by 'reluctant landlords' that were unable or unwilling to sell their home due to drops in property prices at this time.[6] The downturn on this market had an impact on lenders who had increasingly needed to find an alternative to repossessing properties on which the mortgagee had defaulted, and gradually they gained experience in having mortgages repaid on the basis of the rental income obtained from letting the property, eventually finding it

3 Rhodes, D. *The Modern Private Rented Sector* (Coventry, Chartered Institute of Housing, 2006).

4 Todd, J.E., Bone, M.R. and Noble, I., *The Privately Rented Sector in 1978* (London, HMSO, 1982).

5 Kemp, P.A. (ed.) *The Private Provision of Rented Housing* (Aldershot, Avebury, 1988).

6 Crook, A.D.H., Hughes, J. and Kemp, P.A., *The Supply of Privately Rented Homes: Today and Tomorrow* (York, Joseph Rowntree Foundation, 1995).

to be a safe way of lending. In this respect, CML figures confirm that buy to let mortgages are a comparatively safe market for lenders, with a lower proportion of buy to let mortgages being in arrears of three months or more compared with the wider mortgage market.[7]

The third ingredient in the development of buy to let was the recovery following the slump on the owner occupied housing market, which started in the mid 1990s. As activity and prices started to rise, ARLA members began to find that they were losing properties from their lettings registers to the sales market as the previously reluctant landlords became willing vendors, and thereby saw an impact on the amount of lettings business they were conducting. At the same time the agents were beginning to see an increase in demand for rented accommodation, which was largely coming from younger people who were thought to be delaying entry into owner occupation as a consequence of the preceding downturn on the market. It could also be the case that the comparatively low inflation environment of recent years may have increased the attractiveness of renting compared with owner occupation due to lower rates of capital growth.[8]

The fourth component in the development of buy to let was the high level of competition amongst lenders that followed the establishment of the initiative. Many lenders developed products to offer on the buy to let market, with the result that a wide range of mortgages, often differing slightly in their terms and conditions, became available at competitive prices. The level of competition was further enhanced by a number of major building societies de-mutualizing in 1997, which as a result became able to offer a much wider range of financial products than under the more restrictive conditions attached to mutual status. The emergence of buy to let brokers also had an impact on the level of competition in the marketplace. Their knowledge of the market was thought to be an important dimension to the level of competition, as was the fact that some lenders would offer tranches of money at preferential rates through brokers because they were confident that the broker would be able to 'shift it', and also because it can be less expensive for lenders if money is loaned in 'chunks' rather than on a more piecemeal basis.

Although the contextual interviewees recognised the role that ARLA and the panel of lenders had played in establishing the buy to let, many were of the view that the market would have developed along the same lines in the absence of the initiative. The prevalent view was that circumstances alone would probably have led to the development of such a type of lending for property to let. The provisions contained within the Housing Act 1988 were thought to be particularly important in this respect, as was the owner occupied housing slump and the subsequent development of expertise amongst lenders in dealing with mortgages being repaid from rental income.

---

7 CML press release (16 August 2006).

8 Kemp, P.A., 'Private renting in England', *Netherlands Journal of Housing and the Built Environment,* 13, 3, (1998) pp. 233–53.

Characteristics of the Buy to Let Landlords

Thirty of the buy to let landlords that were interviewed were part-time landlords, in that they were either fully or partly employed or self-employed; and a further 14 were full-time landlords, for whom the business was their principal livelihood and occupation. These two types of landlord broadly correspond to what have respectively been referred to as 'sideline landlords' and 'business landlords'.[9,10] The remaining three landlords were fully retired from their employment.

In a reflection of the diversity that characterizes the private rented sector, there was a mixture of legal arrangements amongst the sideline landlords. Most of them were operating as private individuals or couples, although some had set up limited companies under which they traded for some or all of their lettings, and a few had formed partnerships with colleagues, friends or family members. About half of the business landlords were trading as a limited company and about half as private individuals or couples. The retired landlords were also private individuals or couples. Compared with the overall pattern of landlord types found in other research,[11] the business landlords were probably slightly over-represented, a feature that was probably due to one of the three participating lenders focussing its business on the larger, more 'professional' type of buy to let landlord.

The private rented sector has been described as a 'cottage industry', such is the small-scale nature of its ownership structure. Thus in England, 55 per cent of private lettings have been found to be owned by landlords with fewer than ten lettings,[12] and in Scotland the proportion was 49 per cent.[13] In a reflection of this small-scale nature of ownership, the mean portfolio size of the sideline buy to let landlords was six lettings. Not surprisingly, the business landlords tended to have larger portfolios, the mean portfolio size for these being 47 lettings.

Choice of Investment Area

Most of the landlords were living in, or very near to, the area in which their buy to let properties were located. In the small number of cases where this was not the case, they had usually lived in that area until recently. A principal motivation for choosing to invest in a property in this manner was the imperative attached to having a personal knowledge of the area by the landlords. Reflecting the findings of other research on the private rented sector,[14] this was a prevalent attitude that was based on the clear conception that there was a diversity of niche markets within an area, each

9 Thomas, A., Snape, D., Duldig, W., Keegan, J. and Ward, K., *In from the Cold – Working with the Private Landlord* (London, Department of the Environment, 1995).

10 Crook, A.D.H. and Kemp, P.A., *Private Landlords in England* (London, HMSO, 1996).

11 Crook and Kemp, *Private Landlords in England.*

12 Crook and Kemp, *Private Landlords in England.*

13 Kemp, P.A. and Rhodes, D., *Private Landlords in Scotland* (Edinburgh, Scottish Homes, 1994).

14 Rugg, J. Chapter 4, this volume.

with its individual set of characteristics and geographical boundaries. Thus there was seen to be an information need that only a local knowledge could provide in order to make a well-informed investment decision in purchasing property to let, and which made investing in other unfamiliar areas too risky a proposition as a result. As one landlord put it:

> Highfields is effectively the red light district in Leicester, yet it's only 100 to 200 yards that way kind of thing. It's generally how things are, good areas right next to bad areas, but you can see a big rental difference between here and there. You will see a difference of, for example, in this area £48 a week per person, to £35, £36 a week per person 200 yards down the road. [Business landlord]

The few buy to let landlords who had invested in areas other than where they lived, or had recently lived, had usually done so for personal reasons, such as to provide term-time accommodation for a child studying away from home at a university. Although it was not common amongst the landlords as a whole, the business landlords were the most likely to have invested in areas other than where they lived, and usually to spread their risk by not solely investing in just a single area. One of the larger-scale business landlords had invested in areas of the North West of England because rental returns in the region were some of the highest he had found, and in London and the South East regions because that was where he had identified capital growth generally to be at its highest rate. This case was unusual, and even in this instance there was usually some sort of personal connection with, and knowledge of, an area, such as a friend or family member living in a particular area of investment.

Choice of Property Type

The choice of property type purchased by the landlords was generally led in the first instance by their choice of target niche market segment – the two things generally went hand-in-hand. Property that was purchased with the intention of letting to students, for example, was generally terraced housing in specific localities. Thus other research has found that students often favour living in certain localities,[15] and also suggests that they are likely to prefer types of accommodation that allow them to share for companionship or for cost-related reasons.[16,17]

Within the parameters of the type of property preferred by the targeted market segment, the sideline landlords commonly preferred purchasing new or relatively new property where possible, as this was thought to require less maintenance; and in the case of new property was often covered by guarantees for a number of years. The business landlords, in contrast, were more likely to prefer older property that

15 Rugg, J., Rhodes, D. and Jones, A., *The nature and Impact of Student Demand on Housing Markets*, (York, York Publishing Services, 2000).

16 Bretherton, J., Rhodes, D. and Rugg, J., *Accommodation Preferences, A Study for the Accommodation Office, University of York*, unpublished report to the University of York Student Accommodation Office (2005).

17 Kemp, P.A. and Willington, S., 'Students and the Private Rented Sector in Scotland', *Housing Research Review*, No. 7 (Edinburgh, Scottish Homes, 1995).

they could either renovate or modernize, or sometimes convert into smaller units of accommodation, or perhaps into residential units from commercial use. These were seen by the business landlords as ways of enhancing their rental returns, as their overall outlay in relation to the rental value would as a result be comparatively low.

Maintenance and Standards of Accommodation

One of the main areas of concern to emerge from the contextual interviews was that the emergence of buy to let could be encouraging new landlords to enter the market who might have an amateur approach towards the business. In particular, there was a concern that such landlords might, probably through ignorance rather than any deliberate attempt to avoid their responsibilities, give insufficient consideration to the maintenance needs of their lettings. At the time of interview, however, the issue of maintenance by the landlords was almost universally considered to be one of their most important concerns.

Differing reasons were offered for maintaining their portfolios to a high standard, such as an ethical responsibility to provide decent accommodation for their tenants; or for self-interested reasons, such as it allowed a higher level of rent to be charged, or it helped preserve and enhance the capital value of a property. For a number of the sideline landlords, the purchase of new or nearly new property with their buy to let mortgages was one way in which they hoped to deal with maintenance issues, in that it was expected that fewer problems would arise with such property, and the accompanying guarantees were also considered to be an important safety-net by these landlords. The business landlords also generally thought that they were unlikely to have substantial maintenance issues in the short-term because of the refurbishment and conversion works they had often performed on the older property they tended to purchase.

Despite these two scenarios, the wish to keep abreast of the maintenance requirements of their lettings was in fact another common reason given by the buy to let landlords for investing in their home area. Even amongst the landlords who were using an agent for a full lettings and management service, there was still a desire to be nearby, as the landlords ultimately saw themselves as needing to keep a personal check on the condition of their property. A widely-held view amongst the landlords was that agents and tenants were not particularly alert to problems with certain aspects of the maintenance of their accommodation, and that as a result it was important for the landlords themselves to keep a check on the condition of their property.

The importance attached to maintenance issues for the landlords also had other impacts on how some of them had decided to organize their portfolio, such as a widely reported difficulty in securing reliable tradesmen:

> If I've done one thing deliberately and successfully, it's buying a relatively large number of properties in a tiny geographical area. Consequently I only need one electrician, one plumber, one gardener. [Business landlord]

A commonly recurring self-interest theme to emerge was that it was felt to be important to prioritize maintenance and standards of accommodation in order to 'beat the competition', a view that was prevalent in all of the case study areas. At the time of the research there was the view amongst the landlords that there was a degree of over-supply in their area of operation, which was allowing private tenants more choice, and who were as a result being more 'fussy' in choosing somewhere to rent. Thus the market was to some extent being increasingly led by competition in standards of accommodation. This process was summed up by one of the contextual interviewees in his view of the operation of the buy to let market at that time as principally the 'decanting' of tenants from poorer to better quality accommodation. Some landlords made similar comments themselves about buy to let having a positive influence on standards of accommodation, and what they viewed as the desirable impact of this on forcing what they described as the 'older style' landlords out of the market.

Management

Research on private landlords indicates that the usage of letting agents appears to have become more widespread in recent years. Surveys show that a proportion of 63 per cent of private rented English addresses that were being managed solely by the landlord in 1993/94,[18] but that this had reduced to 49 per cent by 2001.[19] This evidence supports the perception of a number of the contextual interviewees that letting agencies were increasingly opening in the most popular buy to let localities within the case study areas.

Letting agents can be used by landlords to provide a lettings only service, which can include finding and vetting tenants, drawing up the terms of a tenancy agreement, and performing an inventory. Alternatively, a full lettings and management service can be obtained, which in addition to the lettings service can include the on-going management of a letting, such as rent collection, organizing repairs and maintenance up to an agreed cost with the landlord, and cleaning and preparing a letting between tenancies.

There was mixed usage of letting agents by the buy to let landlords. Around one third of the sideline and retired landlords had never used an agent, another third frequently used an agent for a lettings only service, and third were using an agent to provide a full lettings and management service. None of the business landlords used an agent for a full lettings and management service, whilst some used an agent for a lettings only service, and others did all of the lettings and management themselves.

The usage of letting agents varied for a number of reasons, but in a reflection of other research on private landlords,[20] one of the most common reasons for using an agent was that the lettings in question were not within the landlord's home locality.

18 Crook, A.D.H., Hughes, J. and Kemp, P.A., *The Supply of Privately Rented Homes: Today and Tomorrow* (York, Joseph Rowntree Foundation, 1995).

19 ODPM (Office of the Deputy Prime Minister) *English Housing Condition Survey 2001 Private Landlords Survey* (London, ODPM, 2003).

20 Thomas, *et al.*, *In from the Cold – Working with the Private Landlord.*

Thus it was often thought necessary to use an agent to manage properties in other areas because of the difficulties of self-managing at a distance. However, a few sideline landlords were using an agent to manage lettings in their own area because they did not have the time to do the management themselves due to their other work commitments.

One of the reservations that financial institutions have been found to have about investing in the private rented market was their view that managing agents were expensive and their standards of service often poor.[21] A number of the buy to let landlords, and especially the business landlords, also refused to use letting agents, and often for these same reasons. One business landlord succinctly summed up the prevalent view: 'I don't want to pay them ten per cent to do a worse job than I do.'

Some of the landlords had quite serious complaints about the agents they had used in the past, but by far the most common grievance was the perception that any management problem that occurred was immediately passed on to the landlord. The landlords who were using an agent had as a result found an agency they were happy with through a process of elimination, but even then were commonly of the opinion that it was necessary continually to monitor the activities of the agent to ensure that they were doing all that was required of them. This view suggests that the use of agents by landlords to manage their property in a different area from which they live might be problematic for the very reason that they were using an agent in the first place, in that they were not near enough to keep a personal check on the agent.

Rent Setting

As a condition of their buy to let mortgage, landlords had usually been required by their lender to obtain a (projected) rental income in excess of the mortgage repayment by a fixed amount. A common figure was for the rental income to be 125 per cent of the mortgage repayment. Within this framework, there were two broad rent-setting strategies, and which have been identified in other research on private landlords.[22] The first of these was generally followed by one group of landlords who were 'rent maximizers', who would charge what they perceived to be the market, or the going, rate for their target market segment and area of operation. If an agent was used by these landlords they had the expectation that the agent would automatically charge the maximum amount that the market could bear.

The experiences of a few of the landlords who were 'rent maximizers', however, suggested that what passed for the market rate could vary under certain circumstances. Two of the sideline landlords, for example, had found that letting agents had been able to obtain a higher rent level for a specific letting than they had themselves. It was not clear exactly why this situation had happened, such as it being due to agents possibly reaching a wider or slightly different market, or perhaps that tenants prefer to deal with agents, who might be considered to be the 'good guys' compared

21 Crook, A.D.H. and Kemp, P.A., *Financial Institutions and Private Rented Housing* (York, York Publishing Services, 1999).

22 Bevan, M., Kemp, P.A. and Rhodes, D. *Private Landlords & Housing Benefit* (York, Centre for Housing Policy, University of York, 1995).

with landlords.[23] However, one landlord had found on more than one occasion that students from the local university had been unwilling to pay him more than £40 per week for a room in a shared house, but that when let through an agency they had been willing to pay £47 for the same room.

The second rent-setting strategy pertained to landlords who were 'turnover minimizers', which is an approach that can still be consistent with a profit-maximization.[24] These landlords aimed to slightly undercut the market rate as a way of encouraging good tenants to stay on for as long as possible, thereby minimizing the costs and 'hassles' associated with re-letting accommodation to a new tenant. Such matters can often be substantial, as it may be necessary to undertake repairs, re-decorations, and the replacement of certain items before the vacancy can be advertized and a new tenant found, and there is also the risk of a void period occurring. Advertizing vacancies with a competitive rent level was also often viewed by the turnover minimizers as an important way of attracting a 'good' new tenant:

> We try and keep our rents a bit below the market level just so that we can get a good choice of people. We know for sure then that when we advertise that we're going to get lots of people come along …We're hoping we'll end up with every house occupied by someone who's going to be there for ever and look after it well, and we're about half way here. So we try and keep rents maybe a shade lower than the market rent because we both know it's important that if we can get the right person we want to keep them. [Business landlord]

Irrespective of the type of rent-setting strategy employed, the sideline and business landlords generally had differing attitudes towards the actual amount of rent they received in relation to their costs. It was usual for the sideline landlords to have a 'break-even' attitude towards their buy to let investments, in that they would be satisfied for their costs – including their mortgage repayments, and the costs of management and maintenance – to be covered by their rental income. Many of the sideline landlords thought that they were about breaking-even, but some were 'subsidizing' the rent at the current time, and a few were doing so quite heavily. Whilst clearly being thought of as an undesirable situation, these landlords tended to view such losses as an accepted risk of being in the business. They were generally willing to continue in this way for as long as they could afford it due to the way in which they were motivated, only rarely suggesting that they might need to sell a property at some stage.

The business landlords, on the other hand, were principally concerned that their properties individually produced a certain current net rental income, and any that were underperforming would generally be removed from their portfolio. In this respect they often applied rigid criteria in their assessment of the expected income from each individual property, and if a potential investment did not 'stack up' in terms of their business plan, then the investment opportunity would be rejected. Thus one business landlord aimed to achieve a net rental yield of 8 per cent, another expected the rent to be 150 per cent of his mortgage repayment costs, and another aimed to make a net annual rental income of £3,500 on each letting.

---

23 Bevan, *et al.*, *Private Landlords & Housing Benefit*.

24 Kemp, P. A., 'Private renting in England'.

Motivations

The motivations of the buy to let landlords were largely reflected in their approaches and attitudes towards setting the rent, and so generally differed between the sideline and business landlords. Almost all of the sideline landlords regarded their buy to let investments as a form of retirement planning, with only a few placing especial importance on the current rental stream from their lettings. Portfolio size, or intended portfolio size, tended to be related to what they saw as being necessary to provide them with a sufficient retirement income in the future.

A few sideline landlords were primarily interested in the capital gains that might be obtained from the lettings in their portfolio, and which they intended to sell some or all of to reinvest elsewhere when they came to retire, such as to purchase an annuity or simply to place in a savings account. Most of the pension planning sideline landlords, however, were primarily motivated by the future rental income that their portfolio would provide for a pension income. It was the long-term view of buy to let as a pension plan that underpinned the sideline landlord's willingness to accept just breaking-even, or even making a loss, at the current time in the expectation of obtaining a future net rental income from their portfolio. Thus the aim of these landlords was to obtain a future net rental income when their mortgages had been largely or completely paid off, and when rent levels would probably have increased also.

As a result of this prevalent view amongst the sideline landlords, most of them viewed capital gains as being of secondary importance to the future net rental income from their portfolio. However, capital growth was of some value to these landlords in that it provided them with a degree of flexibility: the growth in capital value of their portfolio would give them options to reassess their strategy in the light of unforeseen personal eventualities, or changes in the conditions on the local rental market. Thus capital gains might give the landlords the opportunity to liquidate their portfolio to reinvest elsewhere if necessary, or perhaps just sell-off part of it in order to settle the remaining mortgages.

A current rental income was by far the most important motivation for the business landlords, a feature that reflects other research on private landlords.[25] It was not uncommon for these landlords to have initially been motivated to invest in property as a pension plan when they had initially been sideline operators. As they had expanded into being full-time landlords, however, a current net rental income had become the central aim of their business. These landlords still viewed their portfolio as providing a rental income when they retired, however, in that they saw their investments as providing a continual source of rental income into the future. The current rental income stream was of such importance to the business landlords, that they were generally of the opinion that capital growth was not an important factor at all, describing it as simply 'an added bonus', 'something in the background', or 'the wrong reason for being a landlord'.

25 Crook and Kemp, *Private Landlords in England.*

Why Buy to Let?

There were a number of reasons why the buy to let landlords had chosen to invest in property in preference to other available types of investment. These included various 'push factors', such as a dissatisfaction with the performance of alternative mainstream forms of investment, including stocks and shares; and concerns about the poor performance of various types of pension schemes that had been taken out, including fears over the future of employment-related final salary pension schemes. There were also 'pull factors', including the prevalent view that residential property had historically performed well over the medium to long-term (in terms of capital growth), and an existing familiarity, or ease, with dealing with property through having used mortgages for home ownership purposes.

An important attraction of buy to let for many of the landlords was that it was possible to finance a large part of the investment through the use of other people's money: that is, buy to let mortgages for the purchase of property, and the rental income stream to service the mortgage repayments. Some of the landlords had even taken out loans to pay the deposit on their buy to let property. Residential property was also widely viewed as being a particularly flexible way of investing:

> One of the attractions of property is the flexibility, because, you know, if I've got, say, ten properties when I retire and I've got some debt, I could sell five and get a higher income, or I could keep ten, or whatever. I don't think you can really know until you're in the situation. The flexibility of it compared with the flexibility of a pension is very, very attractive. [Sideline landlord]

Market Conditions

The market conditions under which the buy to let investors were operating affected, sometimes quite significantly, how they conducted their business in a number of ways. One important impact for the early buy to let landlords was the favourable market in terms of house prices when they had first begun to purchase property to let. The house price index of HBOS, for example, shows that average house prices in the UK had been on a generally downward trend since 1990, but that this pattern began to reverse in 1996 as prices started to move upwards again.[26] Several of the business landlords first became landlords on a sideline basis shortly after buy to let was introduced, and found that the rising market allowed them to rapidly expand their portfolios through a programme of re-mortgaging the properties they had first bought with buy to let mortgages – sometimes just one or two years after a property was originally purchased – to generate deposits for additions to their portfolio. Due to continued rises in the value of their holdings, some of these landlords had been able to re-mortgage individual properties more than once to raise further funds to invest, and had quickly developed from part-time into full-time operators as their portfolios had grown in size.

26 www.hbosplc.com/economy/historicaldataspreadsheet.asp.

Other landlords, particularly ones who had entered the buy to let market more recently, had a less favourable view of the rises in property values, since the comparatively high rises in property prices meant that they were finding property relatively more expensive to purchase. This problem was seen by these landlords as being exacerbated by the fact that they had not seen rent levels increase in line with property prices, thereby affecting the level of rental return that could be obtained. Some landlords were as a result waiting for property price rises to slow, and some were hoping for them to fall, so that they might be able to afford to increase their holdings.

As well as such broad market conditions and trends that were experienced to varying degrees by the landlords in all areas included in the research, there were localized market features that had certain impacts on the relationship between supply and demand also. The Isle of Dogs was one area where there was widely thought to be over-supply, and which had impacted to restrict and even reduce rent levels, and also lengthen void periods between lettings. This effect was thought to be due to the increase in supply of new property to let as a result of an influx of buy to let investors who had purchased apartments to let in several newly completed developments in the area. Other factors that were thought to have impacted on the local market included building delays in the completion of office blocks in E14, that had led to a lag in the anticipated demand for accommodation from overseas employees. In Leicester, the development of blocks of student accommodation was anticipated as being likely to lead to a reduction in the level of demand for the lettings of several of the buy to let landlords who had been serving this market segment in the area.

Such changes in the relationship between supply and demand at a local level had the greatest impact on the most recent entrants to the business, since they had generally bought property at the highest prices, and on which the net rental returns were the smallest due to rent levels having not increased at the same rate as property prices. The landlords of longer standing were generally of the opinion that they were not seriously affected by such changes in the supply and demand structure within their area, usually considering themselves to be sufficiently 'insulated' as a result of having paid substantially less for their properties, and were therefore obtaining comparatively high net rental returns.

Conclusions

A key point to emerge from the research was that almost all of the landlords were taking a long-term view of investing in private rented accommodation. Despite the two main differing forms of motivation between the business and sideline landlords – respectively for a current (and continuous) net rental income, and primarily for a future net rental income – both types of landlord were expecting to be in the business either indefinitely or for the foreseeable future. A more speculative type of investment, in what had been a rising market, was almost non-existent amongst the landlords who were interviewed. Even the few sideline landlords who were principally motivated by capital growth were taking a long-term view in that the capital so generated was intended to be used to provide for a pension at which time it would be invested in something else.

A second main finding of the research was the importance the landlords attached to the standard of their accommodation. There were usually self-interested motivations in this respect, such as to compete effectively in the marketplace, thereby making it possible for there to be a different attitude amongst landlords if the condition of local markets changed to one of under-supply. Most of the landlords were primarily motivated to look after their properties to protect and enhance the value of their investments, however, which may be something that does not vary substantially under differing market conditions. Perhaps the key issue in this respect will be the future response of the sideline landlords who had bought new property precisely because it did not need any maintenance at that time and had guarantees for a number of years.

Market conditions had clearly had an impact on the growth of buy to let by the time of the research. In particular, steady rises in property prices had fuelled the expansion of a number of the landlords in the study through their programmes of re-mortgaging to generate deposits for further acquisitions. It therefore remains to be seen how existing buy to let landlords will respond to a steadily falling market, such as occurred during the early years of the 1990s, and the extent to which buy to let then continues to attract new investors into the business.

Recent administrations have been keen to encourage institutional investment in private renting, as this has been seen as one way of enhancing the scale and professionalism within the sector. Thus the Business Expansion Scheme was extended to companies letting on assured tenancies towards the end of the 1980s, and legislation for Housing Investment Trusts to be established was introduced in 1996. More recently, Real Estate Investment Trusts have been proposed to allow collective investment in property. This research, however, suggests that although many private landlords do not always act in economically rational ways,[27] they do appear to be responsive to, and well-informed about, often quite subtle market signals and market differentiation in their area of investment in a way in which larger-scale investors perhaps may not. Thus the success of the buy to let initiative to date may rest partly on the fact that its landlords have been local market experts.

---

27 Kemp, P.A. and Rhodes, D., 'The motivations and attitudes to letting of private landlords in Scotland', *Journal of Property Research*, No. 14, (1997) pp. 117–32.

Chapter 4

Housing Benefit and the Private Rented Sector: A Case Study of Variance in Rental Niche Markets

Julie Rugg

Introduction

The private rented sector (PRS) contains a complex, heterogeneous series of niche markets, where demand and supply are framed around the needs of specific groups of renters looking for a particular type of letting. Little research has been completed that charts the characteristics of and interplay between these markets, but the need to map this diversity has become more pronounced. After a long period of relative inattention, policy makers have begun to review the roles that the PRS may play in offsetting difficulties with the two major tenures. For example, the PRS has been seen as a ready-access stop-gap for first-time buyers unable to afford their first owner occupied property; and local authority leasing schemes to secure PRS properties to meet duties under homelessness legislation are becoming commonplace. The capacity of the sector to meet these new demands depends largely on the flexibility of its constituent niche markets. In addition, it is becoming increasingly clear that attempts to regulate the sector, or indeed frame viable policy relating to private renting, must take into account the inherent diversity. This chapter will consider in more detail issues relating to a specific niche market: what will be termed the *benefit market.* This part of the PRS can be defined principally by the willingness of landlords to meet demand for property from households whose rent is supported either wholly or in part by housing benefit payments. Overall, housing benefit lets account for 24 per cent of the PRS; discussion of how this market operates offers a good opportunity to explore wider issues relating to demand and supply in the sector.

The chapter has four principal sections. The first takes a close look at ways in which the PRS has traditionally been defined. There has been a tendency to overlook the existence and operation of niche markets in the sector, although – as will be seen – this approach is useful as a means of reframing issues relating to the sector and its performance. For example, in the ten years between 1991 and 2001, the sector increased in size by 18 per cent. It remains to be asked whether this increase related to a particular market: around a third of students rent privately, and recent years have seen a substantial increase in the number of full-time students.[1] The chapter then discusses the nature of the benefit market, in terms of landlord and tenant characteristics and distinctive letting practices. The third section indicates that the benefit market is itself subject to variation depending on the local housing market in which it is contained. The chapter concludes by discussing the ways in which policy can introduce elements of imbalance into the benefit market.

It should perhaps be noted that much of the discussion in this chapter is based on an extended series of policy evaluation projects that have included qualitative interviews with landlords and letting agents.[2] Much of this work has included questions relating to the way landlords and letting agents 'place' themselves in the sector, and how their management practices have evolved according to the markets they serve. The research has also assessed the impact of policy interventions on consumer and investor behaviour in the private rental market.

The Private Rented Sector: Definitions of Diversity

Few commentators are in any doubt that the PRS is the most diverse housing tenure, and the point is often illustrated by overviews of demand and/or supply side characteristics.[3] With regard to landlords, considerable research has contributed to an understanding of the circumstances in which an individual or an institution lets residential property.[4] Landlords are often characterized in terms of the degree to which letting is their principal employment activity or income source, and the extent to which letting activity is intentional or a consequence of more passive property acquisition – for example through inheritance. Kemp's 2004 review reflected on and updated the classification of landlords in Allen and McDowell's 1989 study of landlordism in London. Kemp recognized eight landlord types including: stewardship landlords; employer landlords; informal landlords; investor landlords; commercial landlords; financial institutions; property dealers and property slump

1 Rhodes, D., *The Modern Private Rented Sector* (York, Joseph Rowntree Foundation, 2006).

2 Including, for example, Rugg, J., *Opening Doors: Helping People on Low Income Secure Private Rented Accommodation* (York, Centre for Housing Policy, 1996); Rugg, J. and Bevan, M., *An Evaluation of the Pilot Tenancy Deposit Scheme* (London: Office of the Deputy Prime Minister). More recently, the author has managed the landlord stream of the Department for Work and Pensions' Evaluation of the Local Housing Allowance. Specific reports from that stream will be cited below.

3 See, for example, Gray, P., Hillyard, P., McAnulty, U. and Cowan, D., *The Private Rented Sector in Northern Ireland* (Londonderry, University of Ulster, 2000); Kemp, P., *Private Renting in Transition* (Coventry, Chartered Institute of Housing, 2004); Rhodes, *Modern Private Rented Sector.*

4 Crook, A.D.H. and Kemp, P., *Private Landlords in England* (London, HMSO, 1996); Kemp, P.A. and Rhodes, D., *The Lower End of the Private Rented Sector: A Glasgow Case Study* (Edinburgh, Scottish Homes, 1994); Thomas, A.D. and Snape, D., *In From the Cold: Working with the Private Landlord* (London, HMSO, 1995).

landlords.[5] Discussion of tenants in the PRS generally takes two approaches. First, large-scale survey work routinely collects information on the types of household who rent property privately. For example, information on households in the PRS is collected in the annual Survey of English Housing (SEH). Regular SEH reports tend to analyse characteristics of private renters by tenancy type, distinguishing between households in assured and assured shorthold tenancies; regulated tenancies; lettings not accessible to the public; and resident landlord and no-security lettings.[6] Second, attention is also paid to the roles and purposes of the PRS in meeting different types of housing need. In 1985, four distinct groups were recognized: the continuing, but declining proportion of renters in old regulated tenancies; tenants in properties that were rented from their employer; households seeking long-term accommodation but unable to secure access to the major tenures; and 'easy access' accommodation to relatively mobile households often requiring short-term tenancies.[7] These groupings have informed much of the subsequent tenant-related discussion of the sector.

The study of demand and supply side characteristics of the sector is an essential tool in understanding the constituent elements of the market. However, in order to understand how the market *operates* in terms of interaction between supply and demand agents, it is useful to distinguish various niche markets that exist within the tenure. In the context of this paper, PRS niche markets are defined largely in terms of special and distinctive characteristics of tenants whose needs are met by landlords and letting agents who have framed their management practices accordingly. Niche markets within the PRS are often not readily identifiable using traditional quantitative methods, but rely largely on the narratives offered by a range of actors and agencies connected with the provision of rented property. This use of expert *rapporteurs* on localized market activity reflects new housing research methods that privilege the accounts of market intermediaries and place an emphasis on 'socially inflected qualitative inquiry' into how housing markets operate.[8]

Explanation of the nature of niche markets is best represented through example. In compiling the following short – and by no means comprehensive – list of niche markets, it becomes evident how little information is available on *parts* of the sector, compared with the growing level of data that describe the PRS as a whole.

Student renters

Research has been completed on characteristics of the student rental market, in terms of the specific requirements of students and indicating the ways that landlords

5 Kemp, *Private Renting in Transition*, p. 102ff; Allen, J. and McDowell, L., *Landlords and Property: Social Relations in the Private Rented Sector* (Cambridge, Cambridge University Press, 1989).

6 Bates, B. *et al.*, *Housing in England 2000/1* (London, Department for Transport, Local Government and the Regions, 2002).

7 Bovaird, A., Harloe, M. and Whitehead, C.M.E., 'Private rented housing: its current role', *Journal of Social Policy*, 14, 1 (1985).

8 Smith, S.J., Munro, M. and Christie, H., 'Performing (housing) markets', *Urban Studies*, 43, 1, (2006) p. 82.

and letting agents adopted their letting practices to meet these requirements.[9] Since 2000, further changes to the student housing market have become evident: private sector property companies have become more involved in opening and managing private halls of residence, or taking over management of halls from higher education institutions.[10] It appears that the competition for student renters may be increasing in some localities, with some areas showing signs of saturation in the student rental market. For example, student landlords operating in Cardiff were being advised to look to 'the social housing market' for alternative tenants following improvements to accommodation provided by local higher education institutions.[11]

'Young professionals'

This term generally refers to the growing numbers of young people, often post-degree and at the early stages of a professional career, who share properties. Young professionals may actively choose to continue renting but there is some concern that this group is over-represented in the PRS because of an inability to afford higher house prices in the owner occupied sector. However, some commentators have recognized that a positive choice has been made by this group, in continuing to rent and so further enjoy elements of a 'student' lifestyle.[12] The characteristics of this market include demand for property in central locations, close to city-centre attractions. Often the properties may have a high specification, with some attention paid to good quality white goods, satellite television and a relatively generous 'room to bathroom' ratio. Management practice will reflect the needs of the group. Landlords might use single and severally liable contracts that include joint responsibility for shared areas in the property. Often, the landlord may give close attention to the selection of tenants for a given property. For example, they would probably house particular professional groups – such as nurses or other kinds of night workers – together, and give existing tenants 'veto' rights over any prospective tenant introduced by the landlord.

Asylum seekers

The niche market with regard to asylum seekers is defined less in terms of the demography of the households and more in relation to the institutional contexts in which they are housed. Under the Immigration and Asylum Act of 1999, a National Asylum Support Service was created to meet the essential needs of destitute asylum seekers. These needs included facilitating access to housing. Public and private sector accommodation providers were invited to enter into contractual arrangements with

9 Rugg, J., Rhodes, D. and Jones, A., *The Nature and Impact of Student Demand on Housing Markets* (York, York Publishing Services, 2000).

10 See, for example, King Sturge, *The UK Student Accommodation Market in 2004/5*. Accessible at www.kingsturge.com.

11 'Social housing future for Welsh landlords', *Residential Property Investor*, January/February (2006), p. 6.

12 Heath, S. and Kenyon, L., 'Single young professionals and shared household living', *Journal of Youth Studies*, 4, (2001).

NASS to provide properties for households supported by the scheme. A complex network of contractors and sub-contractors appears to have developed. For example, The Angel Group is a private sector accommodation provider that was cited by Garvie (2001) as providing accommodation for asylum seekers; part of its operating practices included leasing properties from other private sector landlords.[13] Contracts are reviewed regularly, with the possibility of 'block bookings' of property within tightly defined dispersal areas being either demanded or withdrawn with limited notice.

Corporate lets

A further and largely overlooked niche market is luxury corporate lets. This kind of letting is generally arranged between large businesses and specialist agencies, and includes arranging single or block accommodation for 'inpat' executives commonly from France or Germany. Accommodation is often in exclusive areas of London, and relates to employment in the City. The properties involved have extremely high specifications, including indoor pools and gyms, and may be furnished according to a particular client's taste. Rentals on this type of property can fall in the range of £1500 to £5000 a week or above. For landlords, the risks of letting this kind of property can be high: the possibility of damage to high quality furnishings requires attention paid to inventory and deposit aspects of management; even a short void period can comprise a substantial loss of income; and corporate lets are highly sensitive to fluctuations in the financial markets.[14]

A brief review of these narratives underlines the range of elements is brought to bear to define a niche market, including demand group, landlord type, any statutory involvement in the letting, household characteristics, property specification including its location, and rent. At present, little information is available about the scale of operation of particular niche markets, and how – if at all – it might be possible to define a wider 'open market' within the private sector. Further, and perhaps most importantly, there is limited information available on how particular landlords and letting agents decide to serve a given market. For some niche markets, strategic decisions may have been taken by individuals or institutions to purchase particular types of property in order to serve a given need. This level of decision-marking indicates that some level of market research will have been completed on the needs and preferences of given groups of renters. Television property development programmes frequently advise that 'first-time landlords' should have a particular renter type in view, and purchase and develop their property accordingly. However, elements of choice and constraint are clearly an issue: for example, the student rental market research indicated that landlords in some locations close to higher education institutes found it difficult to let to any other group.[15]

---

13 Garvie, D., *Housing Asylum Seekers in Privately Rented Accommodation* (London, Shelter, 2001). For the Angel Group Plc see: http://www.theangelgroup.com/residential.html.

14 Helen Davies, 'The crying game', *The Sunday Times*, 6 August 2006; 'Beginner's Guide: Corporate Lets', at http://findaproperty.

15 Rugg, *et al.*, *Student Demand on Housing Markets*.

The Benefit Market

A better understanding of the development, characteristics and operation of the benefit market within the PRS has become evident as a consequence of large-scale research to evaluate the introduction of the local housing allowance (LHA). The LHA has been tested in nine Pathfinder local authorities: Blackpool, Brighton & Hove, Conwy, Coventry, Edinburgh, Leeds, Lewisham, North East Lincolnshire, and Teignbridge. This spread of local authorities was chosen to reflect variety in settlement types, housing and labour markets. The new regulations were introduced at varying points by the Pathfinder authorities in the four months following November 2003. At the time that this chapter was written, the evaluation was nearing completion. It is not the purpose of this chapter to comment on either the rationale or features of the LHA, or to describe its implementation.[16] However, the evaluation method included a detailed examination of both claimants and landlords in the private rented sector, where the tenancies were supported by either housing benefit (at the baseline stage of the evaluation) or LHA (in the later stages). The research was both quantitative and qualitative. The claimant stream of the research included contacting recipients of housing benefit in the nine Pathfinder locations by telephone to complete a detailed structured interview. This interview was repeated at intervals during the course of the evaluation period.[17] Quantitative and qualitative work also took place with landlords and letting agents. There were three sources for this group: housing benefit records, contact details provided by tenants on housing benefit, and a small number of randomly selected landlords and agents advertizing in the local newspapers.

Research on the particular characteristics of private renters in receipt of housing benefit indicates that certain key differences emerge in comparison with the wider PRS population (see Table 4.1). Three elements in particular show distinct difference: age of tenant, household type, and incidence of disability or long-term debilitating illness. First, with regard to age, the PRS taken in its entirety is often represented as 'the youthful tenure'. According to the 2001 Census, taking all tenures together, households with household heads aged under 25 comprised 4 per cent of the total. Within the PRS, this proportion was 15 per cent.[18] However, for the benefit market, the proportion was lower: 9 per cent of claimant household heads were under the age of 25.[19] The relatively low presence of young people in the benefit market most probably reflects the operation of the Single Room Rent (SRR). This regulation restricts the level of support offered to younger, single childless claimants. The housing benefit payment for these individuals is based on an eligible rent for a room in a property with shared facilities. This restriction represents the continuation of a

---

16 A series of reports relating to the evaluation is available. For example, Walker, B., *Local Housing Allowance Final Evaluation: Implementation and Delivery in the Nine Pathfinder Areas* (London, Department for Work and Pensions, 2006).

17 For the purposes of this chapter, principal use will be made of the draft report Roberts, S., Beckhelling, J., Phung, V., Boreham, R., Anderson, T. and Nai-lie, *Local Housing Allowance Wave 2* Quantitative Report (Loughborough, Centre for Research in Social Policy, 2006).

18 Rhodes, *Modern Private Rented Sector*.

19 Roberts *et al.*, *Local Housing Allowance Wave 2*.

policy trend that has restricted the help with housing costs given to young people, in the belief that such assistance comprises an encouragement to leave the parental home.[20] Since the introduction of the SRR, the number of recipients has declined substantially. Harvey and Houston's 2005 evaluation of the regulations estimated that the SRR caseload had fallen from around 101,000 live cases in 1997/8 to 34,000 in 2003. This report concluded that since the introduction of the SRR, landlord and letting agents' unwillingness to deal with young people had meant that the PRS was 'increasingly unavailable' to under-25s who looked to the state to help them pay the rent.[21] Thus the benefit market is not necessarily a 'youthful' sector.

Table 4.1 Selected household characteristics compared across all tenures, all PRS and the housing benefit niche

Household type	*All tenures, 2001 census*	*All PRS, 2001 census*	*Benefit sub-market*
Head of household aged under 25	4	15	9
Couples, no children	18	16	6
Lone parents	6	11	30
Long-term sick and disabled	4	6	26

Note: Census material from Rhodes (2006); Benefit sub-market data derived from Roberts *et al.* (2006).

A further difference between tenants in the benefit market compared with tenants overall in the PRS relates to household structure. According to the 2001 Census, single people made up the highest proportion of household types across all tenures. For the wider PRS, the second most common household type was couples with no dependant children. This proportion (16 per cent) was close to the all-tenure proportion for this household type, of 18 per cent.[22] However, within the benefit market, couples with no dependent children comprised just 6 per cent of household types. Within this market, by far the most common group – after single people – was lone parents. Across all tenures, 6 per cent of households were lone parents. Within the PRS this figure increased to 11 per cent. In the benefit market, 30 per cent of households were lone parents. Indeed, this proportion was higher than the proportion of lone parents in social housing.[23] A similar finding was evident in Gray's study of housing benefit recipients in Amagh: in this case, 43 per cent of respondents were

20 See Rugg, J., 'The use and "abuse" of private renting and help with housing costs', in Rugg, J. (ed.) *Young People, Housing and Social Security* (London, Routledge, 1999).

21 Harvey, J. and Houston, D., *Research into the Single Room Rent Regulations* (London, Department for Work and Pensions Research Report No. 243, 2005).

22 Rhodes, *Modern Private Rented Sector*.

23 Rhodes, *Modern Private Rented Sector.*

lone parents.[24] One explanation is offered by Kemp and Keoghan. In their study of movement in and out of the PRS, they found a high number of moves into the PRS from social housing, often following relationship breakdown.[25]

A third substantial difference in the benefit market compared to the wider PRS is the high proportion of household heads who are long-term sick and disabled. Across all tenures, 4 per cent of households were described in this manner in 2001, and this figure roughly equates to the PRS overall, where the proportion is 6 per cent. However, within the benefit market, 26 per cent of claimants were long-term sick or disabled.[26] Kemp and Keoghan comment that both lone parents and long-term sick were 'the very kinds of tenants that New Labour has said should be in social housing rather than private renting.'[27] Gray and McAnulty have also recognized the enhanced role played by private renting in accommodating households who have difficulty in accessing an increasingly restricted stock of social housing.[28] Thus, with regard to some key characteristics, claimants in the benefit market within the PRS are substantially different from the wider PRS tenantry, and presents an image slightly at odds with the 'young and dynamic' image of the sector evident in some accounts.

The demand for accommodation in the benefit market can be clearly defined in quantitative terms. Further study using existing data sets can track this kind of household more closely, and gain a better appreciation of the factors that might lead to a disadvantaged household seeking a private tenancy. Quantitative work to define benefit landlords and agents is a more complex task, and as yet data are not available to draw out basic descriptive elements such as portfolio size, property type and location. How then is it possible to define 'benefit landlordism'? This task is not straightforward, and two factors underlie its complexity. First, it has to be stressed that the simple fact of letting to someone in receipt of housing benefit does not make a landlord or agent a 'benefit landlord'. In many cases, a landlord or letting agent operating largely in the wider private rented sector might find themselves letting to a benefit claimant inadvertently. An individual or household may secure a tenancy whilst they are working, and then – through a change in household or employment circumstances – might find it necessary to apply for housing benefit to help them pay the rent. Few landlords or agents would ask tenants to leave in those circumstances, although any chronic difficulties in meeting rental payments may lead to the termination of the tenancy sooner than would have been the case if the tenant had continued in work. For the most part, the landlord would continue to treat the tenant as if they were still in work, and expect that they would take responsibility for making a housing benefit claim. Generally, the circumstance would be viewed as

---

24 Gray, *et al.*, p. 36.

25 Kemp, P.A. and Keoghan, M., 'Movement Into and Out of the Private Rented Sector in England', *Housing Studies*, Vol. 16, No. 1 (2001).

26 Rhodes, *Modern Private Rented Sector*.

27 Kemp and Keoghan, 'Movement Into and Out of the PRS', p. 31.

28 Gray, P. and McAnulty, U., 'The increased role of the private rented sector in catering for social housing in Northern Ireland', unpublished paper given to the HSA conference (York, 2006).

a temporary anomaly in the tenancy: the tenant would expect to regain employment or otherwise manage their affairs so that receipt of housing benefit would cease to be necessary. Although this train of events is probably not uncommon, no figures are available on the incidence of short-term 'temporary' periods on housing benefit, compared with chronic, long-term reliance on help with rental payment.

Second, it is also the case that landlords and agents rarely express a positive preference for letting to people in receipt of housing benefit. Even amongst the landlords and letting agents at the Baseline stage of the LHA Evaluation – a sample drawn principally from housing benefit records and recipients – just 4 per cent of respondents overall indicated that they actively preferred letting to unemployed people.[29] Even at the bottom end of the rental market, the preference is for a working tenant, largely because of the associated difficulties attached to housing benefit administration which – as will be seen – substantially distorts normal letting practice.

However, despite the fact that benefit landlords rarely declare themselves as such, the qualitative interviews with LHA landlords and agents contained a distinguishable group of landlords and agents whose portfolios tended to be dominated by lettings to households in receipt of housing benefit. The act of classifying a landlord as a 'benefit landlord' did not generally rest on easily quantifiable factors such as whether the landlord operated as a company, or the characteristics of their portfolios. Furthermore, as has been seen, 'benefit landlordism' was rarely an active choice amongst the respondents who were interviewed. Rather, it can be described as an agglomeration of experience, knowledge, attitude and management practice. In order to illustrate this point, it is perhaps appropriate to highlight key elements in a composite picture of the 'career' of a typical benefit landlord. The landlord may have begun letting as a sideline practice initially, started through the purchase of low-value property in a locality dominated by low-income households. The location of the properties was such that it would be difficult to find demand groups other than unemployed households, although there may be some low-income working tenants. Many of the properties initially might be houses in multiple occupation. The landlord initially set the rent by looking around to see what is charged for other, similar properties. Tenants were usually secured through word of mouth recommendation, with the 'pool' of tenants tending to be very local. The initial encounter with the benefit system was a shock, and there could be some confusion on the part of the landlord with regard to the administrative requirements of the system. As experience of the system progresses, the landlord generally accommodates any quirks of the local housing benefit administration, for example, in becoming aware of where an application may be vulnerable to delay. The landlord may, over time, choose to simply set the rent at what appears to be the LRR for that property type, on the understanding that tenants are infrequently able to meet shortfall payments from their other benefit income. For the most part, the management style tends to be flexible. There would be a willingness to take household groups where long-term receipt of housing benefit is likely. An effort would usually be made to keep 'good'

29 Rhodes, D. and Rugg, J., *Landlords and Agents in the Private Rented Sector* (London, Department for Work and Pensions, 2005) p. 16.

tenants who are clearly looking for permanent accommodation, and who look after the property they are renting. For these tenants, the landlord may not increase the rent, or only give limited increases, for extended periods. At the same time, there may be an acknowledgement that – particularly in the HMOs – some tenants may be so chaotic that they are unable to keep a tenancy for any length of time.[30]

In giving evidence to Social Security Committee in 1999/2000, Richard Lambert of the British Property Federation commented that 'It is uncommercial to rent to the Housing Benefit sector.'[31] Rents are often set at levels that fall below the general market level for a property of a particular type. Furthermore, because of the workings of the welfare system, many aspects of benefit landlordism run counter to what might be termed good business practice. For example, landlords and agents generally view the payment of returnable deposit by the tenant as both a good indicator of the financial status of the tenant, and as a means of giving tenants a stake in the smooth running of a tenancy. The Survey of English Housing (SEH) in 1999/2000 found that 78 per cent of tenants in assured tenancies had been asked to pay a deposit.[32] Within the claimant survey, the proportion paying a returnable deposit was 64 per cent. In parts of the benefit market, the practice of asking for a deposit was less commonplace. For example in Glasgow, in the HMO sub-sector, just 30 per cent of tenants said they had been charged a deposit.[33] It should be noted that, since the introduction of the Social Fund in 1988, assistance with the payment of deposits has not been available as either a loan or a grant from the Department for Work and Pensions.

Accepting rental payments in arrears was another marked feature of benefit landlordism that would not be countenanced in other parts of the PRS. The 1999/2000 SEH found that 87 per cent of households in assured tenancies paid their rent in advance. Within the housing benefit system, payment is generally paid to the tenant, four-weekly in arrears. Furthermore, many landlords and agents face long initial delays in the processing of the benefit. According to the regulations, local authorities should make the first payment within 14 days of full receipt of the information. In 2005/06, the national average processing time was closer to 40 days.[34] For landlords dealing with housing benefit claimants routinely, innate flexibility is required. Gareth Hardwick of the National Federation of Residential Landlords indicated that difficulties with housing benefit administration required the employment of different management skills with regard to benefit claimants:

> For example, if your tenant is eight weeks in arrears and you know they are a housing benefit claimant, you can apply for the local authority to have the housing benefit paid directly to

---

30 Composite derived from qualitative landlord material, reported in full in Rugg, J., *Local Housing Allowance Final Evaluation: The Qualitative Evidence of Landlords and Agents Experience in the Nine Pathfinder Areas* (London, Department for Work and Pensions, 2006).

31 Lambert, R., *Social Security Committee Sixth Report Housing Benefit* (London, The Stationery Office, 2000) p. 127.

32 Bates, B., Joy, S., Roden, R., Swales, K., Grove, J. and Oliver R., *Housing in England 1999/00* (London, Department of the Environment, Transport and Regions, 2001).

33 Kemp and Rhodes, *Lower End of the PRS*, p. 66.

34 See http://www.dwp.gov.uk/aboutus/welfarereform/.

> you. But you can only do that if you know that they are a housing benefit claimant. If they are not a housing benefit claimant then you take the normal court action.[35]

As this quotation makes clear, benefit landlordism also generally required a good understanding of housing benefit regulations. Often, landlords and agents dealing routinely with the housing benefit market adjusted their practices as new regulations were introduced. For example, the implementation of the Verification Framework requirements might mean that a landlord would be more proactive in sorting out a tenant's initial application for housing benefit, to the degree of physically taking the tenant and the required supporting documentation to the principal housing benefit administration office, to get a receipt from that office confirming that a full application had been received. Both the level of flexibility with advance payment, and active involvement in a tenant's financial affairs would generally be absent in the wider rental market.

For the majority of landlords and agents in the benefit market, the principal advantage in dealing with the market was not the level of rent that could be charged – which was often regarded as being at below-market levels – but the fact that, once it had been set up, housing benefit payments were made with regularity. This was especially the case if the payments were made direct from the local authority to the landlord or agent. Indeed, landlords and agents with long-term benefit-recipient tenants on direct payments could almost bank on this income and frequently used the steady rental receipts to expand their portfolios.

The Benefit Market in the Wider PRS

It is important to recognize that the housing benefit market is part of a PRS that is itself subject to wider housing market forces. The 2000 Green Paper showed an indifferent and limited grasp of the connection. *Quality and Choice: A Decent Home for All* indicated that in areas of declining housing demand, some unscrupulous landlords were instituting housing benefit fraud, linked to other criminal activities such as drug-dealing and prostitution.[36] Overall, however, there tends to be little acknowledgement that the scale of private renting varies area by area, and – similarly – its principal purposes also differ. Two exceptions are Bone and Walker's study of the PRS in five localities, which aimed to assess any variation in the impact of deregulation in PRS.[37] Rhodes' analysis of the 2001 Census also contributes to the task of charting spatial difference. For example, in 2001 the PRS housed 8 per cent of households in the North East region of England, but 16 per cent of households in

---

35 Hardwick, G., *Social Security Committee Sixth Report Housing Benefit* (London, The Stationery Office. 2000) p. 131–2.

36 DETR/DSS (Department of the Environment, Transport and the Regions; Department of Social Security) *Quality and Choice: A Decent Home for All. The Housing Green Paper*, (London, HMSO, 2000) p. 49.

37 Bone, M. and Walker, E., *Private Renting in Five Localities* (London, HMSO, 1994).

Greater London. Conversely, renting from a relative or friend comprised 8 per cent of the market in Greater London but 13 per cent in the North East of England.[38]

It follows, therefore, that the scale and influence of the benefit market within the PRS will also differ substantially. For example, within the LHA Pathfinder authorities, the proportion of PRS tenants in receipt of housing benefit varied substantially at the Baseline stage, as Table 4.2 demonstrates. Overall nationally, the figure is 24 per cent. However, within the nine Pathfinder areas, this proportion ranged from 74 per cent in Blackpool to 21 per cent in Leeds. As part of the evaluation method, qualitative methods were used as a means of understanding the particular characteristics of each Pathfinder rental market.

Table 4.2 Households on housing benefit in the private rented sector in the LHA Pathfinder areas

Pathfinder area	*Proportion of households in the PRS (1)*	*Housing benefit caseload (2)*	*Proportion of households in the PRS on housing benefit*
Blackpool	18	8,300	74
Brighton & Hove	22	9,000	36
Conwy	13	2,300	38
Coventry	10	4,700	38
Edinburgh	13	6,200	24
Leeds	10	6,500	21
Lewisham	12	4,400	34
NE Lincolnshire	10	4,600	69
Teignbridge	13	2,000	33

Note: (1) Census, 2001; (2) DWP MIS November 2005

Interviews took place with statutory and voluntary sector agencies including the housing strategy officer; the tenancy relations officer; housing benefit administrative staff; environmental health officers; voluntary and statutory welfare advisors and The Rent Service. The respondents were asked a common suite of questions on the nature of the local private rental market, and on the existence and nature of any parts of the market where lets to housing benefit recipients seemed more marked. It became clear that the scale and nature of the benefit market differed from area to area, although it was possible to cluster the nine areas into three broad types.

Within what was called a *housing benefit dominant* market, there was a much higher than average proportion of households within the private rented sector that were reliant wholly or partially on state help to pay the rent. Both Blackpool and North-East Lincolnshire were included in this grouping. In both these areas there was relatively limited alternative demand for rented property from groups such as

38 Rhodes, *Modern Private Rented Sector*.

students or young professionals. Landlords could find themselves competing for tenants. Where the housing benefit dominant market was located in a low housing demand area, landlords may also have to compete with social housing providers as boundaries between the renting tenures could become fluid.

A second classification of benefit market was *concentrated.* Within the Pathfinder areas, both Edinburgh and Leeds fell into this category. In the concentrated benefit market, lettings to benefit claimants comprised a distinctive sector within the PRS, but did not dominate the sector. A number of other competing demand groups existed within the market place, such as students, young low-income professionals (such as hospital staff), asylum seekers and holiday lets. The benefit market may be concentrated within given wards, and these locations may be so located or stigmatized that the landlord may find it difficult to secure a non-benefit tenant. In these circumstances, tenants may find that their only competition for property comes from other tenants reliant on housing benefit. However, where the market becomes over-heated, demand for rental property may spill into previously housing benefit-dominated areas, to the disadvantage of benefit recipients.

In the third classification, demand from housing benefit claimants is *dispersed.* In these circumstances, there is limited evidence of a particular spatial location within the area in which housing benefit lets are concentrated. This may be a result of high demand for property placing pressure on the entire rental market, or housing that is geographically spread, perhaps because of a rural pattern of settlement. In the dispersed benefit market, lettings to claimants do not dominate the rental market, and other demand groups may be evident. In areas of high housing stress, the demand groups may also include households unable to afford owner occupation, but still have incomes above the benefit thresholds. Landlords letting within the PRS in these locations are often able to choose from a variety of demand groups, and are generally not constrained by their property location. Within a dispersed benefit market, claimant tenants are – more so than in any other type of benefit market – open to competition from other demand groups.

It should be stressed that these categories are not strictly contained or exclusive, and it is not always possible to make a categorical judgement about where a particular market might lie. Markets are, by nature, dynamic and often a particular market may be in the process of shifting from one classification to another. A common shift is from concentrated to dispersed benefit market, in the context of increased demand for rental property; or concentrated to dominant markets, in the context of economic downturn. As yet, these assessments are preliminary, and based on material from just nine local authority areas. Further research on housing benefit within the PRS would be useful in testing the analysis. However, it is clear that the existence of these different market types offers a challenge to policy-makers seeking change in the areas of both housing benefit and other aspects of PRS regulation. For example, attempts to create 'shopping incentives' for tenants in receipt of housing benefit will have variable impacts depending on landlords' ability to tap into alternative demand markets.

Policy and Competition in the Benefit Market

The PRS serves diverse purposes, with widely divergent demand and supply characteristics, and is vulnerable to wider housing market trends. These factors mean that there is – as Allen and McDowell recognized in 1989 – 'a need to devise policies which can discriminate between different types of landlords in order to meet the variety of rented housing need in different locations'.[39] This policy challenge is by no means easy to resolve. The long-standing debate relating to the licensing of houses in multiple occupation reflects a desire to separate out a part of the market deemed particularly problematic; the fact that attempts to frame appropriate legislation have been protracted reflects difficulties in drawing sub-sectoral boundaries. This chapter will conclude with some comment on an area where policy development has largely overlooked niche-market operation: the use made of the private rented sector by voluntary and statutory agencies to meet the needs of people in housing need.

Failings in the supply of social rented accommodation mean that more attention is being paid to the possible use of the PRS to meet the needs of households on low incomes and – more particularly – of households to which the local authority holds a responsibility under homelessness legislation. Indeed, the Government strategy report *Sustainable Communities: Settled Homes; Changing Lives* indicates that 'there is scope to make greater use of the private rented sector, either to help households avoid homelessness or to give more settled homes to those in temporary accommodation'.[40] In June 2005, the London Housing Foundation, a charitable organization that seeks to tackle single homelessness, announced a grant programme of £1m to 'stimulate the use of the private rented sector for single homeless people'. According to the Foundation Director, Kevin Ireland, '... in the light of restricted availability of social housing, we feel it is imperative to find more productive ways of utilising the PRS'.[41] The programme aim was to ensure that at least 300 single homeless people will have accessed and sustained a PRS tenancy. Although the programme was aimed at offering financial support for voluntary sector agencies, the work intended to stimulate new approaches to securing a better supply of PRS properties for its client group. Similarly, research on the components of local authority homelessness strategies found that many contained initiatives that included work with private landlords.[42]

At any one time and in any one location there are perhaps up to a dozen different agencies and initiatives seeking to place people in 'sponsored' private sector tenancies. Included amongst these groups are:

---

39 Allen, J. and McDowell, L., *Landlords and Property: Social Relations in the Private Rented Sector* (Cambridge, Cambridge University Press, 1989) p. 160.

40 ODPM (Office of the Deputy Prime Minister) *Sustainable Communities: Settled Homes; Changing Lives* (Office of the Deputy Prime Minister, London, 2005) p. 33.

41 Greater London Authority, 'Homelessness in London 65', *Homelessness Bulletin*, June 2005.

42 ODPM (Office of the Deputy Prime Minister), *Survey of English Local Authorities About Homelessness*, Policy Briefing 13 (2005).

- People seeking assistance with accessing a PRS tenancy, and so falling under the aegis of a local authority or voluntary sector deposit guarantee scheme;
- Housing associations looking to accommodate their clients in accommodation leased from the PRS under HAL or HAMA arrangements;
- Households who have been accepted as statutorily homeless by a local authority, and for whom a *temporary* let has been arranged in a PRS tenancy;
- Those who have been accepted as statutorily homeless by a local authority, and for whom a *longer-term* let has been arranged in a PRS tenancy;
- Asylum seekers being housed under the appropriate dispersal arrangements;
- NACRO-funded resettlement agencies seeking to house offenders leaving institutions;
- Care-leavers looking for settled accommodation, with support packages arranged by the social services;
- Adults with physical and mental disabilities placed in private sector accommodation by agencies using Supported People funding.

The increased use of the PRS for these purposes contains an implicit assumption: that the tenure is flexible enough to cope with increased demand from any source. However, excess demand for rental property at the bottom end of the sector introduces competition for property amongst groups that are already seriously disadvantaged.

One element of concern is the degree to which 'sponsored' tenants may secure assistance that is not available to low-income households who are seeking accommodation in the PRS independently. The ability of these households to find appropriate and affordable accommodation in the sector will vary substantially according to the existence or otherwise in their area of a substantial HB 'sub-market' with landlords willing to meet the needs of low-income groups. These tenants often have little bargaining power in the housing market, beyond the fact that HB payments – once agreed by the local authority – will be made directly to the landlord. If this type of household approaches the local authority, they may be offered little more than a list of landlords who may or may not be accredited.

By contrast, 'sponsored' households – who, for example, may have been accepted as statutorily homeless by local authority, and for whom temporary or long-term lets have been arranged – may be supported substantially by the local authority in the task of securing a privately rented property. Essentially, the local authority may enter into an arrangement with landlords to guarantee that their property is available exclusively to tenants nominated by the authority. Where a formal leasing arrangement has been created, landlords may be offered a lease period of, say, 12 months, during which the local authority will guarantee that the property will be tenanted, with rent paid at a given level and paid directly to the landlord. Even less formal arrangements may include the offer of a deposit or rent in advance, fast-tracking of the processing of housing benefit, a rent guarantee of some description, and mediation to ensure that the course of the tenancy runs smoothly. It is telling that, in its brief summary of activities to engage landlords, the review of homelessness strategies used the word 'reward' to describe services for landlords such as fast-tracked housing benefit and inclusion on accommodation registers to advertize their properties.[43]

Many such initiatives operate in London and in other areas of high housing stress. Indeed, homelessness legislation that is curtailing use of bed and breakfast accommodation encourages local authorities to consider temporary use of private sector tenancies in preference. By the end of June 2005, some 64,000 households had been placed in temporary accommodation by London borough housing departments. In 51 per cent of these placements, the accommodation was leased from a private landlord by either the local authority or by a registered social landlord. Even outside such leasing arrangements, in boroughs such as Bromley, Brent, Hackney and Kensington & Chelsea, the number of direct placements with landlords could be substantial.[44]

These developments constitute good practice with regard to generating property in the PRS, but they can carry unforeseen consequences. The benefit market becomes less 'open', in that some groups become more desirable than others for landlords generally willing to let to people in receipt of benefits. Thus a landlord may be offered a choice between a tenant on low income on housing benefit and a tenant 'sponsored' by the local authority and supported with an incentives package. Amongst the benefit landlords interviewed as part of the LHA evaluation, sponsored tenants clearly comprised a preferred group, particularly since the support usually reduced the substantial difficulties associated with dealing with housing benefit administration. Garvie's work on asylum seekers also indicated the possibility that some landlords 'may see asylum seekers as a lucrative business opportunity' and withdraw property from other disadvantaged groups to meet that demand.[45] 'Unsponsored' households, seeking property independently, are already in a vulnerable position in the rental market, since landlords in many areas are generally unwilling to let to this group. The marginal position of such households is exacerbated when the limited number of landlords willing to take housing benefit cases is drawn into local authority homelessness initiatives or other support programmes for vulnerable groups. Indeed, it may be the case that in some areas, the only way that some households will be able to access a PRS tenancy is to declare themselves homeless.

Conclusion

This chapter has indicated that the complexities inherent in the private rented sector are barely understood, and that the existence and operation of niche rental markets requires full exploration and analysis. Without a detailed appreciation of the ways in which the sector works, it becomes difficult to frame appropriate legislation. Research reviewing the 'cottage industry' nature of private renting has already indicated that traditional law-based approaches are perhaps not the best way to

43 Housing Quality Network Services, *Local Authority Homelessness Strategies: Evaluation and Good Practice* (London, Office of the Deputy Prime Minister, 2004) p. 66.

44 GLA (Greater London Authority), *Homelessness in London,* (London, Greater London Authority, 2006).

45 Garvie, *Housing Asylum Seekers*, p. 30.

regulate the sector.[46] In addition, a failure to understand how the PRS operates can lead to some unfortunate developments. As this chapter indicated, the use of the PRS to house homeless households may create unforeseen market imbalance in some locations.

Murie contends that tenure categories are 'insufficient and obscure difference',[47] and much of this chapter supports this overall view. Indeed, the term 'private renting' covers such a diverse set of housing circumstances as to be meaningless as a single classification. Perhaps the time has come to review the use of the largely unhelpful tenure category 'the private rented sector', at the very least by referring to 'private rented sectors'.

46 Marsh, A., 'Private renting: the regulatory challenge', paper given to the HSA Conference (York, 2006).

47 Murie, A. 'Moving with the times: changing frameworks for housing research and policy', in. Malpass P. and Cairncross, L. (eds), *Building on the Past: Visions of Housing Futures* (Bristol, The Policy Press, 2006).

Chapter 5

Controlling Letting Arrangements in the Private Rented Sector?

Diane Lister

Introduction

> Inasmuch as property is conditional upon the existence of certain types of social relations between people, it is essentially a social phenomenon.[1]

Attempts to regulate, control and govern standards in the private rented sector (PRS) in England have traditionally been based upon conceptualizations of relationships between parties as primarily legal with the economic element of 'consideration' comprising the second factor and social relations between each party receiving limited attention in this context. This chapter considers these issues and argues that legal conceptualizations of relationships between landlords and tenants have not adequately considered the importance of individual agency. The chapter explores the policy and legislative difficulties in regulating the sector and argues that the challenges encountered by successive policy makers and legislators in regulating the sector is in part associated with the diversity of the PRS as well as a lack of recognition and understanding of the social aspects of relationships between landlord and tenant. Control in the sector and the 'currency' of exchange between landlord and tenant are often via social exchange rather than legal and economic mechanisms and it is this social aspect which is often an overlooked aspect of relationships. Drawing on empirical material, this chapter considers alternative ways of conceptualizing relationships between the parties and considers how the sector may be regulated more efficiently if social relationships between the parties (as highlighted in the above quote by Hollowell), with their own internal structure of 'laws', are taken into consideration. This chapter argues that the key orientations, behaviour and motivations of the parties should be considered before developing, delivering and implementing policy and legislative changes. The chapter concludes with a consideration of the Law Commission's recently published plans to reform the sector and whether they are likely to lead to more successful governance.

1 Hollowell, P., (ed.) *Property and Social Relations* (London, Heinemann Educational Books Ltd, 1982) pp. 1–2.

Policy and Legislative Difficulties in Regulating the Sector

Historically, it has proved difficult to control and govern letting relationships and property and service standards in the PRS in England.[2] Over the years successive legislative regimes have produced and reinforced problems under both strict regulatory and more relaxed regimes with ongoing tensions exhibited between landlords' rights as owners of property and tenants' rights as occupiers.[3] Although changes are in evidence (see below), the sector has suffered from a poor image which has often been distorted to focus on bad landlordism because of high profile and well publicized extreme cases involving harassment, unlawful eviction, violence and the death of tenants through fire and carbon monoxide poisoning as a result of inadequate gas safety.[4] Notorious examples of bad landlordism and illegal behaviour are evident in the activities of slum landlord Peter Rachman in the 1960s and more recently landlord Nicholas Van Hoogstraten, who described his tenants as 'filth' and who was involved in a high profile manslaughter case and convicted in 1999. He was released in 2003 but ordered to pay damages in a civil action to the deceased's family.[5] Clearly, these isolated examples of landlords' extreme activities do little for the promotion of a positive image and they mask examples of good landlordism in the sector.

It is well acknowledged that there are difficulties associated with regulatory intervention, balancing the rights and responsibilities of landlords and tenants and maintaining the share of landlords letting properties in the market. There are also challenges associated with the plethora of separate issues which require regulation, the nature of what is being regulated (the property, the landlord and the relationship), achieving a consensus about how these issues are regulated, and what can be enforced, how and by whom. The legislative framework, its volume, lack of coherence and complexity present serious challenges to policy makers and law reformers. The

---

2 See, for example, Daunton, M.J., *House and Home in the Victorian City – Working Class Housing 1850–1914* (London, Edward Arnold Ltd, 1983); Englander, D., *Landlord and Tenant in Urban Britain 1838–1918* (Oxford, Clarendon Press, 1983); Kemp, P., 'Some aspects of housing consumption in late nineteenth century England and Wales' in *Housing Studies*, 2, 1 (1987) pp. 3–16; Cowan, D. and Marsh, A., 'There's Regulatory Crime and then there's Landlord Crime: From Rachmanites to Partners', *The Modern Law Review*, 64, 6 (2001) pp. 831–54; Lister, D., 'Controlling letting arrangements? Landlords and surveillance in the private rented sector', *Surveillance and Society*, 2, 4 (2005) pp. 513–28.

3 Nelken, D., *The Limits of the Legal Process: A Study of Landlords, Law and Crime* (London, Academic Press, 1983); Sharp, C., *Problems Assured! Private Renting after the 1988 Housing Act* (London, SHAC Publications, 1991).

4 Burrows, L. and Hunter, N., *Forced Out!* (London, Shelter Publications, 1990); Jew, P., *Law and Order in Private Rented Housing: Tackling Harassment and Illegal Eviction* (London, Campaign for Bedsit Rights, 1994); *Environmental Health News*, 'Gas safety: a matter of life or death' www.ehn-online.com/cgibin/news/FocusHousing/EEpZVFkFpEGptTQbzN.html (4 February 2005); 'Van Hoogstraten: How the net closed in', http://www.bbc.co.uk/2/low/uk_news/england/2123150.stm BBC News (22 July 2002) (accessed 10 February 2005).

5 BBC News (9 September 2003) 'Van Hoogstraten's life of controversy', http://newsvote.bbc.co.uk/mpapps/pagetools/print/news.bbc.co.uk/1/hi/uk/3301361.stm (accessed March 16 2006).

current legislative framework has been described as a 'labyrinth of technicality, complexity, and difficult concepts'[6] and lacking transparency and clarity in relation to how and where particular aspects of regulatory control, for example, property standards, safety issues and letting agreements, can be enforced, given that much of it is not codified in a coherent accessible way. This complexity inevitably makes it difficult not only for landlords and tenants to understand the law affecting them, but legal advisers often face challenges in disentangling rights and responsibilities.[7] The level of complexity experienced is neatly summed up with a statement made over two decades ago but which still remains true today and serves as a poignant reminder of the slow progress in simplifying rights and responsibilities in the sector:

> The rights and duties of each party were scattered through the housing, public health and rent legislation and varied considerably according to the status of the tenant/licensee … its sheer complexity – seen perhaps at its most developed extent … in Britain.[8]

In addition to the complexity of the legal framework, the volume of statutory and regulatory codes is extensive and attention has recently been drawn to this problematic aspect in relation to the scope for legal reform:

> The *Encyclopaedia of Housing Law*, which contains all the relevant statutes, regulations and government circulars, comprises six volumes that take up twenty-two inches on the bookshelf and weigh well over 10 kilos.[9]

As mentioned above, property standards, service issues, safety and security, management and letting relationship standards often overlap in legislative terms and as a consequence of lack of coherence, complexity and volume there is often a disconnection between both policy and legislative implementation and the transformative intentions and effects of such policies and legislation as they are played out on the ground. This is largely because regulatory measures are initiated politically, expressed in legal terms and are experienced socially, often with little regard for, or consultation with the parties who will be affected by newly implemented measures (but see below). The emphasis upon legal aspects and the assumption of equality between contracting parties can lead to further erroneous assumptions that parties are aware of the legal framework in which they operate and are fully

---

6 Balchin, P. and Rhoden M. (eds), *Housing: The Essential Foundations* (London, Routledge, 1998) p. 241.

7 See, for example, Thomas, A., Snape, D. with Duldig, W., Keegan, J. and Ward, K., *In From the Cold – Working with the Private Landlord* (London, HMSO, 1995); Crook, A.D.H. and Kemp, P.A., *Private Landlords in England* (London, HMSO, 1996); Lister, D., 'Young people's strategies for managing tenancy relationships in the private rented sector' *Journal of Youth Studies*, 7, 3 (2004) pp. 315–30.

8 Harloe, M., 'Landlord/Tenant Relations in Europe and America – The Limits and Functions of the Legal Framework' in *Urban Law and Policy*, 7 (1985) pp. 369–70.

9 The Law Commission, *Scoping Paper* (London, The Law Commission, March 2001).

informed and able to behave as responsible rational actors.[10] These assumptions are problematic as the law often has a limited impact on behavioural outcomes and the legal aspects of contractual relationships may bear no relevance to the lived relationship between the parties:

> … the evidence from empirical studies of contractual behaviour indicates the marginal and sometimes socially disintegrative effects of the law of contract … There is also evidence that whole swathes of the most vibrant parts of the economy … function entirely within their own regulatory system that renders the law almost irrelevant.[11]

Whilst Marx, Durkheim and Weber's respective analyses tended to view the law as a direct reflection of the nature of social relations in modern societies and regarded contracts as the key to sustaining social bonds, as the above quote highlights, contemporary analysis and empirical evidence supports a rejection of these views in favour of a more pragmatic view about what the law can be expected to realistically achieve. Reflecting upon the role of law in contemporary society reveals the gaps between law and practice, the aspirational aspects of the law (rather than it being a reflection of actual practice) and its interpretative relational aspects.[12] By emphasizing the role of the law, social factors of relationships are overlooked which are significant and have a greater impact on behaviour than at first credited with. Furthermore, the diversity of the sector and those operating in it pose problems for regulation and resistance to a 'one size fits all' approach as well as requiring a consideration of individual agency. The motivations of landlords to letting and the increasingly diverse nature of the parties entering into contractual relations in the contemporary market have altered the interplay of legal, social and economic aspects, adding further emphasis to existing claims that an analysis of relationships based solely upon legal criteria is limiting.[13]

The sector has undergone a series of key transformations in recent years and has expanded its overall share of the housing market to 11 per cent of all households in 2003.[14] Ownership and tenureship is currently dominated by two distinct groups –

---

10 Lister, D., 'The nature of tenancy relationships – landlords and young people in the private rented sector' in Lowe, S. and Hughes, D. (eds), *The Privately Rented Sector in a New Century* (Bristol, The Policy Press, 2002).

11 Collins, H., *Regulating Contracts* (Oxford, Oxford University Press, 2002) p. 5.

12 Harloe, 'Landlord/Tenant Relations in Europe and America – The Limits and Functions of the Legal Framework', pp. 359–83; Cotterrell, R., *The Sociology of Law: An Introduction* (London, Butterworths, 1992); Conley, J.M. and O'Barr, W.M., *Rules versus Relationships – The Ethnography of Legal Discourse* (Chicago and London, The University of Chicago Press, 1990); Lister, D., 'Tenancy agreements: a mechanism for governing anti-social behaviour', in Flint, J. (ed.), *Housing, Urban Governance and Anti-social Behaviour* (Bristol, The Policy Press, 2006).

13 Harloe, 'Landlord/Tenant Relations in Europe and America – The Limits and Functions of the Legal Framework', pp. 359–83; Lister, 'The nature of tenancy relationships – landlords and young people in the private rented sector'.

14 Robinson, C., Humphrey, A., Kafka, E., Oliver, R. and Bose, S., *Housing in England 2002/03: A Report from the 2002/03 Survey of English Housing* (Office of the Deputy Prime Minster, London, 2004).

private individuals for whom property letting is not their main occupation and young people comprising the key demand group. The number of private individuals letting property (excluding resident and employer landlords), has increased from just over one million (60 per cent) in 1990 to almost 1.7 million (77 per cent) in 2002/03.[15] For the majority of private individual landlords, letting property is relatively new and not their main occupation but is a small scale 'sideline' or 'part time' activity that does not comprise their main source of income.[16] The sector is characterized by a large number of suppliers providing only one or two properties each often to a particular 'niche' market, for example, students. In 2000/1, 410,000 young people aged 16–24 years old lived in the private rented sector in England, comprising 18 per cent of all private renting households in England.[17] In comparison with other tenures in England, a far higher proportion of household heads are under 25 in the PRS. One in six heads of PRS households are under 25, compared with about one in twenty social tenants and one in a hundred owner occupiers.[18]

Despite the expansion of the sector in recent years, the PRS still has a lack of industry standards and some of the worst conditions in terms of facilities and services, and levels of disrepair and unfitness[19] in comparison to social renting and owner occupation. In 2001 the English House Condition Survey revealed that about half of all PRS dwellings were 'non-decent' compared with a third of dwellings in the stock as a whole.[20] Damp, condensation, overcrowding and inadequate cooking and heating facilities are widespread and have an impact upon the health and well-being of tenants.[21] In addition, Houses in Multiple Occupation (HMOs) have always posed more of a risk in terms of fire and gas safety and the worst conditions tend to be concentrated in the HMO sub-sector. The differential risk to safety in HMOs has been addressed for some time by separate and more stringent regulatory regimes, such as fire safety, as well as accreditation schemes and more recently in the Housing Act 2004 a redefinition of HMO and the introduction of mandatory licensing, and appropriate enforcement action and penalties, for certain types of HMOs.

---

15 Robinson, C. *et al.*, *Housing in England 2002/03: A report from the 2002/03 Survey of English Housing.*

16 Thomas, A., Snape, D. with Duldig, W., Keegan, J. and Ward, K., *In From the Cold – Working with the Private Landlord* (London, HMSO, 1995); Rhodes, D. and Bevan, M., *Private Landlords and Buy-to-Let* (York, Centre for Housing Policy, University of York, 2003).

17 Bates, B., Joy, S., Kitchen, S., Perry, J., Swales, K., Thornby, M., Kafka, E., Oliver, R. and Wellington, S., *Housing in England 2000/1: A Report of the 2000/1 Survey of English Housing* (London, Department of Transport, Local Government and the Regions, 2002).

18 Kemp, P., *Private Renting in Transition* (Coventry, Chartered Institute of Housing, 2004) p. 115.

19 Leather, P. and Morrison, T., *The State of UK Housing: A Factfile on Dwelling Conditions* (York, Joseph Rowntree Foundation/The Policy Press, 1997).

20 Kemp, p. 85.

21 See, for example, Lister, D., 'Unlawful or just awful? Young people's experiences of living in the private rented sector in England' in *YOUNG – The Nordic Journal of Youth Studies*, 14, 2 (2006) pp. 141–55.

In contrast, alongside these conditions, in recent years the sector has appealed to young professionals postponing home ownership and as a result of the gentrification and conversion of city centre buildings into apartments offers a housing choice for more affluent renters wanting a city centre lifestyle.[22] An increase in standards and professional appeal is combined with a new culture of responsibilization which is permeating the sector with landlords' duties given greater emphasis and selective licensing introduced in the Housing Act 2004 and implemented in April 2006. Policy discourse focuses less on discipline and more on an efficient and controlled sector with the onus upon landlords as rational actors in the housing market responsible for the safety and security of their tenants.[23] The implications of more stringent regulatory regimes are far reaching for landlords. On the one hand there is a fear that an increase in regulation of the sector, may result in some landlords exiting the sector. It may be the case that landlords exiting the sector represent the minority of 'bad' landlords and this is a desirable result of registration.

Conceptual Difficulties, Sentiments of Ownership and a Sense of Place

Underlying legislative and policy difficulties in regulating the sector, are a number of conceptual and cognitive issues within the landlord/tenant relationship which contribute to regulatory challenges but are often overlooked because of the focus upon strict legal issues. These conceptual and cognitive challenges give rise to differing interpretations of the nature of the relationship and rights and responsibilities. These challenges are exemplified in the 'hybrid nature' of contemporary letting arrangements between landlord and tenant reflecting the mix of contract with a relationship based on property rights and also influenced by statutory regulation adding a further dimension of complexity as the letting agreement can be, and is, interpreted from differing legal perspectives:

> The modern tenancy relationship reflects the contractual agreement between landlord and tenant, the proprietary nature of the lease and public regulation of leases. The fact that a lease is property as well as a contractual relationship has shaped the development of landlord and tenant law.[24]

The main tension embodied in the letting agreement exists in relation to its dual nature. Competing interpretations exist about whether the agreement is a lease

---

22 Heath, S. and Kenyon, L., 'Single Young Professionals and Shared Household Living', *Journal of Youth Studies*, 4, 1 (2001) pp. 83–100; Allen, C. and Blandy, S., *The Future of City Centre Living: Implications for Urban Policy* (London, Office of the Deputy Prime Minister, 2004).

23 Foucault, M., 'Technologies of the Self: A seminar with Michel Foucault', in Martin, L.H., Gutman, H. and Hutton, P.H. (eds), *Technologies of the Self,* (Amherst, The University of Massachusetts Press, 1988); Deleuze, G., 'Postscript to Societies of Control', *October*, 59 (1992) pp. 3–7; Rose, N., *Powers of Freedom: Reframing Political Thought* (Cambridge, Cambridge University Press, 1999).

24 Bright, S. and Gilbert, G., *Landlord and Tenant Law: The Nature of Tenancies* (Oxford, Clarendon Press, 1995) p. 69.

simply for property, as it was historically, or whether modern day contractual principles apply in relation to the ongoing provision of services throughout the duration of the tenancy relationship. The latter of these interpretations has received some resistance in domestic law (but see discussion of Law Commission proposals below) as it challenges traditional assumptions associated with the ownership of property. As a result of a lack of clarity and consensus in the legal arena about this, combined with some landlords' sentiments of ownership and attachment to property there is inevitably some conceptual confusion about the exact nature of the rights of the owner and the rights of the occupier, and in the absence of legal reform in this area, the interpretation and articulation of these perspectives is likely to depend upon individual tenancy relationships and the subjective orientations and expectations of the parties involved. The distinction between the 'proprietary' and 'contractual' perspectives and their development are as follows:

> The proprietary perspective therefore stresses the possession-rent relationship ... The tenant covenants to pay rent while the landlord covenants to keep the tenant in quiet enjoyment. In this perspective the landlord is expected to keep away. The dominance of the proprietary approach to the relationship between landlord and tenant developed in relation to agricultural land. The tensions begin to emerge when once the lease is used for residential and industrial lettings where 'covenants in the lease form an important part of the bargain and the ongoing obligations of the landlord to supply services and amenities to the tenant and are often as important as the possession of the land'.[25]

Tensions between these two interpretations have arisen in case law and there has been some recognition in domestic law that the application of the 'proprietary perspective' to residential dwellings restrains the law by interpreting it narrowly and does not produce equitable results in line with current expectations of the parties. As a consequence there is a growing tendency to apply ordinary contractual principles to letting agreements,[26] however domestic law is not as progressive as in the USA or other EU countries in this respect (but see below). In contrast to the domestic position, in the USA case law has moved landlord and tenant law to a situation based on contractual principles where tenants do not simply purchase a right to live in property but also purchase shelter and a package of goods and services. This package as Judge Skelly Wright in *Javins v First National Realty Corporation* at 1074 states, includes:

> not merely walls and ceilings, but also adequate heat, light and ventilation, serviceable plumbing facilities, secure windows and doors, proper sanitation, and proper maintenance.[27]

The constraints of viewing the lease as a proprietary interest and not as a contract are clear here, however, when considering the conceptual difficulties involved in

---

25 Quinn, T.M. and Phillips, E., 'The law of Landlord–Tenant: A critical evaluation of the past with guidelines for the future', 38 *Fordham L Rev* 225 (1969) p. 228.

26 Stewart, A., *Rethinking Housing Law* (London, Sweet and Maxwell, 1996).

27 Judge Skelly Wright in *Javins v First National Realty Corporation* at 1074 quoted in Bright and Gilbert, *Landlord and Tenant Law: The Nature of Tenancies*, p. 103.

legal interpretations it is evident why there is confusion and a lack of clarity. In addition, as mentioned above, further constraints can be placed upon the relationship by interpretations of rights and responsibilities which are embodied in sentiments of ownership, attachment to property, attitudes and actions and influence the ways in which landlords and tenants interact. Conley and O'Barr[28] describe situations like this where parties introduce their attitudes, values and social networks into legal relationships, often to the exclusion of contractual, economic and property issues, as a 'relational approach to the law' where social rules are more important than legal rules the emphasis is upon motivations and feelings.[29] This contrasts with a 'rule' oriented approach to legislation where legal relationships are viewed in terms of rules and principles regardless of status or social relationships and society is viewed as a network of contractual opportunities rather than personalized social relationships.[30]

Following on from these approaches to legal relationships, Bourdieu's concept of 'Habitus'[31] is particularly relevant and useful when exploring both the cognitive and embodied aspects of landlord/tenant orientations and provides a useful theoretical tool to analyse the ways in which landlords' and tenants' behaviour is manifested towards property and each other. 'Habitus' offers an insightful way to understand social interaction and raises distinctions between and differentiates between 'a sense of one's place and a sense of the other's place'[32] and relates to both a cognitive sense of place as well as its embodiment in behaviour:

> Actors' behaviours will be related to their position *in* the field (in legal terms and also in terms of the sense of their place and those of other actors in the field). Their behaviours will also be related to the resources available to them and their view *of* the field, including their ideological viewpoint and their perception of which issues are worth fighting for, this last being constructed from their position in the field.[33]

It is evident from this description that individual actors are oriented in particular ways which will dispose them to act accordingly to achieve a desired outcome with regard to their previous experiences, the resources they perceive are available to them '*in* the field' they perceive they are in and in the context of prevailing power relations. Following on from this, landlords' behaviour is contingent upon their perceptions of their own 'sense of place' in legal, social and economic terms, and this is likely to be

28 Conley, J.M. and O'Barr, W.M., *Rules versus Relationships – The Ethnography of Legal Discourse* (Chicago and London, The University of Chicago Press, 1990) p. 60.

29 Allen. J, and McDowell, L., *Landlords and Property: Social Relations in the Private Rented Sector* (Cambridge, Cambridge University Press, 1989) p. 46; McCrone, D. and Elliott, B., *Property and Power in a City – The Sociological Significance of Landlordism* (London, The Macmillan Press Ltd, 1989) p. 143.

30 Conley, J.M. and O'Barr, W.M., *Rules versus Relationships – The Ethnography of Legal Discourse* (Chicago and London, The University of Chicago Press, 1990) p. 61.

31 Bourdieu, P., 'Social space and symbolic space' in *Sociological Theory*, 7, 1 (1989) pp. 14–25.

32 Bourdieu, P. and Wacquant, L., *An Invitation to Reflexive Sociology* (Cambridge, Polity Press, 1992).

33 Hillier, J. and Rooksby, E. (eds), *Habitus: A Sense of Place* (Aldershot, Ashgate, 2005) p. 23.

influenced by and dependent upon, for example, emotional attachment to property, the meaning they attach to it, their ability to control it and the interpretations they attach to their rights and tenants' rights.[34] Given the diversity of parties currently in the sector, the prominence of social rights and relationships, and the conceptual difficulties associated with rights and responsibilities it is unsurprising that there is a considerable degree of confusion and misunderstanding amongst each party about their 'sense of place' and this becomes articulated into an internal set of social 'rules' and 'laws' within the landlord/tenant relationship posing significant challenges for effective regulation of the sector.

The Articulation of Conceptual Difficulties – Landlords' and Tenants' Attitudes to Tenancy Relationships

To highlight how conceptual difficulties are articulated, extracts from qualitative research with landlords and tenants are presented here. The study from which these extracts are taken explored landlords and tenants attitudes to tenancy relationships. The extracts presented here are intended to be illustrative examples, and not generalized accounts, of the varied expressions and articulations of a cognitive 'sense of place' as well as providing indications of the ways in which these attitudes are likely to become manifest in behaviour towards each other. The following extracts highlight some of the ways in which landlords and tenants are oriented towards letting arrangements. The data shows the complex nature of attitudes and expectations and shows the difficulties associated with regulating the sector given the importance of social exchange.

During the landlord/tenant relationship, the disparities between the respective parties' expectations and attitudes are intensified as the conceptual difficulties associated with the 'hybrid nature' of relationships[35] becomes apparent in the mindset and actions of the parties, as relationships are interpreted differently by the respective parties. Theories of social exchange can be drawn upon to highlight conceptual difficulties and the resulting internal structures of landlord/tenant relationships,[36] when they are not based principally upon economic transactions or strict legalities, an exact price for benefits are not stated and are incalculable, as social exchange entails unspecified obligations:

> one person does another a favor, and while there is a general expectation of some future return, its exact nature is definitely *not* stipulated in advance … the nature of the return cannot be bargained about but must be left to the discretion of the one who makes it.[37]

---

34 Allen and McDowell, *Landlords and Property – Social Relations in the Private Rented Sector*; Lister, D., 'Controlling letting arrangements? Landlords and surveillance in the private rented sector', *Surveillance and Society*, 2, 4 (2005) pp. 513–28.

35 Bright and Gilbert, p. 69.

36 Blau, P., *Exchange and Power in Social Life* (London, John Wiley and Sons Inc, 1964); Molm, L.D., *Coercive Power in Social Exchange* (Cambridge, Cambridge University Press, 1997).

37 Blau, p. 94, emphasis in original.

The nature of reciprocity in social exchange takes more or less for granted the ongoing nature of the relationship and the ability of the parties to trust each other to continually fulfil unspecified obligations. This type of reciprocal arrangement deviates from that which is typically contracted for in a letting agreement and where consideration is received and the discrete nature of each exchange is assumed, as obligations are specified in writing. Therefore, the nature of exchange here is incompatible with both proprietary and contractual perspectives as discussed above. These conceptual difficulties are inevitably revealed in the behaviour of the parties and the internal structures of relationships as discussed in detail below.

The data from this study indicates that the attitudes expressed by landlords and tenants towards relationships coincided in only one aspect, that is, each party expected the other to meet their obligations and 'keep their word' when they made promises. However, there was little evidence of shared agreement between the parties about the precise nature of the obligations which were perceived to be part of the contractual bargain, irrespective of whether they were specified in a letting agreement or not. A fundamental disagreement existed between the parties about who was initially obliged to whom, as each party considered that the other party had a responsibility to perform obligations and services before they returned the 'favour'. These attitudes indicate that expectations are not derived from contractual agreements or strict legal arrangements, instead the nature of the bargain is unspecified in advance, and its fulfilment is at the parties' discretion. The complex nature of tenancy relationships becomes evident here as misunderstandings and a mismatch of expectations arise early on in the relationship.

A number of landlords expressed views that tenants should recognize, but often do not, that they have obligations to perform in return for the services that landlords provide, notwithstanding that these services are often basic statutory requirements, for example annual gas safety inspections. One landlord stressed the importance of this approach where young people were left in 'quiet enjoyment' of the property provided they performed their obligations:

> I would like them to move in and the place is theirs for the time they're here and providing they look after it, because I've got responsibilities as well. I've got to be on the ball and make sure, you know, they've got to have smoke alarms fitted and they've got to have the gas fires and boilers serviced once a year, which is fine, I accept all that, but you expect your rent to be paid on time as well (Landlord 11, male).

This view reflects the tensions within the 'hybrid nature' of tenancy relationships with the focus upon mutual obligations during the ongoing relationship. This view contrasts with those expressed by the majority of young people who stressed their role as consumers and expected that landlords would 'take some care and some pride in the house' and provide services throughout the course of the tenancy, including proper maintenance and attention to the property, to which tenants felt entitled by virtue of paying rent. In addition, consumer perspectives support this principle suggesting that tenants' obligations to pay rent and look after the property are, in fact, dependent upon the landlords' compliance with obligations as regards maintenance and repairs.[38]

38 Bright and Gilbert, p. 106.

This perspective was adopted by some young people in expectation of a reciprocal relationship where basic services are provided, engendered by economic exchange:

> I'd much rather feel that it wasn't just a money making exercise and that I wasn't just seen as someone with a bag of money round my neck. I think the ideal landlord would be offering somewhere nice to live as well as some way for them to make a quick pound [and] who's prepared to do the things that you would expect someone who you're paying that much money to. You know, in a way we do them a favour by being here so, they should do us some favours back (Tenant 4, 21-year-old working male).

These two contrasting perspectives highlight the problematic nature of the tenancy relationship in that the basis of economic transactions rest on incomplete contractual arrangements where the precise nature of the services to be performed, the time-scales involved and remedies available for breach of contract are not specified or detailed and do not cover all possible contingencies.

However, although the tenancy relationship involves economic exchange in relation to a commodity – property – it also involves supplying services in relation to the commodity. This type of economic transaction involving the supply of services is, as discussed above, closer to social exchange than economic exchange[39] and rests on the idea that each party provides the other with 'favours' which it is assumed will be returned at some future date. Therefore, in as much as tenancy relationships are based upon social relations, social expectations about the reciprocal nature of these relationships arise. The concept of reciprocity assumes that relationships are entered into voluntarily and that there is a balance between the parties, however, it is evident in these examples that cognitive and embodied imbalances of power exists between the parties. Landlords do not reciprocate for benefits or favours received, as they do not generally consider payment of rent to be a benefit, instead it is a legitimate legal expectation – consideration – which is part of the contractual bargain.

Furthermore, property differs from other commodities as it is not removed from the emotional or sentimental realms attached to it by either party. Although tenants have possession of property, landlords retain ownership and control which become manifest in relation to the supply of services provided and the interpretations of each parties' role in relationships.[40] The tenancy relationship therefore constitutes a distinct form of contractual arrangement which differs from a formal business arrangement. The exact details of the bargain are not stipulated in advance and the nature of social exchange between the parties is based upon trust to discharge obligations. However, a number of young people expressed the view that rather than leaving the observance of rights and obligations to chance or luck, a formal and professional relationship based upon mutually beneficial exchanges and reciprocity would make relations more effective and efficient. Ideally, in order to clarify expectations and achieve reciprocity the relationship should be treated as:

---

39 Blau, p. 93.

40 Lister, D., 'Controlling letting arrangements? Landlords and surveillance in the private rented sector', pp. 513–28; Lister, D., 'Unlawful or just awful? Young people's experiences of living in the private rented sector in England', pp. 141–55.

> ... a normal business and industry where you get a lot more feedback rather than just doing jobs because they've gone wrong. More of a preventative thing and come round and make sure everything is OK and ask if there's anything needs doing and anything that [we] might potentially think needs doing (Tenant 1, male, 24-year-old student).

However, conducting the relationship as a 'normal business' implies equality between the parties but it does not imply a pro-active approach on the part of the landlord to seek out obligations to perform. In addition, the subjective nature of the property relationship removes it from the neutral realms of a strictly business framework. The attitudes described here are characterized by the lack of significance of contractual control which is replaced by the subjective and personal control of landlords based upon specific rights of ownership. This was evident to the extent that almost every landlord in the study expressed emotional aspects of ownership[41] through their views that they expected tenants to treat the property 'with a bit of respect' and

> ... to be sensible enough and old enough to appreciate that it's somebody else's house and what you wouldn't do in your own, you're not expected to do in somebody else's (Landlord 4, female).

The view expressed here highlights the conflict between the legal rights of tenants to exclusive possession of property and the landlord's continuing control of the property, representing the 'social form of the residential property relation'.[42] Although legally the tenant has exclusive possession of the property, and therefore has use rights over it, landlords' rights of ownership provide an important unilateral dimension of control. As discussed above, the social context of tenancy relationships distinguishes them from formal contractual arrangements and gives rise to further complications of an emotional nature, removing tenancy relationships from the realms of a conventional consumer relationship as property is often perceived, by landlords, as being simply on loan to tenants. Landlords' implicit expectation that tenants will 'respect' the property does not form part of the bargain between the parties but instead is part of the landlords' 'psychological contract'[43] with the tenant and plays a significant role in shaping relationships.

From the views expressed here, the overall quality of social relationships with landlords was particularly important in order to establish reciprocity and security in the tenancy relationship. A number of tenants stated that landlords' informal involvement with them and property management, akin to a 'an ideology of service'[44] would indicate a degree of interest in, and commitment to the relationship, as opposed to merely viewing tenants as a source of income. However, tenants acknowledged that they were not legally entitled to 'polite' or courteous relationships with landlords, nor were they entitled to them via consumer principles or economic exchange,

41 Hollowell, P. (ed.), *Property and Social Relations* (London, Heinemann Educational Books Ltd, 1982) p. 12.

42 Allen and McDowell, p. 46.

43 Dale, M., *Successful Recruitment and Selection – A Practical Guide for Managers* (London, Kogan Page Limited, 1995) p. 97.

44 McCrone and Elliott, p. 143.

although, nevertheless, they did 'expect' to be able 'to talk to landlords' and to be treated in an agreeable manner and not to be 'afraid' of them. The dominant attitude expressed by tenants was for a relationship where they were able to exercise some choice and control over their environment and therefore, it was important that the landlord was 'OK' and that the relationship was conducted on a 'friendly', 'honest' and 'open' basis. The views of a full-time student highlight that reciprocity is the key to expectations about relationships:

> I'd want someone that I, well not necessarily liked maybe but, you know, *could* like. I certainly think it's important to have a rapport or fairly good relationship with your landlord/landlady because ultimately it works both ways, doesn't it, and then you know, if you don't like them you're not going to ring them up for things and vice versa (Tenant 9, male, 20-year-old student).

The data highlights the differing and often complex and conflicting attitudes expressed by the parties towards tenancy relationships. The disparities between the parties differing perspectives reflect conceptual differences and indicate the problems associated with the indistinct unspecified nature of social expectations which are often ill matched from the outset of tenancy relationships. The attitudes expressed provide an indication of each parties 'sense of place' and a reference point for expectations and experiences during the course of the tenancy and they influence the nature of interactions during this period. However the unspecified nature of social reciprocation and the reliance upon trust causes additional problems, disappointment and dissatisfaction. Of overriding importance for both parties is a friendly respectful reciprocal relationship and the efficient provision of basic services which contribute towards the maintenance of the ongoing relationship.

Delivering Better Control and Regulation?

At the time of writing this chapter, the Law Commission, after a long consultation period, published their long awaited paper outlining plans for reform and better regulation in both the PRS and the social rented sector. At the outset of the process of reform which began over five years ago, the aims of the Law Commission were to modernize and simplify the law relating to renting homes and to introduce more of a consumer perspective into residential renting.[45] Martin Partington, Law Commissioner for England and Wales, stated:

> Our recommendations deliver better regulation … They also make clear the rights and responsibilities of landlords and renters. This is an historic opportunity to deliver a modern legal framework for renting homes.[46]

---

45 The Law Commission, *Renting Homes 1: Status and Security* (London, The Law Commission, 2002).

46 The Law Commission (website accessed 5 May 2006) *Press Release – A clean-sheet new start for renting homes,* www.lawcom.gov.uk/rentinghomes.htm (London, The Law Commission).

The final report published in May 2006 highlighted 'a clean-sheet new start for renting homes' and recommended a new legal regime built on a consumer approach to the law under which everyone renting a home would have access to a definitive written agreement clearly setting out their rights and obligations. The key feature in relation to the PRS is the introduction of a new form of regulation through the compulsory use of written 'occupation contracts' approved by the Government in the form of a 'model contract' and designed to make private renting 'easier, cheaper and more flexible' by 'setting out the rights and obligations of both landlords and occupiers'. These recommendations, unlike any other housing law reform process, have been arrived at after an extensive period of research and consultation with landlords, tenants, pressure groups, academics, practitioners and policy makers:

> The recommendations result from one of the largest consultation exercises ever undertaken by the Law Commission: over 70 public events were addressed and over 400 written responses received to the two consultation papers.[47]

Informing legislative reforms through a consultation process is a crucial step towards listening to and responding to the ways in which parties behave in the sector as well as framing, shaping and enacting legislation which takes into account the issues as experienced by the parties rather then those as perceived by policy makers and legislators which may be far removed from the real issues. But, to what extent can law and policy be expected to take into account the ways in which people are oriented in the sector and the ways they behave socially? There is a concentrated move in the social sciences and policy oriented research towards evidence based policy initiatives and a greater appreciation of the role of empirical research and consultation in relation to shaping and implementing legislation as well as responding to the information and educational needs of parties when laws are changed. This forward looking approach adopted by the Law Commission which takes into account the diversity of the sector and acknowledges the complexities of the relationship is a dramatic departure from previous reform processes.

The proposals of the Law Commission to introduce compulsory written model contracts for occupation strikes at the heart of the relationship by setting out clear responsibilities and rights. This response appears to balance the interests of both parties by tightening up the landlord's responsibilities and placing the onus upon them to supply a written occupation contract. On the face of it, but without any clear details of what a model occupation contract would look like, how it would be made available or how it would be enforced in the event of non-compliance, it would seem that this approach could aid the smooth running of relationships and if easily enforceable there is little excuse for non-use and non compliance. However, in order to maintain the number of landlords letting property in the PRS, this proposal is offset by reduced security of tenure for tenants with the initial six months security of tenure dispensed with and possession gained at any point during the tenancy. With reduced security of tenure, ease of enforcement is likely to be irrelevant in the event of non-compliance as tenants are unlikely to complain for fear of notice

47 Ibid.

to quit. Therefore, are these reforms likely to improve matters or are sentiments of ownership, control and a 'sense of place' still likely to dominate relationships? Is it feasible to accept that emotional and social aspects of landlord/tenant relationships have an ingrained regulatory resistance and cannot be easily shaped or influenced by regulatory controls and that these aspects are not going to change? And if so, what is the best regulatory response in the sector given that insecurity of tenure is an enduring feature of relationships? Only time will tell whether public consultation exercises and both the content and use of standard 'occupation contracts' as well as the way in which they are implemented will make a difference in the worst case scenarios of bad landlordism.

Conclusion

This chapter has highlighted how difficult the PRS is to regulate given its current diversity in stock conditions and the parties entering the sector. Historically there has been resistance to effective regulation of the sector under both strict and more lenient regulatory and security of tenure regimes as well as challenges posed by the law for lay people and practitioners in understanding and interpreting it. Conceptual and cognitive difficulties are in evidence amongst contracting parties' opinions as highlighted in the empirical research discussed here, where favours, unspecified obligations, trust, and the unwritten expectation of future rewards are often important. These social expectations exist alongside problematic domestic legal interpretations about the precise nature and content of the relationship and rights and responsibilities which have resisted a consumer perspective but which more recently are being interpreted more in line with consumer and contractual principles. Therefore, it is no surprise as highlighted by Hollowell in the introduction to this chapter that relationships between landlord and tenant are subject to social interpretations and rest upon principles of social exchange and are not always or necessarily based upon strict legal criteria. Both landlords and tenants 'sense of one's place and a sense of the other's place' permeate the ways in which relationships are conducted and a range of factors, such as attitudes and assumptions need to be considered in order to be able to develop better and more appropriate regulation. In terms of controlling letting arrangements, social control mechanisms often represent a more viable method of control than strict legal regulatory controls.

The public consultation exercises carried out by the Law Commission in their reform process are a major step forward as they represent a regulatory renaissance with a more responsive and informed approach to the *actual* (rather than *assumed*) behaviour, needs and challenges associated with the ways in which parties operate in the sector. By taking into consideration individual agency, instrumentalism and the real complexities involved in relationships between landlords and tenants, more effective regulation is likely, however, to achieve effective regulatory control which balances the interests of both parties there needs to be recognition that some aspects of the social dimension of relationships are impermeable and cannot easily be eroded by successive policy and legislative regimes. The ways in which legislation is enacted, implemented and communicated to those affected by it is crucial for successful reform. Time will tell how the Law Commission reforms are implemented and communicated and ultimately how well they work in changing the nature of expectations, social exchange and standards in the sector and if they bring about the desired outcome of more effective control of letting arrangements.

Chapter 6

Regulating the Market

David Ormandy and Martin Davis

Introduction: A Decline Halted?

Two of the most common platitudes relating to the state of housing in England are first, that the private rented sector, in terms of its percentage of the market, is in continual and irreversible decline, and second, that the condition of this sector is generally poor.

Until 1989, the truth of the first 'platitude' was beyond argument. Whereas in 1914 80 per cent of dwellings in England were privately rented, by 1951 this had declined to 45 per cent and by 1961 to 25 per cent. By 1989 (the low point) only 9.1 per cent of dwellings were privately rented.[1] The key factors in this decline were usually seen to be the equally inexorable growth of owner occupation (10 per cent of the market in 1914, 65.2 per cent in 1989), the linked sale of much formerly private rented accommodation by landlords as rent controls inhibited investment return, and the growth of a large local authority housing sector catering for many who would formerly have rented privately (1 per cent of the market in 1914, 22.8 per cent in 1985). By 1977 a government housing policy document could state:[2] 'Much of this reduction in the numbers of private rented houses need not give cause for concern – many former tenants – those who might once have become private tenants – have found more suitable long-term accommodation as home owners, or public sector tenants. This process will continue, as the other sectors grow…'

However, as has been widely discussed, both in other chapters in this book, and elsewhere, the decline of the private rented sector has at least been halted, and to some extent reversed since 1989.[3] Numerous influences have underpinned this partial revival but of key significance have been the changes first implemented from

1 Marsh, A. and Mullins, D. (eds), *Housing and Public Policy, Citizenship, Choice and Control* (Buckingham, Open University Press, 1998) p. 102 (Table 5.1).

2 DoE (Department of the Environment) 1977 Housing Policy: A Consultative Document, Cmnd 6851 (London, HMSO) paragraph 8.10.

3 See, for example, Marsh, A. and Mullins, D. (eds), *Housing and Public Policy* (Buckingham, Open University Press, 1998) pp. 112–13; Lowe, S. and Hughes, D. (eds), *The Private Rented Section in a New Century* (Bristol, The Policy Press, 2002); Crook, A.D.H. and Kemp, P. A., 'The Revival of Private Rented Housing in Britain', *Housing Studies* Vol. 11 (1996) pp. 51–68.

15 January 1989[4] which removed anything other than short term residential security from the majority of private sector tenants and replaced 'fair rent' ceilings with a market driven rental system. The tone of the 1987 government White Paper which underpinned the subsequent legislative change could hardly be more different than that of its predecessor 10 yeas before.[5] At paragraph 1.8 the White Paper states, "…the rapid decline of the private rented sector has not been caused by the attraction of owner occupation alone. Rent controls have prevented property owners from getting an adequate return on their investment. People who might have been prepared to grant a temporary letting have also been deterred by laws on security of tenure which make it impossible to regain possession of their property when necessary … yet … private renting offers a good option for people who need mobility … [and] can offer greater flexibility and responsiveness to market demand."

By 2000 belief in the necessity of a 'vital' private rented sector had taken hold across the political spectrum. The Labour government Housing Green Paper of that year[6] stated at paragraph 5.1: 'A healthy private rented sector provides additional housing choices for people who do not want to, or are not ready to buy their own homes. It is a particularly important resource for younger households' and at 5.7 'our objective is to secure a larger, better-quality, better managed private sector'.

Despite such consistent 'official' encouragement of the private rented sector over nearly 20 years, the consequent growth in size and significance of the sector has been relatively modest, even if the decline has been halted. As stated above, the 'low water mark' of 1989 saw only 9.1 per cent of dwellings being privately rented. By 1997 this percentage had slowly increased to 10.2 per cent, since when it has continued to 'hover' around the 10 per cent mark.[7] It may well be that a number of more firmly embedded 'niche' markets, such as students and young 'urban professionals' have steadily replaced more traditional private sector renters during this period[8] and that the long term 'structural' decline has been halted.

Regulating Disrepair: Where Tenants Fear to Tread?

There is more evidence to support the second platitude: that the state of the English private rented housing stock is generally poor. The 1996 English House Condition Survey[9] estimated that approximately 58 per cent of households in the private rented

---

4 Under the provisions in the Housing Act 1988 Part I which replaced Rent Act 'Secure' and 'Regulated' tenancies with 'Assured' and 'Assured shorthold' tenancies.

5 DoE (Department of the Environment), *Housing: The Government Proposals*, Cm 214 (London, HMSO, 1987).

6 DETR (Department of the Environment, Transport and the Regions) *Quality and Choice: A Decent Home for All. The Housing Green Paper* (London, HMSO, 2000).

7 Lowe, S., *Housing Policy Analysis: British Housing in Cultural and Comparative Context* (Houndmills, Palgrave/Macmillan, 2004).

8 See, for example, Lowe, *Housing Policy Analysis: British Housing in Cultural and Comparative Context*, pp. 224–9.

9 DETR (Department of the Environment, Transport and the Regions), *English House Conditions Survey 1996* (London, The Stationery Office, 1998).

sector lived in poor housing conditions by modern standards (so-called 'non-decent homes') the figure was 44 per cent for households overall. The criteria that a decent home[10] is required to meet are that it:

- Meets the current statutory minimum standard for housing;
- Is in a reasonable state of repair;
- Has reasonable modern facilities and services;
- Provides a reasonable degree of thermal comfort.

The 2001 EHCS shows that the private rented sector remains in a poorer condition than the rest of the total English housing stock, with 49 per cent being found non-decent (33 per cent for the total stock), and this sector is more likely to fail the pre-2006 minimum standard for housing (10 per cent).

Of course, as much of the rest of this book suggests, the private rented sector market is an increasingly heterogeneous one and this is particularly marked in relation to housing standards. Standards, as might be expected, are particularly poor in relation to pre-1919 properties (most typically old terraced houses). In the 2001 EHCS approximately 10 per cent of all pre-1919 properties was seen to be unfit and over 91 per cent in need of repairs. By comparison only 1 per cent of post-1964 properties was classified as unfit and only 50 per cent required repairs.

The common perception is that the private rented sector is characterized, disproportionately, by such older properties. The reality is that the market is as segmented in relation to property type, as it is in relation to tenant and landlord 'type'. The deregulation of this sector since the Housing Act 1988 Part I has, in part, resulted in a more 'fluid' pattern of tenure – with a more rapid turnover of properties. In general, properties moving into the sector in the 1990s, or (increasingly) being specifically constructed for this purpose, were in a better state of repair than those already in it. The underlying problem, however, is that the problems of ageing properties and poor maintenance management by landlords tend to be mutually reinforcing. Disrepair is particularly associated with Houses in Multiple Occupation (HMOs), bedsits and hostels, in which (according to the 2001 EHCS) 2.6 million people lived (1.3 million households) one third of these in London, and over half in urban areas. A moment's reflection indicates that here not only is there a concentration of old properties and often 'absentee' or unresponsive landlords but also low income transient and insecure tenants.

There is little in the 1987 White Paper,[11] which (of course) provides the 'template' for the current tenure regime in the private rented sector, about improving standards. It appears to be assumed that deregulation alone will drive standards up – 'better' properties would command higher rents and this would encourage landlords to invest accordingly. In reality it appears that rents do not vary much with conditions.[12] This

10 ODPM (Office of the Deputy Prime Minister), *A Decent Home: The Definition and Guidance for Implementation* (London, ODPM, 2004).

11 DoE, *Housing: The Government Proposals*, 1987.

12 Crook, A.D.H., 'Housing Conditions in the Private Rented Sector within a Market Framework', in Lowe S. and Hughes, D. (eds), *The Private Rented Sector in a New Century: Revival or False Dawn?* (Bristol, The Policy Press, 2002).

might, at first, seem surprising but it must be remembered that the market is a highly mobile and transient one comprising many who will take whatever is on offer, are unable to exercise meaningful choice or are predominantly influenced by location rather than price.

However, it is equally true that the worst stock (typically in HMOs or hostels) is invariably occupied by those with least resources and unable to access other types of housing. The 2000 Housing Green Paper[13] recognized that although this sector had a key role to play in the provision of housing, 'the quality of our private rented stock and its management is not always what it should be', and that 'too many privately rented homes are in poor condition, and we need to make sure that the worst landlords also improve their housing or get out of the business altogether'.

Traditionally legal responses to substandard private rented housing have centred on one of three approaches:

- Civil action by the tenants themselves, via such routes as a claim for damages, an 'injunction', specific performance, or even 'self help' measures, for example withholding rent to pay for repairs;[14]
- Private prosecutions using section 99 of the Public Health Act 1936 by tenants concerning dwellings that were statutory nuisances;[15]
- Intervention by the local authority using a range of duties and powers under the Public Health and Housing Acts concerning property seen to be a statutory nuisance, unfit[16] or in need of substantial repair, or in the pursuit of some form of area action such as 'clearance'. Local authorities also have additional powers to deal with unsatisfactory conditions in HMOs such as poor management, lack of amenities, and inadequate fire safety measures.

Actions by tenants

Civil actions by tenants are crucially affected by the terms of the contractual agreement between the tenant and the landlord.[17] Prior to 1890 there was little, if any, legislative interference with a landlord's 'freedom of contract' and (unsurprisingly) tenancy agreements were drafted in the landlords favour, minimizing the latter's responsibility for the condition and on-going maintenance of the property rented. Eventually, Parliament decided that it needed to interfere in the contractual arrangements between landlords and tenants.The Housing of the Working Classes

---

13 DETR, *Quality and Choice: A Decent Home for All*, para 5.3.

14 Legislation such as s4 of the Defective Premises Act 1972 and s11 of the Landlord and Tenant Act 1985 underpins a tenant's contractual and other private law rights. Cases such as *Lee Parker* v *Izzel* [1971] 1 WLR 1688 confirms (with limitations) a tenant's right to exercise 'self-help'.

15 See now the Environmental Protection Act 1990, ss79–82.

16 'Unfitness' and allied issues were, until 6 April 2006, dealt with under a variety of provisions under the Housing Act 1985 and associated codes and circulars. The new provisions are dealt with below and form the centre of this chapter.

17 On this, see: *Landlord and Tenant: Responsibility for State and Condition of Property* (1996) Law Com No. 238.

Act 1890 introduced a requirement that at the commencement of a letting the dwelling should be '*in all respects reasonably fit for human habitation*'.[18] This had several weaknesses, many of which were dealt with over the years. But one serious weakness, one which makes the obligation almost pointless, remains – that it only applied to dwellings let at a low rent.[19] This provision remains in the Landlord and Tenant Act 1985,[20] but the rent levels, of £50 per annum outside London and £85 per annum in London, ensure it is useless.[21]

In 1961, Parliament introduced another implied covenant.[22] This imposed an obligation on landlords of lettings for a term of less than seven years, that they must:

(a) keep in repair the structure and exterior (including drains etc); and
(b) keep in repair and proper working order installations for:
    i) the supply of water, gas and electricity, and for sanitation; and
    ii) space and water heating.

This provision was re-enacted in 1985[23] and then extended in 1988[24] for dwellings contained in larger buildings (i.e., flats and maisonettes) to cover installations serving the dwelling but outside its curtilage.

A major flaw of the implied covenants was highlighted by the case of *Quick v. Taff-Ely BC*[25] when the Court of Appeal held that, as the cause of the problem, severe condensation dampness, was inherent, resulting from design deficiencies in the property, no state of 'disrepair' existed. 'Disrepair' implied that the cause was some deterioration/damage to the existing fabric of a building, not merely that the building fell short of modern design standards. As there was no disrepair, there was no breach of the general repairing covenant.

An alternative line of action taken by tenants (more often by public sector tenants[26]) was under the statutory nuisance provisions of the Public Health Act 1936.[27] Such actions were a private prosecution and, as the majority of actions were

---

18 Housing of the Working Classes Act 1890, s75.

19 Less than £20 per annum in London – based on the rate assessment made under the Poor Rate Assessment and Collection Act 1869, s3.

20 Landlord and Tenant Act 1985, s8, the Standard of Fitness being repeated at s10.

21 For a review of this obligation see *Legislation to Secure Fitness for Human Habitation of Leasehold Dwelling-Houses* JPL (1986) pp. 164–73.

22 Housing Act 1961, s32.

23 Landlord and Tenant Act 1985, s11

24 Housing Act 1988, s116, inserting s11(1A), (1B) and (3A).

25 [1986] QB 809. The Court of Appeal did note that where there *was* disrepair (for example in a 'condensation' case by perishing of plaster, or the rotting of wooden window frames) amelioration of the disrepair could involve improvements to the property (for example by installing UPVC windows).

26 Council tenants of local authorities lacking the protection of the local authority environmental health department – see *R v Cardiff City Council, ex parte Cross* (1982) 1 HLR 54.

27 Public Health Act 1936, s99, subsequently Environmental Protection Act 1990, Part III.

being taken against local authorities, considerable pressure built up to prevent or at least limit these actions.[28]

The provision proved quite effective, and filled gaps in the repairing obligation by covering inherent defects including those excluded by the *Quick* case. It also appeared to cover dangerous design features that could lead to physical injury (matters not covered by the Fitness Standard – on which see below) as it dealt with matters likely to be 'prejudicial to health' – defined as '*injurious, or likely to cause injury, to health*'.[29] The term 'health' had usually been interpreted by public health 'professionals' as including physical injury. However, the courts held that the concept was limited to 'disease' and related matters and did not extend to the risk of physical injury.[30] This decision meant that inherent features such as very steep stairs, low window sills, and low guarding to balconies, although potentially dangerous, were outside any legal controls.

The role of local authorities and standards in the private rented sector

Even before the changes to the private sector 'security' regime in the Housing Act 1988 Part I, it was often the case that local authority intervention (through their environmental health officers) was likely to be more effective to secure property improvement for a tenant than the piecemeal and sometimes time consuming use of the civil law (although 'self help' could often be effective in practice). Civil actions and private prosecutions have also been affected by changes to the Legal Aid regime and to the role and practice of expert witnesses.[31]

Today, relatively few private sector tenants remain in properties long enough to be credibly willing or able to 'mount' a private action even if they find lawyers willing or able to represent them. Moreover, even should they be so disposed, the lack of security of tenure means that they may feel disinclined to 'rock the boat' by challenging their landlord. It is, therefore, unsurprising that the 2000 Green Paper saw an improved 'public' regulatory regime as the way forward for improving

---

28 See *The Use of Section 82 of the Environmental Protection Act 1990 Against Local Authorities and Housing Associations* (HMSO, 1996).

29 Environmental Protection Act 1990, s79(7).

30 *R v Bristol City Council, ex parte Everett* [1999] 2 All ER 193, [1999] 1 WLR 1140. The Court of Appeal was particularly influenced by the fact that the report presented to Parliament in support of the Bill which became the 1936 Public Health Act had explained that the Bill was confined to 'provisions of a strictly public health character, relating to the prevention and treatment of disease' (1936) (Cmnd 5059).

31 See *Access to Justice* (July 1996), the so-called 'Woolf' report after its author Lord Woolf, and the subsequent changes to civil procedure in the Civil Procedure Rules 1998. The core aim of 'Woolf' was to 'streamline' court procedure, above all by giving judges greater power to manage/control the way cases developed through the courts. The Civil Procedure Rules give effect to this. As regards the use of experts, the rules (last amended March 2006) give the judge a power to direct that expert evidence may be given by one expert only (Rule 35.7(1)), a *de facto* joint expert for the use of the court, rather than, *per se*, for the use of either of the parties. This embodies the general principle in Rule 35.1 that it is the primary duty of the expert to help the court.

housing standards in this sector. Local authorities might not be willing to 'rush in' where tenants would be fearful of going but their intervention at least carried some promise of being effective. The question then arose as to what changes were needed to local authority powers to make control of standards by them more effective.

Local Authorities' Powers and Duties to Deal with Unsatisfactory Dwellings

As early as the 1860s Parliament was persuaded that the relationship between landlord and tenant was imbalanced and that there was a need for some form of state intervention to protect the health and safety of tenants. This acceptance of an interference in property rights followed considerable pressure from various sources including the report on the Sanitary Conditions of the Labouring Classes.[32] This pressure may not have been from pure altruistic reasons, but may have been influenced by fear and, as industry was labour-intensive, the need for a healthy labour force – fear of diseases spreading from the overcrowded slums occupied by the labouring population, and the finding that the poor, the 'labouring population', died younger.[33]

Reacting to this pressure, Parliament placed duties on the newly formed local authorities to identify and deal with dwellings that were 'in a Condition or State dangerous to Health so as to be unfit for Human Habitation'.[34] Where they identified such dwellings, authorities were empowered to require repairs or closure, and where there were areas of such housing to require demolition. This same principle continues today, and although the criteria to trigger or justify intervention and the enforcement regime are inextricably linked, they have to some extent developed separately.

Criteria for Intervention Prior to the Housing Act 2004

Originally, in the 1860s, there was no statutory definition of the term 'unfit for human habitation', and interpretation was by reference to local building codes and decisions of the higher courts.[35]

It was not until 1919, that an 'official' definition of fitness for human habitation was proposed (by the Ministry of Health[36]). This was based firmly on the 'Sanitary Idea' of the previous century and recommended that a house should be regarded as unfit if it was not: (i) free from serious dampness; (ii) satisfactorily lighted and ventilated; (iii) properly drained and provided with adequate sanitary conveniences

---

32 Report to the Home Secretary from the Poor-Law Commissioners, on an inquiry into the *Sanitary Condition of the Labouring Classes in Great Britain.* Presented to both Houses of Parliament in July 1842.

33 Finer, S.E., *The Life and Times of Sir Edwin Chadwick* (London, Methuen, 1952) p. 154.

34 Artisans and Labourers Dwelling Act 1868.

35 See, for example, *Jones v Green* [1925] 1 KB 659, *Wilson v Finch Hatton* (1877) 2 ExD 336 and *Chester v Powell* (1885) 52 LT (NS) 722.

36 *Manual of Unfit Houses and Unhealthy Areas* (Ministry of Health, 1919). See also *Rural Housing Manual* (Ministry of Health, 1938).

and with a sink and suitable arrangements for the disposal of waste water; (iv) in good general repair; and if it did not have: (v) a satisfactory water supply; (vi) adequate washing accommodation; (vii) adequate facilities for preparing and cooking food; and (viii) a well-ventilated store.

In 1946, an up-dated and extended definition was proposed by the government's Central Housing Advisory Committee. However, it was not until 1954 that the first statutory definition was introduced.[37]

This 1954 definition of Fitness (re-enacted in 1957[38]) was more limited and weaker than those previously proposed. It gave a list of only eight requirements, and a dwelling was deemed unfit if in the opinion of the local authority it was so far defective in one or more of those requirements as to be not reasonably suitable for occupation. The requirements covered: (a) the state of repair; (b) stability; (c) freedom from damp; (d) natural lighting; (e) ventilation; (f) water supply; (g) drainage and sanitary conveniences; and (h) facilities for storage, preparation and cooking of food and for the disposal of waste water.

Initially, interpretation of this Standard was left to local authorities and the courts (although no cases were brought to give the higher courts an opportunity to set out their views). Then, in 1967, central government issued guidance on what each of the eight requirements covered,[39] this being the first time that there was both a national statutory definition and national guidance to assist in a consistent interpretation.

There were only two minor changes to the Standard of Fitness in the 36-year period between 1954 and 1990 – the removal of the requirement for food storage facilities, and the addition of a requirement dealing with internal arrangement.[40] The removal of food storage facilities could be put down to a recognition that built-in larders were old-hat and occupiers were more likely to want space for refrigerators. However, this also meant a shift of responsibility. The Standard had placed the responsibility to make provision of food storage on the landlord and by deleting that requirement, responsibility to provide for the safe storage of food shifted to the occupier.

Introducing internal arrangement into the Standard was aimed at inherent (design) faults that could interfere with the 'safe and unhampered passage through the dwelling' or could cause inconvenience.[41] Examples were steep and winding stairs, trip steps (small and awkwardly sited changes of levels) and bedrooms entered only through another room.

The 1985 Housing Act consolidated the various Acts since 1957 and repeated the Standard of Fitness.[42] That same year a Green paper was issued, 'Home Improvement – A New Approach',[43] proposing a major revision of the Fitness Standard, both in

37 Housing Repairs and Rents Act 1954, s9.

38 Housing Act 1957, s4.

39 Ministry of Housing and Local Government Circular No. 69/67. This repeated guidance given in *Our Older Homes: A call for action*, Report of the Standards of Fitness Sub-Committee of the Central Housing Advisory Committee (the Dennington Committee), 1966.

40 Housing Act 1969, s71.

41 Ministry of Housing and Local Government Circular No. 68/69, Appendix para 2.

42 At s604.

43 Cmnd 9513, HMSO, May 1985.

content and approach. In the event, when introduced in 1990,[44] the new Fitness Standard was really an up-dated version of the previous one. However, while it introduced for the first time requirements for the provision of artificial lighting and for heating, facilities for personal washing and hot water, it made no reference to internal arrangement.

Link between state intervention and the obligation of landlords

Until 1985, the Standard of Fitness was both the trigger for intervention by local authorities and one of the implied covenants imposed on landlords.[45] The consolidation process in 1985 started the processes of severing this link. First, the albeit weak (and in practice almost completely useless) implied covenant that a dwelling was to be fit was re-enacted in the Landlord and Tenant Act 1985,[46] and the Standard of Fitness was repeated, word for word, in both the Housing and the Landlord and Tenant Acts.[47]

Severing the link was completed when the new 1990 Fitness Standard was introduced only in the Housing Act; leaving the almost pointless duty on landlords[48] that their dwellings be fit for human habitation referring to the pre-1990 standard.

Deficiencies in the Pre-Housing Act 2004 Approach

The original concept of what was the minimum necessary for a dwelling to be fit for its purpose – that of providing a safe and healthy shelter for the occupiers – could be said to be grounded in the 'Sanitary Idea' movement of the 1850s. However, the phrasing of the Standard when introduced into the legislation (in 1954) was building focussed, the emphasis being on what was necessary to achieve the result. This was equally true of the Guidance when that appeared (in 1967).

Although it was claimed that the approach of the new Fitness Standard introduced in 1990 was to be different, the language of the Standard itself remained building focussed. While the Guidance[49] alluded to the health basis underlying the requirements, the appraisal of the dwelling was primarily an assessment of the structure and amenities of the dwelling – the assessment of defects and deficiencies. The effect of this 'building focus phrasing' encouraged the severity of the condition to be judged in terms of the cost or extent of the remedial work necessary to make the dwelling fit.

44 By the Local Government and Housing Act 1989, Sched 9, para 83.

45 See Housing Act 1957, s6, although the rent levels were set absurdly low to have any real use.

46 At s10.

47 As Housing Act 1985, s604 and Landlord and Tenant Act 1985, s8.

48 Landlord and Tenant Act 1985, s8.

49 Department of the Environment Circular 6/90, Annex A.

A 1993 study into the interpretation and application of the new Fitness Standard[50] suggested some improvements to the Guidance on certain requirements,[51] and identified matters outside the scope of the Fitness Standard that local authorities considered should be covered. These included: internal arrangement (or dangerous design features); thermal insulation; sound insulation; threats to health or safety from the immediate locality; fire precautions and means of escape in case of fire; and threats from Radon. The study also commented that the second stages in the assessment under the Fitness Standard was clearly subjective and a source of confusion.[52] This second stage was, having determined whether the conditions meant that there was a failure of one or more of the requirements, whether the dwelling '... *by reason of that failure, is not reasonably suitable for occupation.*'

In 1995, other research reviewed evidence of the relationship between building design and condition and the health and safety of users.[53] It also checked the extent to which legal controls gave protection to users, primarily the controls applying to all buildings, but also a brief overview of those applicable to existing dwellings.[54] This research also used a simple risk assessment approach to rank threats to health and safety and this showed that many of the most serious potential housing hazards were not covered by the Fitness Standard. This finding complemented that from the 1993 study, citing the omissions as including: threats from excess cold (poor energy efficiency, heating and thermal insulation); fire safety; threats from Radon; and potential fall injuries (internal arrangement or dangerous design features).

Following these two studies, the government commissioned further work with three prime aims.[55] First, to identify and review all the legal provisions controlling minimum standards in existing housing with particular reference to such matters as anomalies, overlaps, and gaps. Second, to investigate options to cover the omitted hazards highlighted by the previous studies. And finally, to investigate whether a risk assessment approach could be devised for housing conditions. The study concluded that such a system could be developed, could cover all potential housing hazards, could grade the severity of hazards, and, by assessing the likelihood of a hazardous

50 Burridge, R., Ormandy, D. and Battersby, S., *Monitoring the New Fitness Standard* (London, HMSO, 1993).

51 For example, although the new Standard had introduced a requirement for the provision of heating, the Guidance (DoE Circular 6/90, Annex A) stated that this could be satisfied by the existence of a dedicated 13-amp electric socket in the living room. The report recommended that there should be means of producing heat.

52 This obvious subjective element led to some inventive terminology among officers. One requirement of the Standard was that there should be a wash-hand basin with a supply of hot and cold water (Housing Act 1985, s604(1)(d), as amended). If this requirement was not met because of a lack of a supply of hot water, officers may not be convinced that it made the dwelling unsuitable for occupation. So, unable to feel justified in declaring it unfit for the purposes of the Housing Act, they would use the term '*technically unfit*'.

53 *Building Regulation and Health* (London, CRC, 1995), *Building Regulations and Safety* (London, CRC, 1995), and *Building Regulation and Security* (unpublished).

54 Although not attributed, this overview was carried out by members of Warwick Law School.

55 *Controlling Minimum Standards in Existing Housing* (Coventry, LRI, 1998).

event and potential health outcomes, would shift the attention from the building to the effects of defects so giving the assessment a human focus.[56] Based on this conclusion, central government issued a Consultation Paper seeking views on proposals and options for change to the Fitness Standard.[57] There was overwhelming support for the concept of a risk assessment approach, and in July 1998, the Minister for Housing announced that work had been commissioned to develop such a system.

Towards the Housing Act 2004 'Regime'

In July 2000, the first version of the Housing Health and Safety Rating System was released.[58] Further work reviewing and refining the evidence base[59] underpinned the second version published in November 2004. The HHSRS identified 29 potential housing hazards that were attributable to a greater or lesser degree to housing conditions (it did not include potential hazards attributable solely to human behaviour).

In November 2004, Parliament passed the Housing Act 2004, Part 1 of which included the replacement of the Fitness Standard and a new enforcement regime. This new regime, together with the introduction of the HHSRS as the prescribed method for assessing housing conditions as the first stage in determining whether enforcement action should be taken, was brought into force in April 2006.[60]

The Enforcement Regime of the Housing Act 2004

The powers and duties associated with the 1954 Fitness Standard were contained primarily in the Housing Act 1936. These included duties on local authorities to deal with unfit houses, which in outline, gave the following options:

- Serve a Repair Notice requiring the works to render the dwelling fit for human habitation. Non-compliance was a criminal offence and the local authority also had the power to carry out the works and recover their costs;

---

56 Ibid., Appendix 1.

57 *Housing Fitness Standard: Consultation Paper* (London, DETR, February 1998) – http://www.odpm.gov.uk/index.asp?id=1152850 (accessed 1 November 2005).

58 *Housing Health and Safety Rating System – The Guidance (Version 1)* (London, DETR, 2000), and *Housing Health and Safety Rating System – Report on Development* (London, DETR, 2000).

59 Carried out by Warwick Law School working with the London School of Hygiene and Tropical Medicine. See: *Statistical Evidence to Support the Housing Health and Safety Rating System, Vols I, II and III* (London, ODPM, 2003). *Housing Health and Safety Rating System – The Guidance (Version 2)* (London, ODPM, 2004), http://www.odpm.gov.uk/index.asp?id=1152820 (accessed 3 November 2005). See also *Project Report – Preparation of Version of the Housing Health and Safety Rating System* (London, ODPM, 2004), http://www.odpm.gov.uk/embedded_object.asp?id=1152842 (accessed 3 November 2005).

60 Housing Health and Safety Rating System (England) Regulations 2005 (SI 2005 No. 3208), and *Housing Health and Safety Rating System: Operating Guidance* (ODPM, 2006) (statutory guidance issued under Housing Act 2004, s9).

- Where the local authority considered that the dwelling could not be made fit at 'reasonable expense', then the authority could serve a Closing Order. Where the rest of a dwelling could be made fit if a part of it was closed (e.g., a basement or an attic) then the Order could be made on the specified part. Such an Order made it a criminal offence for the dwelling to be used for human habitation and the authority was responsible for ensuring that any occupier displaced was properly rehoused.

This regime was re-enacted unchanged in the Housing Act 1957.[61] In 1969 a new option was added, the power to deal with serious disrepair,[62] which was intended to allow authorities to act to prevent a house deteriorating into unfitness. The 1985 Housing Act repeated this extended regime. However, it limited the Closing Order provisions, removing the option to close a part of a dwelling.[63] The enforcement provisions associated with the 1990 Fitness Standard[64] (with some minor changes to reflect the change to the definition) remained much the same as those under the 1936 Act.

In the main, the enforcement toolbox introduced by Part 1 of the 2004 Act is much the same as before.[65] Repair Notices[66] have been replaced with *Improvement Notices*, including a power to suspend all or part of the requirements.[67] Similarly, Closing Orders[68] were replaced with *Prohibition Orders*,[69] and the option of prohibiting the use of a part of a dwelling or building was re-introduced together with a power to suspend the Order.[70] However, two new options were introduced. First, power to take Emergency Action, either to carry out remedial work or to prohibit the use of the dwelling (or a part of it).[71] And second, a *Hazard Awareness Notice*,[72] a formal procedure informing and advising the owner and occupier of a Hazard, but with no sanctions for ignoring the advice.

Houses in Multiple Occupation (HMOs)

Although HMOs make up a relatively minor part of the English housing stock, it is, as already discussed, in these houses that some of the worst conditions are found. Recognizing this, the legislation has always given local authorities additional powers to deal with the special problems found in such houses.

---

61 Part II Housing Act 1957.

62 Housing Act 1969, s72.

63 Housing Act 1985, s266.

64 By the Local Government and Housing Act 1989.

65 This regime followed, in principle at least, that suggested in Appendix 2, *Controlling Minimum Standards in Existing Housing* (Coventry, LRI, 1998).

66 Housing Act 1985, ss189 and 190 (as amended).

67 Housing Act 2004, ss11, 12 and 14.

68 Housing Act 1985, s264 (as amended).

69 Housing Act 2004, ss20 and 21.

70 Housing Act 2004, ss22(4) and 23.

71 Housing Act 2004, ss40 and 43.

72 Housing Act 2004, s28.

Definition

Prior to 1969, an HMO was defined by reference to whether it was 'let in lodgings' or was occupied by more than one family.[73] Following several decisions, in particular one excluding a house occupied by members of the same family but living as two separate households,[74] references to 'lodgings' and 'family' were dropped, and the simpler definition of '... a house which is occupied by persons who do not form a single household' adopted.[75]

There were still problems with this definition. The central difficulty lay in the deceptively simple concept of a 'single household'. Understandably, but mistakenly, many local authorities equated this with the existence (or otherwise) of a joint tenancy – i.e. a joint tenancy was seen as amounting to a single household, but a number of individual tenancies to a number of 'households'. In fact, although the existence of joint (or single) tenancies might have made a finding of a 'single' household more (or less) likely, the concept was suggestive less of the formal tenancy arrangements and more of the realities as to how the property was used and occupied. This was borne out by the case law.[76] There was therefore considerable uncertainty in practice as to where the line should be drawn between 'single' and 'multiple' occupation. However, the definition was retained until the 2004 Act, when a new set of provisions was introduced[77] primarily for licensing purposes (on which see below). The 2004 provisions retain the concept of a 'single household', whilst overlaying it with other key criteria,[78] but provided for the first time some attempt at a statutory definition of the concept, linking it to membership of a 'family'[79] or being a 'live in' employee or carer.[80] Further elaboration on the issue is beyond the scope of this chapter.

Conditions in and management of HMOs

In the Housing Act 1957, local authorities were able to require works at what was then known as houses 'let in lodgings' to make the house suitable for the numbers of individuals and/or households at the house having regard to five of the matters

---

73 See Housing Act 1961, s12.

74 *Holm v RB of Kensington and Chelsea* [1968] 1 QB 646.

75 Housing Act 1969, s58. See also MHLG Circ No. 67/69, para 5.

76 For example *Barnes v Sheffield CC* (1995) 27 HLR 71 and *Rogers v Islington LBC* (2000) 32 HLW 138. In *Rogers* Nourse LJ stated (at p141) 'where a house is occupied by more than one person I do not think that the occupants can be said to form a single household unless there is between them a relationship which provides a particular reason for them living in the same house'.

77 Housing Act 2004, ss254–260.

78 For example the size of the property and numbers of those living in it – three storeys or more and five or more persons, respectively (The Licensing of Houses in Multiple Occupation (Prescribed Descriptions) (England) Order 2006 (SI 2006 No. 371) paragraph 3.

79 Housing Act 2004, s258(3) and (4). 'Family' includes cohabitants, close relatives and stepchildren.

80 The Licensing and Management of Houses in Multiple Occupancy and Other Houses (Miscellaneous Provisions) (England) Regulations 2006, paras 3 and 4.

listed in the Fitness Standard. These matters were: natural lighting, ventilation, water supply, drainage and sanitary conveniences, and facilities for the storage, preparation and cooking of food and for the disposal of waste water. This direct link between fitness for multi-occupation and the Fitness Standard was broken in 1961 and the matters to be considered were extended to include artificial lighting, personal washing facilities, and space heating.[81]

As well as adequate amenities for the numbers of households, three other aspects of multi-occupation were considered important in the 1960s – the management of the common parts and shared rooms, tenant welfare, and fire safety. As it has been estimated that there is around a ten times greater risk of a fire in HMOs, local authorities have, since 1961 been given specific powers to require fire precautions and safe means of escape at any multi-occupied house.[82]

The problem of poor management and exploitation of tenants of HMOs received wide press coverage in the late 1950s and early 1960s. Stories of harassment, illegal evictions and appalling conditions were numerous, and it became apparent that some (maybe a minority) landlords owned large numbers of such houses from which they derived a large income.[83]

As a reaction to these stories, local authorities were given new powers in the Housing Act 1961 to deal with the management generally and with the protection of tenants. First, where they found poor standards of management, authorities could make an Order[84] applying regulations which imposed duties on the manager.[85] Any breach of the regulations was a criminal offence, and authorities also had the power to require works to make good the neglect.[86] Under the 1985 Act, the need to make an Order (termed a 'Management Order') to apply the Management regulations was dropped, and the regulations were made to apply to all HMOs[87] and this remains the case under the 2004 Act.

In 1964, a more draconian procedure was introduced enabling local authorities to make a 'Control Order' and so take possession of a house for up to five years where they considered this was necessary to protect the safety, health and welfare of occupants.[88] Perhaps confusingly, the Control Order provisions of the 1985 Act[89] were replaced in the 2004 Act with provisions enabling local authorities to take control of an HMO using Interim and Final Management Orders.[90]

81 Housing Act 1961, s15, re-enacted as Housing Act 1985, s352.

82 See for example Housing Act 1985, s365.

83 One such landlord was Peter Rachman, whose name became synonymous with gross exploitation, harassment and illegal evictions – see Green, S., *Rachman* (London, Hamlyn, 1981).

84 Housing Act 1961, s12, re-enacted as Housing Act 1985, s370.

85 The Housing (Management of Houses in Multiple Occupation) Regulations 1962.

86 Housing Act 1961, s14, re-enacted as Housing Act 1985, s372.

87 Now The Management of Houses in Multiple Occupation (England) Regulations 2006 (SI 2006 No. 372).

88 Housing Act 1964, ss73–91.

89 Housing Act 1985, ss379–94.

90 Housing Act 2004, Part 4.

Registration and licensing

> The landlord has always been the spoilt child of the law; it is time his rights and duties were re-defined, with special reference to working-class property. The ownership of all such property should be entered in a public register, and there should be a tightening up of enforcement of by-laws.[91]

In 1961, local authorities were given powers to declare a Registration Scheme, requiring the registration of certain types of HMOs.[92] These powers were extended in 1969, enabling local authorities to impose requirements as a condition of registration.[93] (These powers were in addition to the requirement that local authorities keep a register of all HMOs subject to Management Orders.)

In 1997 the Labour Party's manifesto stated that '*We value a revived private rented sector. We will provide protection where most needed: for tenants in houses in multiple occupation. There will be a proper system of licensing by local authorities which will benefit tenants and responsible landlords alike.*' This led to the provisions in the 2004 Act requiring the licensing of certain types of HMOs.[94] (Other provisions were also introduced for declarations to require the selective licensing of other types of residential properties.[95])

A detailed discussion of mandatory and selective licensing is beyond the scope of this chapter, but clearly effective 'policing' of the management of HMOs should lead to better 'health and safety' standards in them and reduce the need for other forms of local authority intervention. Indeed, key potential licence restrictions can include 'conditions requiring … facilities and equipment to be kept in repair and proper working order' and conditions requiring the carrying out of works.[96] However, none of this precludes other forms of Part 1 local authority intervention. A HMO is specified in the legislation as 'residential premises'.[97] Moreover it is specifically stated in the legislation that, presumptively, the removal or reduction of HHSRS Hazards should be achieved via the exercise of Part 1 functions, and not by means of licence conditions.[98]

---

91 *Our Towns: A Close-up. A study made in 1939–42 with certain recommendations by the Hygiene Committee of the Women's Group on Public Welfare.* (Oxford University Press, 1943).

92 Housing Act 1961, s22.

93 Housing Act 1969, s64.

94 Housing Act 2004, Part 2.

95 Housing Act 2004, Part 3.

96 Housing Act 2004, s67(2)(d) and (e).

97 Housing Act 2004, s1(4). Moreover none of the exceptions/exclusions found elsewhere in the Act apply to Part 1.

98 Housing Act 2004, s 67(4).

Controlling Standards in the Private Rented Sector – Will the New Regulatory Regime Work?

As discussed above, the current lack of any real security of tenure means that private sector tenants are in no position to challenge their landlord, and that they are unlikely or unwilling to 'mount' a private action however unsatisfactory the condition of their accommodation. Moreover, as also discussed, the private sector market is, now, relatively mobile, and property selection by prospective tenants is influenced by location, services and transport as much (if not more) than by the quality of the property.

There is probably a significant percentage of 'good' landlords, those who make every effort to provide good quality accommodation, and who take a 'professional' approach to management of their properties and the welfare of their tenants. It is these landlords who are encouraged and supported by initiatives, such as local authority run accreditation schemes (as discussed in Chapter 8). However, there is also a body of either unscrupulous or just incompetent landlords who are providing badly managed properties.

The issue is not, primarily, about maintaining an asset (the building), and it is not, merely, about ensuring that there is a need for sufficient accommodation in the right place to satisfy the demand. Above all, the issue is that accommodation should provide a safe and healthy environment for the occupiers. Unsatisfactory housing is not just uncomfortable and unpleasant, it is well established that it has a negative impact on health[99] which not only has consequences for the individual, but also for society affecting the economy and creating demands on the health services.

Once again the imbalance between landlord and tenant means that the market is failing, and will continue to fail, to drive housing conditions up. Indeed, to some extent it may be doing the opposite. This suggests that intervention by public authorities is, at present, the only way to ensure that conditions in this sector can be controlled. To this end, Parliament had now provided in the Housing Act 2004 Part 1 and associated Guidance, both a comprehensive method for assessing conditions and a potentially effective enforcement regime, and in Part 2 it provides for the control of HMOs. However, the concern must be to what extent local authorities will embrace this new approach. Historically local authorities have adopted a primarily reactive approach, responding to complaints from tenants about their conditions. Only in some cases, for example in relation to HMOs (and particularly in relation to fire safety), have they taken a pro-active approach, searching out those failing to meet current standards. There now needs to be a more general change in attitude, and a recognition of responsibility. Local authorities need to be encouraged to become

---

99 See, for example, Raw, G.J., Aizlewood, C.E. and Hamilton, R.M. (eds), *Building Regulation, Health and Safety* (Watford, Building Research Establishment, 2001); Ranson, R., *Healthy Housing: A Practical Guide* (London, E & FN Spon, 1991); Burridge, R. and Ormandy, D., *Unhealthy Housing: Research, Remedies and Reform* (London, E & FN Spon, 1993); British Medical Association, *Housing and Health: Building for the Future* (London, BMA, 2003); Howden-Chapman, P. and Carroll, P., *Housing and Health: Research, Policy and Innovation* (New Zealand, Steele Roberts, 2004); *Reviews on Environmental Health*, Vol. 19, Nos. 3–4 (Tel Aviv, Freund Publishing House, 2004).

more pro-active and to make full use of the range of legal tools to drive up standards in the private rented sector.

Health and safety not structural integrity

At the heart of the Housing Act 2004 Part 1 scheme is an emphasis on intervention to secure or enhance an occupier's health and safety rather than merely to maintain the fabric of the building occupied. Of course if the fabric of a building seriously deteriorates, the health and safety of its occupants is inevitably threatened. However the conceptual framework underlying the 'old' law was lacking in clarity and coherence and enforcement was patchy. As discussed above, many of the determining requirements concerning 'fitness' in the 'old' law did relate implicitly to health and safety, such as freedom from damp, ventilation and 'sanitary' issues but the overall appraisal as to whether intervention was required turned more on the cost/extent of the remedial work required, i.e. it was building focused. The new emphasis is explicitly on the ability of a tenant to occupy their home healthily and safely. Although concerned with the 'social'/public tenants of Sheffield Homes[100] rather than the private sector the philosophy clearly outlined in the report *Decent Homes: Better Health*[101] exemplifies this shift in emphasis. As the report states, the aim is '[to] make a major contribution to improving the health and quality of life of Sheffield residents'. It even goes so far as to specifically claim (*inter alia*) that 'improved kitchens and bathrooms … will reduce falls, trips, scalds and burns, with substantial savings to the NHS', and 'new windows and doors … will improve security, promote feelings of safety and have a major impact on mental health and well being, with cost savings to the NHS'.[102] Of course, the impact on the private rented sector will inevitably be more patchy, and less focused, but the message behind the new legislation is clear: poor housing is a major contributor to poor health and this should guide local authority practice.

Attitude of local authorities

It should be clear from all the above that the effectiveness of the new approach crucially depends on the attitude of local authorities towards it. Some signs are encouraging, for example the 'joined up thinking' implicit in the Sheffield report already discussed involving the local authority and the NHS. It would be nice to think that this would be replicated nationally, and across the 'public/private' tenure divide. Some concerns, however, do remain. The 'Sheffield' report also states that '*… in reality local partnerships have found it difficult to integrate housing and public health policies and programmes. Sheffield has one of the more dynamic strategic*

100 The Arms Length Management Organisation (ALMO) which in 2004 took control of 52,000 properties of Sheffield City Council's housing stock.

101 A joint report (July 2006) written by Gilbertson J., Green, G. and Ormandy, D. on behalf of Sheffield City Council, Sheffield Homes, and the Sheffield (NHS) Primary Care Trusts.

102 Ibid., foreword and executive summary.

partnerships and the overarching Sheffield City Strategy goes further than most in integrating diverse policy and programme domains yet the chapter highlighting the contribution of housing to neighbourhood regeneration makes little mention of health and the chapter on health does not refer explicitly to housing as one of its wider determinants.'[103] Moreover, local authorities themselves do not have a track record of being consistently 'pro-active' when it comes to substandard housing. SSRC research carried out by Neil Hawke and Gillian Taylor in the 1980s[104] discovered substantial variations in practice between local authorities when it came to using their statutory powers to deal with unfitness and statutory nuisance. Unsurprisingly, issues concerning the difficulties in supervizing new or on-going work and the recovery of costs weighed heavily with many local authorities. Some of them mentioned that the presence of a nearby law centre 'encouraged' a more 'pro-active approach'. Again, unsurprisingly, the size and staff resources of the department and the commitment of the authority to neighbourhood/area regeneration also played their part.

Of course much has changed since the 1980s, but it is doubtful if better resourcing of environmental health departments/teams is one of those changes! It is possible that authorities will not universally embrace the new approach. Some have even argued[105] that the legislation itself might facilitate a less than whole-hearted attitude, for example by allowing the use of the warning Hazard Awareness Notice (HAN) as a possible response to an unacceptable Category 1 Hazard.[106] Might a 'stretched' local authority work initially via a generalized system of HANs rather than moving swiftly towards Improvement Notices? If so, is there a danger that excessive 'consensualism' will partially undermine the effectiveness of the new health and safety oriented procedures, particularly as anyone wishing to challenge the appropriateness of such a response would need to demonstrate that it was a decision which no reasonable authority could have arrived at. Systematic local and national monitoring of the implementation of the new standards seems essential if a truly innovative approach is to be embedded.

This new territory and putting 'health' at the centre of tools to deal with housing conditions offers new possibilities. It gives the opportunity for local authorities and the health services to work together to identify priorities for action. Where the health service sees a high demand for treatment of fall injuries, the local authority could target those fall related housing hazards. Where the police identify a particular district as suffering numerous burglaries, the authority could target housing security features. And, rather than monitoring the activities of the local environmental health

103 Ibid., p. 1.

104 Hawke, J.N. and Taylor, G.A., 'The Compulsory Repair of Individual and Physically Substandard Housing: The Law in Practice', *Journal of Social Welfare Law* (1984) p. 129.

105 Hughes, D., Davis, M., Jones, A. and Matthew, V., *Text and Materials on Housing Law* (Oxford, Oxford University Press, 2005) p. 594.

106 Housing Act 2004, s28. The Guidance (paragraphs 4.14 and 4.15) states that the use of HANs is to be regarded as only an 'exceptional' response to a Category 1 Hazard and 'in most cases ... will not be a suitable response to a hazard that can do harm …'. Authorities must take account of this, but, of course, can depart from it in appropriate cases. Successful challenges to the use of HANs only really seem credible in the somewhat unlikely event of them becoming the 'default' response to a Category 1 Hazard.

departments by looking at housing conditions, the monitoring could be health and safety based, looking at the demands on the health services. Although attempts to prove that poor housing causes ill health have often been inconclusive, the recent Scottish House Conditions Survey[107] showed that amongst households with children, over one in four had a child with symptoms of respiratory health problems, often attributable to damp housing conditions. The 'Sheffield' report discussed above seems to embody good practice, and expresses clearly the potential for significant housing-linked improvements to the health and well being of tenants in general. The Housing Act 2004 Part 1 reforms give the green light for similar initiatives in the private rented sector.

107 Scottish Executive, *Scottish House Conditions Survey 2002* (Edinburgh, Communities Scotland, 2002). The 2002 survey, for the first time, included questions on the health of occupants.

Chapter 7

Landlords and Fair Trading: All Consumers Now?

Martin Davis and Rachael Houghton

Introduction

Even in 2007, it is not an instinctive reaction for most lawyers to consider tenants as 'consumers' (or, correspondingly, to think of a landlord as a 'seller or supplier'[1] to consumers). In 1977 it would probably have been seen as eccentric to conceptualize tenants in this way. However, in that year a piece of legislation was passed which can, 30 years later, be seen as the starting point for the current concern with 'fair trading' and 'balanced' markets. The legislation in question was the Unfair Contract Terms Act (UCTA) 1977. In 1977, housing lawyers, whilst acutely aware of the importance and intricacies of the consolidating Rent Act 1977, would probably have given UCTA little thought. However, while the Rent Act 1977 is today, outside London, largely an historical artefact[2] which has little to say about the current state of the PRS in England and Wales, the themes first legislatively promulgated in UCTA are becoming central to much of the discussion on how the PRS should be regulated.

In a formal sense it is unsurprising that housing lawyers paid little attention to UCTA, in that Schedule 1, paragraph 1(b) of the Act specifically excludes from its ambit 'any contract – so far as it relates to the creation or transfer of an interest in land'. Although this does not necessarily wholly remove tenancies from the reach of the Act,[3] it 'signals' that tenancies, as 'interests in land', are not generally the concern of the legislation. However, the probability that UCTA would not have been 'on the radar' of the typical housing lawyer would have been for more fundamental reasons than this. Although it was self evident that a tenancy was, in part, a contract as well as an 'interest in land', it was the latter which dominated the thinking of most lawyers. No doubt a 'mere' licence had had to be understood as inherently contractual in nature, but a tenancy was not – it was a 'status'-based entity, conferring rights derived from that status rather than in essence because of any contract which

1 To adopt the language of Regulation 4 of the Unfair Terms in Consumer Contracts Regulations (SI 1999/2083).

2 Not merely in that those tenants still protected by the security and fair rent provisions of the Rent Act 1977 are relatively few in number, but above all that the strict and formal regulatory protection central to the Act seems from another world when reflecting on the PRS today.

3 For example, s. 8 UCTA, concerning pre-contract misrepresentations would still apply, see *Walker v Boyle* [1982] 1 WLR 495.

might have been made.[4] If, then, a tenancy was barely perceived as 'contractual', it is hardly surprising that tenants were not seen as 'consumers'. 'Consumers', as the name would suggest, 'consumed' goods and services – tenants did not.

By 2004, things had begun to look very different. In *R (Khatun and others) v Newham London Borough Council,*[5] Laws LJ stated, '[Some] tenants or prospective tenants are especially vulnerable people. For most consumers, the acquisition of a home, to rent or buy, is a key event in their lives. If the house is bought rather than rented, it will most likely be the biggest purchase the buyer has so far ever made. I recognize, of course, that sales of private houses are most often effected between consumers, rather than between a consumer and a trader. But not all are. And it is a commonplace that tenancies are let by landlords who are in business as such.'[6] As a further indication of the strength of the 'consumer' tide, a year earlier the Law Commission had viewed a consumer-based analysis of tenancy relationship as central to its proposals for reforming the relevant legal framework.[7] The thrust of the Commission's 'core' principles was that '… a clearer consumer perspective should be brought to housing law, that would emphasize both the rights and the obligations of both landlords and occupiers'.[8]

Of course, numerous objections can be raised concerning the appropriateness of a consumer analysis of tenancy relationships, and the advisability of applying consumer law principles to them. For example, the Law Commission itself noted that criticisms had been made of its earlier proposals to this effect.[9] In particular, it was argued that, unlike the position with other consumer contracts, a residential occupier could not easily go to another supplier to purchase 'goods' or 'services', particularly in areas of the country where there is an excess of housing demand over supply.[10] Even assuming a consumer analysis was appropriate, others had argued that the relatively 'soft' and 'consensual' regulation implicit in much consumer protection would not be an adequate response to the 'power imbalance' implicit in many landlord–occupier relationships.[11] This issue is discussed in more detail later. Perhaps even more fundamental is the criticism that to focus on a contractual/

4 Of course, initial protection under the Rent Act 1977 was contractual in nature (the 'protected' tenancy), but once this was brought to an end, rights were inherently 'status'-based (the 'statutory' tenancy). Lord Browne-Wilkinson in *Hammersmith LBC v Monk* [1992] 1 AC 478 at 491 made reference to the 'tension' between contractual and 'property-based' analyses of a tenancy, but most lawyers in 1977 would have begun with a tenancy as a species of 'landed property'.

5 *R (Khatun and others) v Newham LBC* [2005] QB 37, [2004] EWCA Civ. 55.

6 *Khatun*, at 67.

7 Law Commission, *Renting Homes*, Law Com. no. 284 (November 2003).

8 Law Commission, para. 2.11.

9 In Law Commission Consultation Paper (CP) no. 162.

10 Law Commission, para. 4.6 (2003).

11 Law Commission (2003), para. 4.7. Such an analysis of 'consumer protection' is, in itself, contentious. Some 'consumer protection' is far from 'soft' in nature – involving, as it may, consumer rights to terminate contracts forthwith, or prosecutions by local authorities of those supplying unsafe products or publishing misleading advertising. The point is discussed more fully later in this chapter.

'consumerist' analysis of a tenancy is to succumb to a philosophy of 'choice and individualism', and to lose the benefits, individual and collective, which a 'status'-based analysis can confer. The usual response to such criticism is that the nostrums of the market have advanced so far in relations to the PRS since 1977 that little of use can come from arguing for a return to a different 'age'. Nevertheless, the point is a serious one.

However, although numerous criticisms can be made and objections raised concerning a consumer-based analysis of tenancy relationships, it is an analysis now taken as axiomatic by both the courts and bodies such as the Law Commission and the Office of Fair Trading. It is to the crucial work of the latter that we now turn.

Modern Landlords, Confident Tenants?[12]

Although UCTA, as discussed above, may have had mainly symbolic importance in the development of a 'fair trading' approach to tenancy regulation, the same cannot be said of the Unfair Terms in Consumer Contracts Regulations (UTCCR).[13] The UTCCR are the 'translation' into our law of Council Directive 93/13/EEC on Unfair Terms in Consumer Contracts. This directive was the product of nearly 20 years' work by the European Commission. The Commission's initial exploratory activity in the 1970s and early 1980s helped inspire numerous individual legislative developments around the community, including UCTA in 1977. However, the 1993 directive was aiming for far greater uniformity of practice around the EC, enabling 'non-negotiated' terms in consumer contracts to be (presumptively) challenged as 'unfair'. This development was seen as necessary both to protect consumers against exploitation and to create a 'level playing field' for businesses around the Community.[14] Although they are not specifically excluded from the UTCCR, some commentators suggested that the original 1994 version of the regulations did not apply to tenancies.[15] As originally drafted, the regulations only applied to the sale of goods, or the provision of services by businesses. From this, it was argued that they were not apt to apply to any contract for the sale or disposition of an interest in land, since real property could not properly be described as 'goods', given the crucial distinction in English law between real and personal property. Such views were far from universal, particularly given the fact that the original (French) version of the directive referred simply to 'biens', which in French law could encompass land. Crucially, the view of the Office of Fair Trading (OFT) was always that land transactions (including tenancies) fell within the purview of the regulations. The above debate is now largely irrelevant, as the current (1999) version of the regulations

12 The title is a 'reworking' of the Department of Trade and Industry (DTI) White Paper, *Modern Markets: Confident Consumers* (Cm 4410, 1999).

13 These regulations, originally enacted as the UTCCR 1994 (SI 1994/3159), were more recently re-enacted in amended form as the UTCCR 1999 (SI 1999/2083), in force 1 October 1999.

14 As the preamble to Directive 93/13 indicates.

15 For example Treitel, G.H., *Law of Contract*, 10th edition (London, Sweet and Maxwell, 1999) p. 246.

simply applies to contractual terms 'imposed' by business 'seller(s) or supplier(s)' on consumers,[16] so bypassing the above difficulty. Any lingering doubts on this have now been dispelled by *R (Khatun and others) v Newham London Borough Council.*[17] The defendant authority had operated a policy under which London applicants would be required to accept offers of accommodation, and sign tenancy agreements, without having had the opportunity of viewing the property. Khatun argued (*inter alia*) that the UTCCR 1999 and (as relevant) Council Directive 93/13 applied to the terms on which accommodation was let by the authority pursuant to its 'homelessness' obligations.[18] The Court of Appeal held that firstly the regulations and the directive did apply to tenancies, secondly that they did extend to public authorities such as the authority, and thirdly that the authority was a 'seller' or 'supplier' and the applicants were 'consumers' for the purpose of the regulations. In coming to this decision, the Court of Appeal was influenced by the fact that the Commission,[19] the Department of Trade and Industry (DTI)[20] and the OFT all took the view that the directive and/or regulations applied to 'land' transactions, and therefore to tenancies. The views of the DTI[21] are worth reproducing, in particular its statement that the 1999 amendments to the UTCCR were '... intended, in particular, to remove any uncertainty that the Regulations are, not capable of applying to contracts relating to land ... Some of the most vulnerable consumers live in rented accommodation, and there is much evidence of exploitation and onerous conditions imposed, by landlords ... Revising unfair terms, in tenancy agreements would improve the rights of tenants'.

The central role of the OFT in 'steering' law and practice in relation to unfair terms in general, and unfair terms in tenancy agreements in particular, has already been alluded to. In *Khatun*,[22] Law LJ referred to them as the 'lead regulator', and this leading role is borne out in practice as well as in theory. Under the 1999 UTCCR, the OFT has a duty to consider complaints that a contract term is unfair, the power to seek injunctions to prevent continued use of unfair terms, and to obtain relevant documents and information to help it 'rule' on a complaint, and a duty to arrange for the 'appropriate' publication and/or dissemination of undertakings given by and court orders made against organizations and individuals utilizing 'unfair' terms.[23] In theory, similar powers and duties exist in relation to other 'qualifying bodies', such as trading standards 'authorities' and various utility regulators[24] (although generally only in liaison with the OFT).[25] However, in practice the role of the OFT is central and crucial.

---

16 See UTCCR 1999, regulations 3 and 4.

17 See notes 5 and 6.

18 Under Part VII Housing Act 1996.

19 In its report of 27 April 2000 *On the Implementation of Council Directive 93/13/EEC* at p. 46.

20 In para. 11 of the Regulatory Impact Assessment (RIA), produced in conjunction with UTCCR 1999.

21 RIA, para. 11.

22 *Khatun* [2005].

23 UTCCR 1999, regulations 8, 12, 13 and 15.

24 UTCCR 1999, Schedule 1 part I.

25 UTCCR 1999, regulations 11, 12 and 14.

Reference was made earlier to the debate as to whether 'consumer'-focused regulation is too 'soft' to adequately counter the potential 'power imbalances' in landlord and tenant relationships.[26] The general approach of the OFT brings this issue into sharp focus. In one sense, the regulatory approach *is* 'soft', rarely involving the use of litigation. On paper, the OFT has extensive powers to seek what are termed 'enforcement orders' to compel businesses to amend their standard forms of contract if these are adjudged 'unfair'.[27] Alternatively, in relation to unfair terms it may seek an injunction to prevent their continued use.[28] In practice, applications for such orders or injunctions are rare, the OFT preferring to work through a process of undertakings whereby businesses judged to be using unfair terms agree to amend or delete offending provisions. Initially this may be seen to be a largely consensual and 'co-operative' process. However, it needs to be remembered that the ultimate sanction of an enforcement order may await a business which fails to amend or delete terms as agreed. Moreover, the governing legislation[29] envisages the OFT initially working via a system of undertakings, and provides that a court must 'have regard' to the existence (or otherwise) of an undertaking and (any) failure to comply in deciding whether to make an order.

In addition to its direct regulatory role, the OFT has a crucial role in providing information to consumers and businesses.[30] In relation to unfair contract terms, regulation 15 of the UTCCR provides that the OFT 'shall arrange for the publication in such form and manner as it considers appropriate' of undertakings given to itself or other 'qualifying bodies'. As discussed below, regular OFT 'bulletins' contain relevant details of undertakings given by businesses. This information is a crucial informal source of law, in the absence of much case law, and of course provides vital information for consumers. In addition, the OFT publishes guidance both on unfair contract terms generally, and unfair contract terms in tenancy agreements specifically. The most recent guidance on tenancy agreements was issued on 7 September 2005, replacing guidance issued in 2001. Again, as well as 'guiding' good practice by landlords, it serves as a useful source of information on the types of term the OFT at least is likely to consider 'unfair'.

Since the implementation of the 1999 UTCCR in particular, sufficient undertakings have been given by landlords to begin to build a picture of how 'interventionist' the OFT appears to be in relation to tenancy agreements. From this, some conclusions can be drawn about the effectiveness of a 'fair trading' approach towards the regulation of landlord and tenant arrangements in the private rented sector (PRS). The remainder of this chapter will focus on the 'core' provisions of the UTCCR,

26 See note 11.

27 Under the provisions of the Enterprise Act 2002, in particular ss. 217 and 218. Prior to the Enterprise Act similar powers existed, the so-called Stop Now Orders. In addition to the OFT, local authority trading standards departments can also apply for enforcement orders. However under s. 216 of the Act, the OFT is given the lead role of co-ordination – it may direct that only itself or a specified enforcer may apply for an order.

28 UTCCR 1999, regulation 12.

29 Enterprise Act 2002, s 217(4).

30 Enterprise Act 2002, s 229(1).

their theoretical impact on tenancy agreements and the likely practical impact on tenancy agreements (particularly in the light of OFT attitudes).

The Theoretical Impact of the Unfair Terms in Consumer Contracts Regulations

The UTCCR do not apply to all contracts, and certain criteria must be met before they are invoked. First, the parties entering into the contractual agreement must encompass a business and a consumer, as contracts agreed between two businesses (or indeed two consumers) are outside the scope of these regulations.[31] 'Seller or supplier', as defined by the regulations, includes 'any natural or legal persons ... acting for purposes relating to his trade, business or profession'. 'Consumer' means simply 'any natural person ... acting ... outside his trade, business or profession'.[32] Landlords and tenants (as already discussed) clearly fit the respective 'seller or supplier' and 'consumer' definitions. Secondly, the terms contained in the contract must be 'non-negotiable'.[33] Once these criteria have been met, the OFT or other qualified bodies are able to (potentially) intervene. The second criterion needs further discussion.

Individually Negotiated

The inclusion of this requirement in the UTCCR is of fundamental importance to consumers, as it embraces the notion of fair trading through its recognition of the fact that consumers are often the disadvantaged party, particularly at the stage of negotiating a contract. This is certainly the case with tenancy agreements. Tenancy relationships '... may be characterized as relationships that are founded on power – the power of property' – set against the weakness and insecurity of those who do not have that property.[34] This inherent tension between 'market' power and 'need'-based vulnerability illustrates the fact that despite traditional theory focusing on landlords and tenants 'freely' negotiating the terms of the tenancy agreement, tenants are in the weaker bargaining position at the negotiation stage, and thus may not agree to terms in their favour. Traditional assumptions on freely bargained contractual negotiations between landlords and tenants have resulted in '... liberal conceptions of contractual arrangements ...',[35] a presumption that landlords and tenants enter into 'free' negotiations which result in a broadly equal and mutually satisfactory contract. These assumptions are based upon the focus of 'classical' contract law on individualism, and above all on the doctrine of 'freedom of contract'. The classic text concerning

31 UTCCR, regulation 4(1).

32 UTCCR, regulation 3(1).

33 UTCCR, regulation 5(1).

34 Partington, M., *Landlord and Tenant*, 2nd edition (London, Weidenfeld and Nicholson Ltd, 1980) p. 2.

35 Lister, D., 'Young People's Strategies for Managing Tenancy Relationships in the Private Rented Sector', *Journal of Youth Studies*, 7/ 3 (2004) p. 316.

the ideology underpinning 'freedom of contract', Atiyah's *The Rise and Fall of Freedom of Contract,*[36] states that it rests on 'the traditional liberal values of free choice', which are 'inescapably [compromised by the fact] that some individuals are better equipped to exercise free choice than others … and the greater … the scope for the exercise of free choice, the stronger … the tendency for … original inequalities to perpetrate themselves by maintaining ever increasing economic inequalities'.[37] Atiyah further notes[38] that the freedom of contract 'model' presupposes that parties bargain 'at arm's length' – neither owing any kind of fiduciary obligation to the other – and that in reality, in most cases, true bargaining negotiation does not take place. As the title to the book would suggest, Atiyah saw the twentieth-century rise of state intervention to regulate the economy and/or 'corporatism' as presaging the 'fall' of classical freedom of contract. Ironically, the election in the same year the book was published (1979) of a Conservative government ostensibly committed to breaking up the post-World War II corporatist consensus saw a renewed vigour in at least some aspects of 'freedom of contract'. 'Freedom' and 'choice' now appear to be the bywords for mainstream political discourse. Current theorizing in relation to consumer protection appears to seek to mitigate the most unfair consequences of 'freedom of contract', and to provide a degree of regulation over it rather than to challenge it directly.

Nevertheless, it is a common perception that this ideology of freedom and equality '[is] … a legal fiction that ignores power relations …'.[39] The landlord–tenant relationship has been identified above as a relationship essentially based upon the power and control of the landlord, and to achieve meaningful contractual equality requires a fundamental change in the way in which landlord–tenant relationships are formed. The extent to which the UTCCR 1999 have this impact is discussed below.

Regulation 5(1) of the UTCCR recognizes that, although parties to a contract require freedom to negotiate terms of (for example) a tenancy agreement, where the agreement creates an imbalance between the parties' respective rights and obligations and places the consumer or tenant at considerable disadvantage, he or she may need protection. The substantive issue of when, or indeed if, intervention is likely is discussed next. However, we first examine what appears to be meant by 'not individually negotiated' in the regulations.

Regulation 5 continues, 'A term shall always be regarded as not having been individually negotiated where it has been drafted in advance, and the consumer has therefore not been able to influence the substance of the term.'[40] Moreover, it states[41] that a particular term having been 'individually negotiated' does not preclude the application of the regulations to the remainder of the contract. The burden of proof

36 Atiyah, P.S., *The Rise and Fall of Freedom of Contract* (Oxford, Oxford University Press, 1979).

37 Atiyah, p. 6.

38 Atiyah, generally but most specifically at pp. 402–5.

39 Blandy, S. and Goodchild, B., 'Tenure to Rights: Conceptualising the Changing Focus of Housing Law in England', *Housing, Theory and Society*, 16/1 (1999) pp. 31–42.

40 UTCCR, regulation 5(2).

41 UTCCR, regulation 5(3).

is on the 'seller or supplier'.[42] We would suggest that it is unlikely that most private sector tenants are in a position to 'individually negotiate' with their landlord or their landlord's agent.[43] Indeed, we doubt if many of them actually get to see the contracts they sign up to significantly in advance of signature. Further, most landlords, through their agents, tend to operate on the basis of contracts 'drafted in advance'[44] – what the regulations term 'pre-formulated standard contracts'. Therefore, it seems clear that the vast majority of tenancy agreements in the PRS are now potentially subject to UTCCR control and OFT scrutiny. One possible exception could be in relation to small/'niche' landlords with one or two properties, who may not use letting agents and/or have their own 'standard' forms of agreement. In some cases, particularly with student 'lets', and if some form of accreditation process is in place, there may be a willingness on the part of the landlord to accept an agreement presented by the tenant (albeit no doubt supplied by the tenant's university accommodation service). A literal reading of regulation 5(2) might render the UTCCR applicable even in such cases (that is to say, where the tenant had not *himself/herself* played any part in 'influencing the substance' of the contract). However, it is at least arguable whether the OFT would feel it appropriate to intervene in such cases.

Once the regulations do 'bite', two further provisions are of 'key' significance: first there is the 'core' requirement that all terms falling within the UTCCR should be 'fair', and secondly the allied requirement that all terms should be 'expressed in plain, intelligible language'.

Fair or Unfair?

The UTCCR states that '... a contractual term ... shall be regarded as unfair if, contrary to the requirement of good faith, it causes a significant imbalance in the parties' rights and obligations arising under the contract to the detriment of the consumer'.[45] It should be immediately apparent that there are three distinct, albeit interrelated, elements here:

- 'Significant imbalance'
- Detriment to the consumer
- Lack of 'good faith'.

The first two factors are clearly 'case'-dependent, and probably do not lend themselves to overly elaborate analysis. This seems to be confirmed by the comments of Lord

42 UTCCR, regulation 5(4).

43 A view reinforced by the earlier research of Diane Lister: see notes 35, 73 and 77. Taken together, Lister's work creates a strong impression that to expect or anticipate that tenants will seriously negotiate with their landlords over the content of their tenancy agreements is highly unrealistic.

44 UTCCR, regulation 5(3).

45 UTCCR, regulation 5(1).

Bingham in *Director General of Fair Trading v First National Bank,*[46] where he stated, 'The requirement of significant imbalance is met if a term is so weighted in favour of the supplier as to tilt the party's rights and obligations under the contract significantly in his favour'. This both confirms the essentially factual nature of the test and the interpendency of 'significant imbalance' and 'detriment'. In a landlord–tenant context, this means that the tenancy agreement will need to be examined to see how far it prioritizes/promotes a landlord's interests at the expense of those of the tenant.

If the first two criteria are essentially concerned with 'product', the third is more about 'process'. 'Good faith' has an unfamiliar ring to a common lawyer's ears, but is familiar enough to lawyers in the rest of Europe: it involves 'transparency', fair dealing and the absence of 'sharp practice'. In the *First National* case, Lord Bingham stated, 'Fair dealing requires that a supplier should not, whether deliberately or consciously, take advantage of the consumer's necessity, indigence, lack of experience, unfamiliarity with the subject matter of the contract [or] weak bargaining position …'.[47] Earlier, the (then) Bingham LJ had put matters even more graphically in *Interfoto Picture Library Ltd v Stiletto Visual Programmes Ltd:*[48] '[Good faith] does not simply mean that [parties] shall not deceive each other … [Its] effect is perhaps most aptly conveyed by such metaphorical colloquialisms as "playing fair", "coming clean", or "putting one's cards upwards on the table". It is, in essence, a principle of fair and open dealing.' The OFT *Guidance on Unfair Terms in Tenancy Agreements*[49] states (simply) that '… the requirement of good faith embodies a general principle of fair and open dealing', but tellingly (in the light of OFT practice discussed below) then puts emphasis on the clarity/legibility issue: '… [It] means that terms should be expressed fully, clearly and legibly, and that terms which might disadvantage the consumer should be given appropriate prominence'.

In addition to the generality of regulation 5(1), Schedule 2 of the UTCCR contains a (so called) indicative and non-exhaustive list of terms which may be regarded as unfair. It is clear that this list is for guidance only, 'indicative' *and* 'non-exhaustive', but the inclusion of the type of term in question in the list does reinforce the argument that it should (presumptively at least) be seen as unfair. The schedule includes a classic disclaimer of liability clauses, one-sided cancellation clauses, clauses allowing unilateral varieties of contract terms and 'disproportionate' fixed penalty clauses.

---

46 *Director General of Fair Trading v First National Bank plc*, 2001 UKHL 52 [2002] 1 AC 481, at 414 (c–e).

47 Ibid. at p. 494 (f–g).

48 *Interfoto Picture Library Ltd v Stiletto Visual Programmes Ltd* [1989] 1 QB 433, at 439.

49 *Guidance on Unfair Terms in Tenancy Agreements*, OFT 356 (September 2005) at para. 2.5.

Plain, Intelligible English

The UTCCR require that 'A seller or supplier shall ensure that any written term of a contract is expressed in plain, intelligible language',[50] and that '[If] there is doubt about the meaning of a written term, the interpretation which is most favourable to the consumer shall prevail'.[51] Moreover, the usual exemption from scrutiny of terms which 'define ... the main subject matter of contract' does not apply if the term in question is not expressed in 'plain, intelligible language'.[52] The OFT has often expressed the view that the test of 'intelligibility' should be that of the 'ordinary consumer' who has not received legal advice.[53] Aside from its impact on the 'core terms' exemption, there is no specific penalty in the regulation for not using 'intelligible' language, which tends to reinforce the impression that 'intelligibility' is, in essence, a key aspect of the general 'fairness' requirement. As already discussed, this is certainly the OFT view. This was expressed vividly in an address given in 1997 by Pat Edwards (then Director of Legal Affairs at the OFT). She stated, 'It seems likely that the use of plain language, and the dropping of substantial unfairness tend to go hand in hand ... once terms are seen in the cold light of ordinary language unfairness, which was decently veiled by jargon and complexity, stand out ...'.[54]

The Practical Impact of the Unfair Terms in Consumer Contract Regulations 1999 on Tenancy Agreements

In order to establish the effectiveness of the UTCCR 1999 in relation to terms in tenancy agreements and, in particular, the agreements made between landlords and students, a detailed analysis of the undertakings obtained by the OFT in the PRS under the UTCCR between May 1996 and May 2006 has been undertaken. During this ten-year period, approximately 70 tenancy agreements have been declared by the OFT incompatible with the UTCCR. The majority of these agreements have either had a number of their terms modified or deleted. However, a few have been totally replaced with model tenancy agreements previously approved by the OFT.

Analysis of the OFT's undertakings identifies that OFT intervention concerning unfair tenancy terms had a slow start, as it was not until the fifth bulletin that the first declaration of incompatibility arose. Given the significance of Regulations 5 and 7, we were surprised to find that Regulation 5 was rarely invoked before 2002, and Regulation 7 before 2003.[55] Moreover, analysis of the bulletins also demonstrates either inconsistencies or a changing pattern in the way the OFT classifies terms. An illustration evidencing this relates to a term removing a tenant's right to assign a tenancy. In issue 21,[56] this type of term was placed in the 'unclassified terms' category.

50 UTCCR, regulation 7(1).
51 UTCCR, regulation 7(2).
52 UTCCR, regulation 6.
53 For example, see OFT bulletin No. 3 at p. 19, and bulletin 2.12.
54 Cited in OFT, bulletin No. 4, at p. 26.
55 A surprising finding in light of the views of Pat Edwards already mentioned (note 54).
56 OFT bulletin No. 21 (July–September 2002).

However, the same type of term in Bulletin 23[57] was seen to be incompatible with the requirements laid out in Regulation 5.

The majority of declarations of incompatibility have arisen in relation to Regulations 5 and 7 and Schedule 2, paragraphs 1(b), (e) and (i). The period of greatest OFT 'activism' was between 2002 and 2004: during this period some 40 tenancy agreements were subject to intervention. Since then the number of tenancy agreements scrutinized by the OFT has gradually declined, and indeed from late 2005 to May 2006, not one tenancy agreement received OFT intervention.

We found that over the ten-year period from 1996 to 2006, 17 references were made specifically in respect of student tenancies. Some 310 terms were either deleted or modified as a result. Of these reported references, ten applied to halls of residence provided by universities themselves, but only one related to a commercial provider of student accommodation.[58] (At present, approximately 400,000 students reside in halls of residence; of these, about 100,000 are in commercially-provided halls of residence.)

Typical Examples of Terms Modified or Deleted by the OFT

Amongst the terms most often seen as incompatible with the UTCCR 1999 by the OFT are:

- Terms binding tenants to documents they may not have had a copy of, or indeed read, prior to signing the tenancy agreement. These may include, for example, insurance documents, 'student residence handbooks' and 'tenants' handbooks';[59]
- Terms concerning the access landlords have to the property. Many tenancy agreements contain a term permitting the landlord or his/her agents access to the property at all times. It is 'trite' law that during the currency of a tenancy, a tenant has the right to exclusive possession to the exclusion of all others, including the landlord.[60] However, many landlords are under the misconception that they can enter the property at any given time, as they 'own' the property and this confers special rights on them. The OFT recognizes that this type of term places an unfair burden upon a tenant, and invariably changes then to include a requirement for at least 24 hours' notice to be given before the

57 OFT bulletin No. 23 (January–March 2003).

58 This somewhat surprising finding *might* be simply the result of large-scale 'private' student housing providers being relatively late 'on the scene' (mainly since 2000). However, the current size of the 'market' should by now have led to more references if that is the only reason. Our research is currently pursuing this very question. One possibility is that an increasing 'short-term' outlook amongst students might reduce the likelihood of complaints to bodies such as local Trading Standards and the OFT. As long as the accommodation seems generally satisfactory, the 'fine print' of the tenancy agreement may be of less concern to the student than the rent payable.

59 See, for example, OFT bulletins 18 (2001) and 27/28 (2004).

60 See, for example, *Street v Mountford* [1985] AC 809 and many other cases.

landlord (or his or her agent) enters the premises, except in circumstances of extreme emergency;[61]

- Terms whereby landlords have complete control over the return of deposits, including terms whereby the whole deposit can be retained if a student changes his or her mind about attending a particular university, withdraws from a course or is asked to leave by the university;[62]
- Terms with the potential of transferring a landlord's obligations to the tenant in such matters as the repairing of guttering, windows and/or doors;[63]
- Terms giving the landlord unlimited right to vary the terms in the contract;[64]
- Terms withholding vital information, such as the fact that the landlord is required to obtain a court order before a tenant can be evicted.

As we are specifically looking at student tenancies here, we have closely analysed some of the terms modified or deleted by the OFT in the tenancy agreement of the only commercial provider of student accommodation whose agreement has been under OFT investigation. These include:

- A term making the student liable for all damage and undue wear and tear, regardless of his or her fault in causing the damage;
- A term requiring the student to open, or leave ajar, the window in his/her room every day for ventilation purposes. The original term required the student to ensure the window was open during his/her absence. The OFT considered this to be 'an unreasonable ancillary obligation', in particular in that it excluded the landlord's responsibility for the tenant's loss through compliance with this obligation;
- A term which gave the impression that a landlord could evict without a court order. This term was changed to specifically include the requirement to obtain a court order;
- A declaration of incompatibility was imposed (under Regulation 7) requiring that the definition of 'private parties' be changed so as to provide for a specific procedure to be followed for students wishing to make plans for a 'social event' at the halls of residence.[65]

Overall, the OFT looked at 32 of the terms in this tenancy agreement. The landlord currently provides 4,062 bedspaces for university students, with other developments currently in the pipeline. Of these 32 terms, four were not changed, two were deleted and the remainder were modified.

As already discussed,[66] Regulation 7 requires that tenancy agreements are laid out in 'plain and intelligible' language, and the OFT is rigorous in ensuring that

61 See, for example, OFT bulletins 18 and 27–28.

62 See, for example, OFT bulletins 8 (1999), 15 (2001) and 27–28 (2004).

63 See, for example, OFT bulletin 8.

64 See, for example, OFT bulletin 18.

65 <www.crw.gov.uk/Undertakings+court+action/Publish+Public/20521.htm> (January 2005).

66 See notes 50–54.

agreements referred to them do indeed comply with this regulation. The OFT's unforgiving stance concerning legal jargon in consumer contracts[67] has led to the removal of words not likely to be understood by the average consumer, unless clear and comprehensible explanations are provided. Terms removed from contractual agreements include 'joint and several liability', 'lieu', 'time is of the essence', 'indemnify', 'liquidated damages', 'determine', 'vitiate', 'void'/'voidable' and 'estoppel':[68] these may not be understood by the ordinary consumer, and their removal aims to create clearer contracts for tenants.

The OFT's *Guidance on Unfair Terms in Tenancy Agreements* now provides full and clear guidance on Regulation 7. It is clear that the OFT will look at both the wording *and* the layout of contracts, placing further emphasis on creating clear contractual documents: agreements should contain short sentences, the layout must be systematic, with sub-headings where necessary, and '... statutory references, elaborate definitions, technical language and extensive cross referencing between terms' should be avoided.[69] There is even guidance on size, colour, background and quality of paper.[70] The OFT perspective is that when a tenant receives a copy of a clearly laid-out tenancy agreement without any legal jargon, he or she is more likely to understand his or her rights and obligations. Tenants will then not only be able to protect their interests, but also exert choice and freedom over contracts they enter into, as they have the opportunity to understand the true implications of terms.[71] Moreover, the OFT view is that if both parties understand the tenancy agreement from the onset, there will be less scope for disputes. The Guidance also suggests that if a term is not to the tenant's advantage, it should be brought specifically and very clearly to the tenant's attention, and such parts of the contract should be clearly highlighted. Unavoidable technicalities should be explained, and a summary or additional information provided about the tenancy agreement.[72] This is aimed at helping the tenant understand at least the majority of the contract. However, it might also be suggested that it may still not be acceptable for terms to be to the tenant's disadvantage, even if supporting information or an adequate explanation is provided.

Nevertheless, even though the initial impression conveyed by the above is impressive, if the UTCCR 1999 are to become truly effective, both landlords and tenants require greater awareness of the expectations these regulations purport to place upon them. The regulations themselves recognize that landlords are in the stronger bargaining position, and that this enables them to draft contracts in their favour. The UTCCR require that a landlord considers the legitimate expectations of a tenant, and balances these against his own self interest when drafting a tenancy

---

67 Albeit a rather belated 'stance' in relation to tenancy agreements – see note 54.

68 *Guidance on Unfair Terms in Tenancy Agreements* (note 49), para. 5.4.

69 *Guidance*, para. 5.6.

70 *Guidance*, para. 5.7.

71 We return to this in the conclusion to this chapter. Some might feel that the OFT are overly sanguine that greater 'transparency' will lead to the more meaningful exercise of tenant/'consumer' choice.

72 Generally, see *Guidance*, paras 5.8–5.9.

agreement. However, we would suggest that this can create a number of problems for the tenancy relationship and tenancy agreements. Firstly, as already discussed, Lister has established that when forming a tenancy relationship, '… the legal, social and financial arrangements were rarely discussed'.[73] Our research has further indicated a general unwillingness on the part of landlords and/or their agents to negotiate the terms of the contract. In fact, one tenancy agreement obtained during the course of the research has a clause imposing a £50 fee if a tenant wishes to change any terms in the contract, thus acting as a disincentive for tenants to negotiate.[74] Generally, a tenant is presented with a pre-formulated contract which he or she is expected to sign without question. He or she has two choices – sign the agreement without negotiation and secure a home, or attempt to discuss the contents of the agreement and possibly lose the tenancy. Many tenants are in such a vulnerable position at this stage of the tenancy relationship that it is arguable whether they would put their potential home at risk by attempting to negotiate. This places the onus on the landlord to be upfront and scrupulously fair in the negotiation process. We question later how realistic this is.

Another difficulty arising from these expectations is the fact that landlords and tenants are often ill-equipped to negotiate the terms of the agreement, due to their inadequate negotiation skills and knowledge of the law. An increasing percentage of the PRS (particularly outside London) now consists of young people, often students. Given their age and vulnerability, they are less likely to feel willing or able to discuss the contents of a tenancy agreement with their landlord or their landlord's agent. They instinctively believe they have little status as students, and although they are aware of their right to negotiate terms, they are unwilling to. The transient nature of student life enables, perhaps even encourages, them to move to another property or halls of residence if they are unhappy with their current agreement or landlord.[75] If they are unhappy at, for example, a commercial hall of residence, they will migrate into some other part of the PRS during the next academic year. If dissatisfied with this agreement or landlord, they will then migrate back to the hall of residence, or to another landlord providing student accommodation within the PRS. In other words, as they are only bound to the terms of the agreement for one academic year, they do not attempt to negotiate as they know they can move elsewhere.

Small, 'niche' landlords may often operate without the use of agents or lawyers, and may also experience difficulties with the OFT's guidelines on Regulation 7. Inadequate knowledge on their part of phrases or terms in a tenancy agreement means they may have difficulty providing explanations or summaries of tenancy agreements, and will need to seek legal advice if they are to avoid 'unfairness' in the end product of the final agreement. If they do not seek legal advice, there is

73 Lister, D., 'The Nature of Tenancy Relationships: Landlords and Young People' in Hughes, D. and Lowe, S. (eds), *The Private Rented Sector in a New Century: Revival or False Dawn?* (Bristol, The Policy Press, 2002).

74 Houghton, R., *The provision and governance of student accommodation with reference to the impact of fair trading and consumer protection* – a forthcoming PhD thesis.

75 See note 59.

every possibility that they will misinterpret the meaning of a word, and create further confusion for their tenants.

The UTCCR 1999 theoretically constitute a significant legislative turning point, in providing for the partial regulation of tenancy agreements in an otherwise deregulated PRS. The creation of 'fairer' agreements is a laudable objective, in an often confusing and chaotic marketplace. However, is a theoretical change in the law – even one supported by OFT intervention – enough? Nelken's classic study[76] emphasized that landlords' practices had little directly to do with the law. Lister's research[77] establishes that the most influential factor in a tenancy relationship is the social and economic relationship between the landlord and tenant, and not the legal one. If the day-to-day relationship is of fundamental importance, how does this leave the 'fine print' of the tenancy agreement, fair or unfair? How closely is the agreement followed on a daily basis? If, for example, a landlord visits the property without 24 hours' notice, or asks a tenant to fix the guttering, will the tenant refer to his or her tenancy agreement or simply permit it to happen?

Our research is, as yet, incomplete. However, even preliminary findings call into question whether changing the law *in theory* is enough to change practice 'on the ground', even if 'the law' is enforced through direct OFT intervention and scrutiny. To date, as noted, some 70 tenancy agreements have been examined by the OFT. This sounds impressive but is, of course, just a 'drop in the ocean'. The real question is not the impact on the relatively small number of tenants whose agreements have been scrutinized, but the likely impact of such scrutiny on the rest of the sector. 'Soft' regulation does, at the very least, require that central guidance and public 'undertakings' are widely publicized and have a significant 'deterrent' effect on other 'traders'. Is this true in relation to the PRS? It is to that question that we now turn.

Conclusion: Is 'Soft' Regulation of the PRS Merely 'Self' Regulation?

As should be clear from all the above, a strong tide is now running in support of a 'consumerist'/fair-trading approach to the regulation of tenancy agreements in the PRS.[78] Much can be said in support of this. At the very least, it is true that a significant number of tenants in the PRS (unlike those in the 'social' rented sector) do have the classic 'exit' option[79] if things do not work out for them with a particular

76 Nelken, D., *The Limits of the Legal Process: A Study of Landlords, Law and Crime* (London, Academic Press, 1983).

77 Lister, D., *Negotiating the Impossible? The Pursuit of Fair and Equitable Relationships between Landlords and Under 25s in the PRS* – unpublished PhD thesis (2002).

78 Of course not all landlord and tenant initiatives (in the PRS or the social rented sector) are susceptible to a 'consumerist' analysis. For example, the mandatory and selective licensing provisions in the Housing Act 2004 are clearly *regulatory* rather than consumerist in focus.

79 The extensive literature on choice 'exit' and 'voice' in relation to tenants largely pays homage to the original work of Albert Hirschman in 1970, Hirschman, A.O., *Exit Voice and Loyalty: Responses to Decline in Firms* (Cambridge, Massachusetts, 1970). As Karn, V., Lickiss, R. and Hughes, D., *Tenants' Complaints and the Reform of Housing Management*

landlord. This is particularly true for students who have (now) a clear choice between some form of 'hall' accommodation (whether provided by their university or college or by one of the relatively new large-scale student housing providers). As noted above, it may be that this goes some way to explain the relatively low incidence of references to the OFT concerning potentially unfair terms by student tenants.[80] Students can, and indeed do, exercise the 'consumer' option of taking their 'custom' elsewhere – at least at the end of a particular tenancy term.[81] However, at the heart of the 'consumerist' approach lie two dilemmas, one theoretical and one practical. Firstly, is the relatively 'soft' regulation it envisages an adequate response to an increasingly diffuse and diverse market, with widely variable standards and landlord attitudes? Secondly, even if it is theoretically appropriate, will it work in practice? Is an inevitably selective regime of OFT intervention likely to be a sufficient deterrent and/or a sufficient 'good practice' guide to landlords who are not directly the subject of the intervention? Alternatively, is such 'soft' regulation inevitably (in most cases) merely 'self' regulation of questionable effectiveness?

Some of the principal criticisms of 'soft' consumerist regulation of the PRS were addressed in the introduction to this chapter.[82] Few would argue that there is no need for some 'hard' regulatory control of the sector, for example in relation to houses in multiple occupation, fire safety and general fitness standards.[83] The Law Commission in *Renting Homes*[84] accepts that '... there is an inherent imbalance in the relative bargaining power of landlords and occupiers', and that 'for key issues, such as ensuring that occupiers get value for money, and an appropriate level of security of tenure, there is always the possibility of exploitation'.[85] As a result, the Commission accepts that '... [There] is a [need for] a comprehensible and practical regulatory framework ... to minimize such exploitation'.[86] However, aside from distinct areas where 'hard' regulation is still seen to be necessary, such as the law on harassment and unlawful eviction, the general approach of the Commission is a contractual 'fair trading' one, emphasizing principles of 'fairness' and 'transparency'. The overall aim seems to be the encouragement of a thriving and diverse PRS by not seeking to put traditional regulatory 'obstacles' in the way of the private landlord, whilst, at the same time, deterring any exploitation or unfairness which such a relatively deregulated market might produce. We now ask whether this seems an appropriate theoretical 'model', and whether it is likely to prove effective in practice.

(Aldershot, Dartmouth, 1997) and Alder, J. and Handy, C., *Housing Associations, Law and Practice,* 4th edition (London, Sweet and Maxwell, 2002), the 'exit' option is limited in relation to 'social' tenants, although the 'voice'/complaint option is of some significance. With students in the PRS the reverse seems to be broadly the case.

80 See note 58.

81 It must not be forgotten that most student tenants are required to sign 'fixed-term' tenancy agreements, typically of nine to ten months' duration with very limited opportunity to exit early without breaching the agreement.

82 Notes 10–12.

83 See Housing Act 2004, and note 78.

84 2003, note 8.

85 Law Commission, para. 2.2.

86 Law Commission, paras 2.1 and 2.2.

Is 'soft' regulation workable in theory?

If the Law Commission's proposals were ever to be legislatively adopted,[87] the application of the UTCCR to the PRS would be expressly legislatively underwritten. However, more significantly, 'model' tenancy agreements would be legislatively prescribed. Such 'model' agreements would contain four categories of terms:

- *Key* terms – such as the names and addresses of the parties and the property;
- *Compulsory minimum* terms, prescribing (for example) the duties of the parties and circumstances in which a landlord would be entitled to seek possession – any departure from these terms could only be so as to enhance them in the tenant's favour;
- *Special* terms, for example any relating to anti-social behaviour;
- *Default* terms – further terms needed to make the particular contract work.

It is clearly envisaged that such 'model' agreements would be in clear and straightforward language, and would not contain any terms that would unfairly disadvantage tenants. On that basis, if adopted by a landlord, terms of such an agreement would be presumptively 'fair' in relation to the UTCCR.[88]

Even if a landlord chose not to use one of the 'model' agreements, it would still be incumbent on him to at least provide the tenant with a written statement of the tenancy agreement.[89] The agreement would not be binding until such a written statement of terms was provided.[90] However, the Commission does not take the further step of recommending that the agreement itself needs to be signed, with a specific 'cooling-off' or 'consideration' period for tenant reflection prior to signature.

The above proposals would go some way to counter criticisms of the uncertainty and lack of rigour in a general consumerist 'fair trading' approach. 'Model' agreements would have an obvious attraction for well-intentioned landlords (particularly perhaps the 'small' or 'hobby' landlord), and if a landlord chose not to adopt them this might, over time, result in a presumption of unfairness developing in relation to the agreements they did use. However, given that there is no immediate prospect of the proposals becoming law, how far do *existing* 'fair trading' controls in the UTCCR represent an adequate response, even in theory, to the irregularities in bargaining strength and potential for tenant exploitation which even the Law Commission concedes exist? 'Hard' regulation, even given the normal doubts concerning interpretation and application of the law, has the virtue of relative consistency, and the attendant sanctions (criminal and civil) give teeth to the regulatory process. In relation to the UTCCR, even in the most obvious cases, there must always be some doubt as to whether a particular term is 'fair' or 'unfair' (unless it has already been referred to and considered by the OFT). It is difficult for even an experienced adviser to be sure

87 At the moment there seems little immediate prospect of this. Nearly three years have now passed since *Renting Homes* was published.

88 Law Commission, paras 3.2.9 and 4.4–4.19.

89 Law Commission, para. 7.5.

90 Law Commission, para. 7.20.

whether any given term would be seen as unfair by the OFT if referred to them.[91] Even if a term is successfully challenged, the only sanction appears to be that it is 'struck out' – there are no specific sanctions in the UTCCR to fine landlords for the use of unfair terms, or even to compensate tenants for any loss caused by their use.[92]

Is 'soft' regulation workable in practice?

As should be clear from the above, we have serious reservations about centring the regulation of the PRS on a 'consumerist'/'fair trading' model. Moreover, even the strongest advocates of this approach will, of necessity, concede that it cannot work adequately without widespread awareness amongst landlords and tenants of the existence of potential OFT intervention, and a willingness in tenants to refer agreements to the OFT. We would seriously question whether either of these requirements is likely to be fulfilled in practice.

Our research into student tenancy agreements suggests that awareness of the UTCCR and their potential amongst tenants is low. Few student tenants have the inclination to scrutinize their agreements in detail, and they do not put their tenancy agreements on the same instinctive 'consumerist' footing as (for example) retail purchases. In the latter case, a long history of media focus on 'rogue traders' has embedded a degree of consumer awareness. We are not aware of a similar media focus on 'rogue landlords'. In any event, however much a tenancy agreement might be conceptualized as a species of consumer agreement, it initially has a different 'feel' from, say, the purchase of an iPod or a pair of shoes. The Law Commission may wish to 'downgrade' the importance of land law concepts in relation to tenancy agreements, but to a tenant an agreement may well have the permanence and 'status' attaching in the popular mind to 'property', rather than the relatively ephemeral nature of a consumer 'good'. The large-scale 'student' landlords we have interviewed do seem to be aware of the UTCCR and (in a general way) of their significance, but have no real understanding of the importance of 'fairness' and 'balance' in tenancy agreements as advocated by the OFT *Guidance*.[93] We wonder whether small 'niche' landlords have even this degree of awareness.

We would further query whether most tenants would wish to challenge terms in their tenancy agreements on the basis of 'unfairness', even if they were aware of their right to do so. As discussed earlier,[94] most are unwilling to 'rock the boat' by discussing the 'fine print' of their agreements with their landlords, as long as they are broadly content with the property and the rent. Our research suggests that this is even more the case with student tenants, who are, simultaneously, likely to be

91 Of course, in theory, a tenant can challenge contractual terms directly before the courts. In practice, however, such challenges are likely to be few and far between.

92 Indeed, even the Law Commission in *Renting Homes* is at pains to play down any suggestion that 'punitive' sanctions might flow from its proposals. Whilst acknowledging that 'power imbalances' might continue to exist in relation to tenancy agreements, even if its proposals become law, it merely notes that there will be a further requirement 'to [encourage] good practice … and [discourage] inappropriate behaviour'!

93 See note 49.

94 Particularly in relation to the work of Diane Lister, notes 35 and 73.

deterred by the notion of raising detailed queries with their landlords, and far more concerned with other matters, as long as the property is adequate for their needs. The idea of making a formal reference or complaint to the OFT would be improbable in most cases. Our view would seem to be borne out by the statistics: as noted earlier,[95] in the ten-year period to 2006, only 70 tenancy agreements had been referred to the OFT, a mere 17 of these 'student' tenancies, and only one concerning the new 'mass' providers of student housing. We suggested earlier that a combination of deference, indifference and an end-of-tenancy 'exit' option are likely to make references to the OFT concerning 'hall-type' accommodation (whether university owned or privately owned) unlikely. We repeat that view again, and wish to reinforce our earlier conclusion that such fragmentary and partial 'referencing' makes it highly doubtful that the UTCCR are likely to have much 'deterrent' effect. Indeed our research has uncovered many clauses in ongoing student tenancy agreements which seem highly unreasonable and one-sided, and yet the large-scale landlords concerned continue to use them. It may be that in the other parts of the PRS, more 'committed' 'long-stay' tenants might have more of an 'interest' (in both senses of the word) in making references to the OFT. However, this is far from certain and, in any event, outside London the student tenancy market often dominates the PRS.

Our conclusions about the overall impact of the UTCCR may not seem unduly positive. It is certainly true that we are highly sceptical about how widespread awareness of its provisions is amongst tenants – in particular how willing young tenants would be to mount an 'unfairness' challenge. Equally, in the absence of generalized 'hard' regulation of the PRS[96] and sufficiently widespread accreditation schemes, it may be 'the only show in town'. One proposal which would undoubtedly have given 'consumerist'/'fair trading' regulations more 'bite' – the Law Commission proposal for model tenancy agreements – seems unfortunately some way from legislative realization. At present, despite its theoretical potential, our general conclusion about 'soft'/consumerist regulation in this area is that it lacks teeth in practice – amounting to little more than self regulation. To conceptualize tenants as 'consumers' is theoretically coherent, but to base regulation of the PRS on an assumption that they are 'consumers' like other 'consumers' is questionable.

The further our research delves into this area, the more concerns we have about both the theoretical 'model' of 'tenants as consumers' and the practical implications this has for regulation of the PRS. Amongst the key issues for further exploration in the future (by ourselves and others) are:

- The conceptual nature of tenancy agreements, and the extent to which they are governed by property law or contract law. The conflict in analysis has been a major bone of contention in recent years.[97] Although a 'consumer' analysis

---

95 See notes 58, 79 and 80.

96 Recent legislation on housing standards, licensing and tenancy deposits notwithstanding.

97 See, for example, the discussion surrounding cases like *Bruton v London and Quadrant Housing Trust* [2000] 1 AC 406 and *Islington LCB v Green and O'Shea* [2005] HLR 35, [2005] EWCA Civ. 56.

points to a 'victory' for contract law, our research indicates that a 'land law'/ 'property' perception of tenancies still features in tenants' thinking;
- The dissonance between the law's assumption of 'free' negotiation between equal parties and the reality of deference by would-be tenants towards their landlords. Does this render the apparent protection provided by the UTCCR and the OFT illusory?
- The extent to which landlords are aware of the significance of the UTCCR and the role of the OFT, and the degree to which those who are aware (to some extent) of the OFT are likely to modify their behaviour (or at least their written agreements!) as a result. Wider research on *this* issue seems to be urgently required.

The authors wish to thank Alwyn Jones of the School of Law, De Montfort University, for his numerous helpful comments and suggestions concerning this chapter.

Chapter 8

Accreditation

David Hughes and Rachael Houghton

What is accreditation and how does it fit into the overall scheme of governance of the private rented sector (PRS) of housing? 'Governance' is used in contra-distinction to 'regulation'; for the latter implies a system of 'command and control' regulation operated by an enforcing central or local government body with powers to punish those who do not comply with a set of legal rules. Accreditation, which began with early pioneer schemes in the 1990s[1] is based on voluntary compliance by landlords with codes of standards and practices relating to the standard of their properties and their relationships with tenants. The 'carrot' based approach of accreditation centres on the argument that it encourages landlords to adopt 'good' management practices by conferring on them a market advantage. Insofar as there is a 'stick' element in accreditation, it is that those who having sought accredited status and who then fail to comply, can lose it, maybe with consequent bad publicity. This might be embarrassing to larger scale landlords operating on a regional or national basis: it is more questionable whether small local landlords feel subject to the same constraints, particularly in areas where there is no lack of demand for accommodation and only a limited supply.

The Origins of Current Policy on Accreditation

These are found in the 2000 Housing Green Paper *Quality and Choice: A Decent Home for All.*[2] Chapter 5 was concerned with promoting a 'healthy private rented sector' in housing. It was acknowledged that while the rented sector provides an additional source of housing choices, particularly for younger people, the quality of both the rented stock and its management is deficient in too many cases, with a small minority of landlords actively exploiting their tenants and flouting legal requirements. The private rented sector was acknowledged to have a poorer image than is deserved and to be performing below its potential. The Green Paper argued this should be reversed by encouraging a larger, better quality and better managed stock of privately rented housing which retains existing 'good' landlords, encourages new investment by both

1 Leather, P., Revell, K. and Appleton, N., *Developing a Voluntary Accreditation Scheme for Private Landlords: A Guide to Good Practice* (London, Department of the Environment, Transport and the Regions, 2001).

2 DETR (Department of the Environment, Transport and the Regions), *Quality and Choice: A Decent Home for All. The Housing Green Paper* (London, HMSO, 2000).

existing landlords and incomers to the sector, and forces existing 'poor' landlords either to improve their standards or to leave the sector altogether.

A number of policy initiatives were proposed: one was the encouragement of self regulation by the sector. It was pointed out that a number of local authorities and universities already operated local landlord accreditation schemes which establish their members in a competitive market position and encourage others to join and accordingly raise their standards of management and provision. It was, however, acknowledged that these schemes had grown up independently of each other and varied considerably as to their requirements. The Green Paper accepted that there was a need to establish which types of accreditation are the most productive, and also to move towards commonality of standards. To this end research had been commissioned and good practice guidance would be published.[3]

The subsequent Housing Policy Statement *Quality & Choice: A Decent Home for All – Housing Policy in England*[4] announced that, *inter alia*, the development of accreditation schemes would be a 'Key Measure' in the promotion of a healthy private rental sector.[5] The Office of the Deputy Prime Minister (ODPM), which had taken over responsibility for housing from the erstwhile Department of the Environment, Transport and Rural Affairs (DETR) (and is, as from 2006, subsumed in the Department of Communities and Local Government) had already published a summary of responses to the Green Paper which stated that some 480 respondents had replied with 50 per cent supporting the development of accreditation schemes, including the National Federation of Private Landlords and a number of local authorities with large private sector stocks.[6]

The research commissioned from the Centre for Urban & Regional Studies at the University of Birmingham (CURBS) was published in 2001.[7] This revealed two principal means of fostering voluntary improvement of standards by landlords, landlord forums and accreditation schemes. The former, which involve meetings between authorities and landlords to discuss issues of common interest, were more common than the latter. One hundred and forty-six local authorities then had local forums while only 57 had active accreditation schemes, while nine had schemes in suspension and 21 had a scheme in planning. Some authorities which had accreditation schemes saw them as a principal means of influencing private rented sector standards; others considered them to be of use only outside the Housing in Multiple Occupation sector and only where landlords were otherwise responsible. The research established that a viable scheme has to have local political support and should be part of authorities' wider corporate housing objectives, while in practice most schemes also focused on the accreditation of individual properties rather than

---

3 DETR, *Quality and Choice: A Decent Home for All. The Housing Green Paper*, para 5.12.

4 ODPM (Office of the Deputy Prime Minister), *Quality & Choice: A Decent Home for All – Housing Policy in England* (London, ODPM, 2000).

5 ODPM, *Quality & Choice: A Decent Home for All – Housing Policy in England*, Chapter 3, para 3.3.

6 http://www.odpm.gov.uk/index.asp?id=1150269.

7 DETR, *Voluntary Accreditation for Private Landlords*, Housing Research Summary No.144 (London, Department of the Environment, Transport and the Regions, 2001).

landlords. Some schemes applied only to student lettings while others covered the whole rented sector; yet others applied only to parts of authorities' areas or only to particular property types. It emerged that accreditation schemes were aimed at those who managed their properties well and without complaints rather than those with a history of mismanagement.[8]

Landlords were motivated to join schemes for a variety of reasons, including finding tenants and to secure recognition of their level of service, though they might be less motivated to join in areas of high demand.

Most schemes were found to be run by authorities with some involving local Higher Education Institutions, and a variety of staffing levels were discovered together with variations in the provision of training and administrative support. The survey further discovered inconsistencies of standards between schemes and differing strategies to improve standards. Some schemes set high standards from the outset while others allowed for gradual improvement, yet others allowed provisional accreditation to landlords who would not meet targets initially. Some schemes featured regular monitoring of properties while others depended on self certification by landlords. The majority of schemes had an incentive for landlords to join, principally that of giving help in securing tenants via advertizing or listing. The survey concluded then it was too early to conclude whether schemes were effective in improving standards as most authorities with schemes had not yet monitored this. It was, however, argued that schemes can:

- Secure improvements to the condition and safety of stock;
- Encourage confidence that private landlords are able to meet housing needs;
- Reduce complaints from tenants;
- Free up resources to concentrate on landlords who flout the law;
- 'Badge' good landlords;
- Enable tenants and potential tenants to identify better quality properties.

It was, however, again stressed that accreditation is essentially voluntary in nature, works by persuasion, and is attractive only to responsible landlords whose stock is in reasonable condition. Schemes do not attract landlords with poor quality stock and those who are unwilling to comply with voluntary standards. Landlords who join do so only where they see a clear market advantage in doing so; however, accreditation was considered to be a cost effective alternative in appropriate cases to forms of legal enforcement.

Following this the DETR published *Developing a Voluntary Accreditation Scheme for Private Landlords: A Guide to Good Practice*[9] dealing with issues such as developing a scheme, recruiting appropriate staff, standard setting and compliance, incentivizing schemes for landlords, and the provision of information and publicity. This again stressed the key features of a scheme as:

- Its voluntary nature;
- The creation of standards relating to the condition and management of stock;

8 DETR, *Voluntary Accreditation for Private Landlords.*

9 Leather, Revell, and Appleton, 2001.

- Administration by an independent body such as a local authority or university;
- Incentives for landlords to join.

It was further stressed that schemes depend on two essential pre-conditions:

- Genuine commitment to co-operative working by both landlords – who must be sufficiently numerous and unanimous in their support – and the administering body;
- Inclusion of the 'right' sort of landlords and properties: schemes are inappropriate for the private sector as a whole and for landlords who have no intention of complying.

Voluntary accreditation was considered most likely to work with well-intentioned landlords who perceived benefits in receiving advice and practical help from the local authority and valued accredited status, or the increased likelihood of attracting tenants consequent on being accredited. It was further emphasized that in high demand areas landlords may require strong incentives to join a scheme, and that once a scheme is set up it must be run in an effective way so as to attract and retain members and to ensure compliance with standards set.

The role of schemes in assisting local housing authorities to take forward their various functions, for example accommodating the homeless, was examined by Jill Stewart in 'A Step in the Right Direction'.[10] This concluded that in addition to assisting with the homelessness function, where some authorities had found landlord accreditation schemes a more acceptable and viable option than the use of bed and breakfast hotels as temporary accommodation, schemes could also assist local strategies of increasing the supply and quality of the private rented stock, particularly regarding bringing vacant property into use, anti-poverty measures and urban regeneration. Stewart, however, emphasized once again the need for strategic planning in the development of a scheme, particularly the need to involve landlords from the outset, for example by means of a landlords' forum, and counselled that it is likely to take 12 months to develop a scheme and a further six months to launch it, additionally pointing out that the cost of a scheme will not be insignificant, while there may be an unfavourable ratio between the amount of acceptable property entering a scheme and the resources taken to set it up. Stewart pointed out particular issues to be addressed:

- All interested parties, for example housing allocations and advice sections, environmental health officers and potential landlords and tenants need to be in agreement on the aims and objectives of a scheme;
- Concerns that exist as to who may be held liable should a local authority place a tenant in accredited accommodation that subsequently proves to be injuriously defective;

10 Stewart, J., 'A Step in the Right Direction', *Environmental Health Journal,* (April 2002) pp. 104–7.

- Landlords' concern over the payment of rent by tenants, for example where this is to be met by housing benefit.

Stewart argued that accreditation was a step towards licensing in the private rented sector, but warned that the establishment of schemes required considerable resource input with no guarantee that the supply of accommodation would be increased and, once again, the participation only of better landlords being likely.

We now turn to consider more recent developments and research findings in relation to this issue. Initially we shall consider the particular issue of accreditation of student accommodation, especially with regard to its large scale provision by commercial providers.

Provision of Accreditation Schemes by ANUK

Over recent years students have become a key demand group in an increasingly commercialized sub-sector of the PRS. The shortfall in university provided accommodation was traditionally met by private landlords, often under head tenancy schemes.[11] More recently a new phenomenon has emerged in the student housing market – namely the commercial provider of student accommodation. Commercially developed student accommodation currently accounts for about 100,000 bed spaces[12] with another 25,660 bed spaces in the pipeline for 2006.[13] The increasing level of participation of commercial landlords in this specialist housing market prompted our research in order to establish the potential impact accreditation schemes might have on the student housing market and the PRS.

Though there are local providers of new build/converted student accommodation, in England the market is dominated nationally by five companies who are very often in competition with each other within individual university towns and cities. In Leicester, for example, four of the companies operate developments catering for both Leicester and De Montfort University students.[14] Other cities with similar developments include Sheffield, Leeds, Manchester, Liverpool and Nottingham.

The research underpinning this portion of the chapter, which consisted of interviews with relevant bodies, including a selection of local authorities, was undertaken at an opportune time due to the Housing Act 2004, the issue of the *Consultation Paper on Codes of Practice for Student Accommodation: Approved Codes under Section 233 of the Housing Act 2004* and the subsequent responses to

---

11 See Hughes, D. and Davis, M., 'Student Housing: a cautionary tale of one city', *Journal of Social Welfare and Family Law*, 24(2) (2002) pp. 135–55.

12 ODPM, *Codes of Practice for Student Accommodation: Approved Codes under Section 233 of the Housing Act 2004 – Consultation* (London, ODPM, September 2005) para 33.

13 King Sturge Newsletter, *The UK student accommodation market 2005/2006* (September, 2006) p. 2.

14 Davis, M. and Hughes, D., 'Changing Rooms: the legal and policy implications of a burgeoning student housing market in Leicester' in Lowe, S. and Hughes, D. (eds), *The Private Rented Sector in a New Century: Revival or False Dawn?* (Bristol, The Policy Press, 2002).

this *Consultation Paper, Codes of Practice for Student Accommodation: Responses to Consultation on Approved Codes under Section 233 of the Housing Act 2004*.[15]

Perhaps the most prominent bodies contributing to the development of accreditation schemes are Unipol and Accreditation Network UK (ANUK). More recently Universities UK (UUK) has become involved in the development of an accreditation scheme for university provided halls of residence at the request of the former ODPM. It can thus be seen that even within the student housing sub-sector there are a variety of accreditation bodies.

The Development and Role of Unipol and ANUK

The charitable body Unipol was formed in 1973. Its task was to help students in Leeds find accommodation. This service was subsequently extended to students in Wakefield and, until recently, Bradford. The primary functions of Unipol have since expanded and nowadays the charity is involved in the provision of accommodation for 2,000 students, property management, running training programmes for landlords, the development of accreditation schemes, rent collection and property inspection.

Unipol's first accreditation scheme was not developed until the mid-1990s. A new interest in accreditation schemes arose in response to the decision in *Barnes v Sheffield City Council*[16] (which determined that where students occupy a property as a cohesive family-style group they occupy as a 'single household' taking the property outside the definition of 'House in Multiple Occupation') coupled with a perception that tenants required protection from unscrupulous landlords.

In recognition of a growing trend towards self-regulation in the PRS and accreditation, the current Chief Executive of Unipol and an employee of Leeds City Council formed an umbrella company, Accreditation Network UK (ANUK), in order to provide annual accreditation conferences, the first of which was held in 2000. Unipol remains the secretariat for ANUK and is responsible for ANUK's funding through its finance department and the organization of the conferences. Numerous conferences are held throughout the year covering topics ranging from current legislation such as the Housing Act 2004 and the impact on student accommodation through to student lifestyles.

ANUK and its codes are owned by a consortium comprising of the National Union of Students (NUS), ANUK and Unipol. There is a Committee of Management which comprises representatives from accredited accommodation providers, professional bodies and parties involved in the consortium. The main responsibility of the Committee is to oversee the development of the codes. Four meetings are held each year, one of which is devoted to establishing whether the codes require updating. It is envisaged that this process will continue on a yearly basis 'approving revised codes

---

15 ODPM (Office of the Deputy Prime Minister), *Codes of Practice for Student Accommodation: Responses to Consultation on Approved Codes under Section 233 of the Housing Act 2004* (London, ODPM, March 2006).

16 (1995) 27 HLR 719.

that offer significant improvements over their predecessors'.[17] Our respondents emphasized that it is necessary to take a flexible approach when developing good practice benchmarks as this enables the codes to change as management practices and/or student requirements alter. Examples of developments that may be introduced in the future include updates on security standards, requirements for the provision of broadband facilities, and a separate energy efficiency supplement.

The growing trend towards self-regulation and accreditation schemes has been formally recognized in the Housing Act 2004, and particular provision has been made with regard to student accommodation. In relation to students, ANUK had previously developed a code of practice for large student halls of residence provided either by universities or commercial providers of student accommodation. This code was the model mainly followed by the ODPM in the Codes of Practice for Student Accommodation. The initial Consultation Paper and subsequent response papers leading to the Codes included ANUK's models for student accommodation 'managed and controlled' by both universities and those commercial bodies who are not exempted from HMO licensing.[18] This emphasized ANUK's place at the forefront of the accreditation movement. We shall return to the development and detail of the codes later; for the moment a brief outline of their applicability needs to be given.

During the consultation phase it was suggested that approved codes would apply only to property management, and not to any other issue. The reasoning was that where students reside in university or commercially provided halls of residence, their academic and disciplinary relationship with their institution is essentially separate from the tenancy relationship, though only as long as they remain students are they able to reside at the halls of residence. The ANUK approved codes of practice nevertheless cover the pre-contractual, contractual and post-contractual elements of a tenancy relationship. At the pre-contractual stage guidance is provided on, for example, the tenancy agreement and the fact that it must comply with the Unfair Terms in Consumer Contract Regulations[19] as well as issues such as advertizing and misrepresentation of the accommodation through advertizements, transparency on issues such as rent payments, insurance, deposits and any other costs associated with the tenancy. During the currency of a tenancy the ANUK code has provisions with regard to health and safety and management issues, and a complaints procedure is also in place which includes the ability to refer unresolved disputes to a Unipol Tribunal. This is particularly relevant where the landlord has committed a breach of health and safety or management related issues. Poor management practices and unnecessary retention of deposits are examples of matters that have been referred to

17 ODPM, *Codes of Practice for Student Accommodation: Responses to Consultation on Approved Codes under Section 233 of the Housing Act 2004*, p. 28.

18 ODPM, *Codes of Practice for Student Accommodation: Responses to Consultation on Approved Codes under Section 233 of the Housing Act 2004*, p. 16.

19 HMSO, The Unfair Terms in Consumer Contracts Regulations 1999 (SI 1999 No. 2083) (London, The Stationery Office Limited, 1999).

the jurisdiction of the tribunal and it has been effective in reaching resolution.[20] The post-contractual guidance covers matters such as the fate of deposits.

The primary functions of ANUK have included the facilitation, development and support of good practice in accreditation. While ANUK's accreditation schemes were initially developed for traditional 'small' landlords renting properties in the PRS, this function was extended with the launch of ANUK's Code of Standards for Larger Developments on 2 November 2004. The introduction of this code was arguably of fundamental importance in the accreditation movement as it was the first code that applied to a particular defined group within the PRS – the student housing market.

The purpose of this code was to provide good practice benchmarks laying down criteria for health and safety, and management practices for properties with a large concentration of students living within them. The size criterion under the code is properties with 25 or more students residing in a building with self-contained or cluster flats. The number of relevant properties in the first published list was some 150.[21] This has subsequently increased to over 200 properties supplying specialist accommodation for students.[22] In general universities, commercial providers of student accommodation and Housing Associations have agreed to abide by this code, which demonstrates a growing trend towards compliance with voluntary codes of practice and also a perceived need to obtain a market advantage by providers in such a competitive housing market.

Further Developments in Accreditation

Our research indicates there are, in mid 2006, 76 different accreditation codes, mainly administered by local authorities. Twelve of these codes have been specifically designed for student housing. These codes aim to provide realistic guidelines as to how both parties to a tenancy agreement should operate their daily relationship from the beginning of the tenancy. This is particularly important for young tenants such as students who have little or no experience in managing a tenancy relationship. Likewise, a high proportion of traditional landlords operating in the PRS are side-line or 'hobby' landlords and '… it is not only lack of knowledge of legal procedure that typifies individual landlords but also generally low levels of management expertise ad skill'.[23] It is, however, not only small-scale landlords who lack the appropriate skills required for managing tenancies. Other research we currently have in progress indicates that local hall managers responsible for the day-to-day tenancy

20 www.unipol.leeds.ac.uk/Leeds/COS/Tribunal_Minutes_and_press_release_index/Chairs_Action/13Dec04.asp?sch=tribunal+action.

21 www.anuk.org.uk/News/Largec=Codelist.asp (no longer available).

22 www.anuk.org.uk/LargeCode/list.asp?sch=list+of+accredited+student+accommodation.

23 Lowe, S., *Housing Policy Analysis: British Housing in Cultural and Comparative Context* (Houndmills, Palgrave/Macmillan, 2004) p. 231.

relationship in commercially provided student accommodation do not necessarily have a background in managing tenancy relationships.[24]

Landlordism is traditionally 'under-professionalized',[25] thus management skills training in conjunction with guidance on conducting tenancy relationships becomes part of a necessary skills training programme in order to ensure the protection of tenants in both the 'traditional' and emerging commercial student accommodation markets.

The evidence provided by our local authority respondents on the flexibility of accreditation codes indicated that landlords are not required to include all of their properties when joining a scheme. This may be due to the fact that some properties may not meet the standards required by an accreditation scheme or the landlord may simply decide against including all properties. What this does mean, however, is that landlords have the opportunity to include other properties within accreditation at a later date or as their property profile increases. This level of flexibility is preferred generally to an 'all or nothing' approach. Such an option would hinder the improvement of the PRS as it would only attract landlords providing high standard accommodation and exclude completely those who aspire to improve their accommodation but are only able to do so on a gradual basis. To assist landlords in bringing properties up to the standards required by accreditation schemes, some local authorities provide grants or loans.[26]

Some landlords have opted out of accreditation schemes as their properties have not met required standards. Our respondents indicated that these landlords would generally reapply about a year later, during which time they would have brought the property up to standard. This highlights the growing attraction for landlords in joining accreditation schemes; they are aware of market forces and although improvement entails financial outlay, the long term reward through enhanced tenant flow outweighs the burden of expenditure.

When landlords enter an accreditation scheme, it appears they can generally do so with minimal expenditure. Setting unrealistically high benchmarks in an attempt to create an immediate impact on the standards within the PRS would act as a disincentive for some landlords as compliance would be a time-consuming and costly exercise. As suggested above, it is more productive in the long-term if the overall aim is a gradual improvement in standards of tenanted housing. An example which illustrates the effectiveness of gradual improvement of conditions and standards is an accreditation scheme in Bradford. Here, over a period of the three years, the accredited student housing market moved from a code of standards lower than those being met in the more mature student housing market in Leeds to the same level of standards.

---

24 A doctoral thesis by Rachael Houghton, supervised by Professor David Hughes, examining the provision and governance of student accommodation by large commercial providers.

25 Lowe, *Housing Policy Analysis: British Housing in Cultural and Comparative Context*, p. 49.

26 www.alliance-leicestercommercialbank.co.uk/bizguides/full/lettings/parkes-loan.asp?version=graphical.

Accreditation also provides a further mechanism that can lead to the improvement of standards within the PRS, albeit in an indirect fashion. This is a consequence of the employment of 'aspirational' standards. This is a means whereby landlords can aim to improve on the minimum standards required, with the objective of supplying accommodation to a standard above and beyond the requirements laid out in legislation such as the Housing Act 2004. As the provisions of the Housing Act 2004 and the Codes of Conduct for Student Accommodation are, however, still in their infancy, further empirical research would need to be undertaken in order to establish the long-term impact of such aspirational provisions on the standards of housing provision and housing management practice.

Who May Be Involved in the Development of Schemes and the Issue of Effective Enforcement

During the development phase of accreditation schemes ANUK and Unipol found that input from landlords was essential to the success of a scheme. The importance of external input was further reinforced during consultation on the development of the national codes approved under the Housing Act 2004. Input was obtained from, for example, the National Union of Students, the Chartered Institute of Environmental Health, Association for Student Residential Accommodation, and private providers of student accommodation. The Consultation Paper on the Codes of Practice for Student Accommodation[27] indicated that current members of the ANUK network such as local authorities, higher education institutions (HEIs), commercial providers and registered social landlords (RSLs) were consulted during this period. However, individual students as consumers of this specialist accommodation, were not. Maybe this indicated a degree of paternalism on the part of the framers of the codes and unwillingness to involve specifically the recipients of a service in formulating the terms on which it is offered, or it may simply reflect difficulties in consulting so large and diverse a group of people.

Weaknesses in the effectiveness of accreditation schemes may arise, for example, as a result of failure to inspect properties at the time they receive accredited status and the consequent policing methods currently relied upon by ANUK and Unipol. The enforcement methods include following up tenants' complaints and annual compliance checks. The former mechanism relies on tenants following the complaints procedure if their landlord is in breach of any of the accreditation conditions. The latter involves a questionnaire sent to tenants. This questionnaire requires tenants to declare whether the property has relevant health and safety features and enquires into management practices, responses to repairs requests and other tenancy related issues. The response rate to these questionnaires is between 15 per cent and 30 per cent. It may be asked whether an improvement in response rates needs to be sought. As membership of schemes increases, reliance on tenant responses and complaints procedures may not be the most appropriate way of ensuring that landlords meet

---

27 ODPM, *Codes of Practice for Student Accommodation: Responses to Consultation on Approved Codes under Section 233 of the Housing Act 2004*, para. 25.

required standards. There may well be passive tenants who live in sub-standard properties or who are subject to unscrupulous management practices despite the fact that the landlord is accredited and who neither complain nor return questionnaires. The problem faced by Unipol and ANUK in this connection relates to resources for initial inspection of properties and monitoring continued compliance.

Throughout the development of accreditation schemes the voluntary nature of accreditation, as opposed to a compulsory membership, has always been a fundamental requirement. When accreditation schemes were initially introduced, compulsory compliance with a code of conduct was not felt to be desirable as this would apply a form of coercion to landlords who did not want to be part of such a scheme or could not comply due to the level of improvement required to properties. This could drive some landlords out of the market. The involvement of central government, however, questions the future longevity of voluntaristic accreditation. This seems to follow from the provisions of the Housing Act 2004 which lay down that universities who are part of an approved accreditation scheme are exempted from Housing in Multiple Occupation regulation, while commercial landlords (who are subject to such licensing) but who are also accredited, will receive favourable treatment such as reduced license fees.[28] These provisions arguably initiate an indirect move towards compulsory accreditation of certain providers of student accommodation. Landlords will have no choice with regard to licensing and may join an accreditation scheme but the 'true' choice will have been taken away as accreditation here will give no exemption from control, merely some easing of the regulatory burden.

To ensure the continued success of accreditation schemes as an important initiative aimed at improving the conditions of the PRS, membership needs to continue expanding and, to encourage this, landlord incentives are necessary. The most obvious incentive relates to market recognition by an external body that the landlord is a good practitioner. Where there is a high level of demand for accommodation, for example in a university town, the promotion of accredited status does give such landlords a market advantage. Our respondents emphasize the importance of this, and Unipol/ANUK have found that landlords secured tenants for accredited properties faster. The future success of accreditation is thus dependent on increasing scheme memberships and promoting the advantages of membership. So far as the student sector is concerned, national events aimed at informing HEIs about accreditation schemes and how these fit into the pattern of legislation have been carried out by the former ODPM. Leaflets from the National Union of Students and the former ODPM are available to educate students about accreditation and its benefits. Students need to be aware of accreditation schemes if these are to be truly effective – a comment that, of course, applies to tenants generally. Such an awareness should be accompanied by a greater degree of knowledge and understanding of all the terms and requirements of tenancy agreements, but experience generally indicates that this desirable state of affairs is probably incapable of being brought about. Despite accreditation, therefore, there is a continuing need for external regulation of landlords.

---

28 ODPM, *Codes of Practice for Student Accommodation, Consultation Paper* (London, ODPM, 2005) p. 12, para. 35.

It must, however, be pointed out that some of the large commercial providers derive many, and indeed in some cases all, of their tenants from nomination schemes operated by universities. De Montfort University in Leicester, for example, has a block booking, primarily for first year students, on one commercially provided hall of residence. Where such an arrangement exists it is clearly in the interest of the university to promote and maintain its links with the commercial provider and it must be asked whether such a relationship might act as a disincentive to a company from joining or remaining in an accreditation scheme unless, of course, relevant university authorities made it a requirement of their nomination arrangements that the provider should be accredited so as to demonstrate overall commitment to good management practices. That would operate as a somewhat different 'carrot and stick' within the world of landlord accreditation.

Memberships of Unipol's accreditation schemes are renewed on an annual basis and the number of landlords who are members of the scheme varies from year to year. For the period 2006/07, there are over 400 members.[29] Landlords whose tenants remain in situ after the year in which they entered an accredited property do not need to re-join the scheme until those tenants leave that property. This suggests that landlords may become accredited merely in order to secure long-term tenants rather than to achieve recognition as an accredited landlord who follows good practice.

Accreditation in the East Midlands: Local Schemes

Because of the large number of accreditation schemes in operation nationally, our research focused on schemes in the East Midlands in the counties of Leicestershire, Nottinghamshire, Northamptonshire, Lincolnshire and Derbyshire in order to provide a snapshot of accreditation in the PRS.

Currently only three local authorities – Derby, Kirby-in-Ashfield and Broxtowe – are members of ANUK's general accreditation schemes, one of which is a student-orientated scheme.[30] As our research primarily focused on the student housing market, particular reference was made to properties registered under ANUK's National Code of Standards for Larger Developments as this relates to high density student housing. It was established that most of the university towns in the East Midlands had properties registered under this code.[31] The only exception to this was University College, Northampton, which only secured university status in 2005.[32] It was further discovered that the majority of relevant properties accredited under this code included those of the major providers of student accommodation to whom earlier allusion was made: the only variation was the inclusion of halls of residence owned by Nottingham Trent University.[33] In Leicester the major commercial providers and

29 Unipol, *Code of Standards Members 2006/2007* (Leeds, Unipol Student Homes, 2006).

30 www.anuk.org.uk/Directory/eastmidlands.

31 www.anuk.org.uk/LargeCode/list.asp.

32 Education Guardian, 11 July 2005, http://www.educationguardian.co.uk/newuniversities/story/0,,1526142,00.html.

33 www.anuk.org.uk/LargeCode/list.asp.

one Housing Association are accredited through ANUK's specialist student codes of practice. However, one other Housing Association in Leicester provides large scale student accommodation but currently is not a member of an accreditation scheme. What we have found in the East Midlands generally confirms that accreditation schemes are attractive to some landlords who wish to market a particular type of property and who desire to enhance their market position by gaining the recognition that accredited status confers.

Further information obtained from desk-top research and telephone interviews with respondents indicates that each region may have local authorities with greater or lesser involvement in the accreditation movement. In the East Midlands generally some accreditation schemes have been in existence for about 10 years and currently have between 1,500 and 1,600 accredited landlord members. By way of contrast an area such as East Lincolnshire's accreditation scheme has only been in force since 2004 and has a membership of only 13 landlords. Other developments include:

- A student accreditation scheme implemented in May 2005 at De Montfort University, Leicester. This scheme is run in partnership with Leicester City Council who have the responsibility of monitoring properties;
- A new student accreditation scheme developed between Northampton Borough Council, the University of Northampton and the Northampton branch of the National Landlords Association;
- The City of Derby is currently updating its student accreditation scheme in order for it to comply with the Housing Act 2004 for the September 2006 intake of students.

Throughout the development and implementation of these accreditation schemes, a multi-agency approach has often been adopted. The parties involved include landlord associations, employees of councils, numerous councils working together, cabinet members, university accommodation offices, student unions and universities themselves. However, one group was consistently excluded from the consultation phase – the consumers of private rented accommodation, i.e. tenants. Landlords have not always been included in the development of accreditation schemes, though the experience of ANUK is that such involvement is crucial to the successful implementation of a scheme.

Because of the large number of either university or privately owned halls of residence (and the relevant implications of the Housing Act 2004) this sub-sector of the market must have an important role to play in the future development of accreditation schemes. The majority of the local authorities we investigated have a student accreditation scheme in force. In one area where there is not a specific accreditation scheme for students, the reason was that the authority did not have a large student population. However, another area whose student population was less than that of Leicester or Nottingham did have a scheme for student properties, indicating local awareness of the importance of this sub-sector of the market, though this clearly varies from area to area.

The standards required by accreditation schemes are variable: they range from a single generally applied standard to, for example, a tiered three star rated system.

Variations are also encountered with regard to inspection under schemes. In some areas all properties are inspected at the initial registration stage, whereas others select only a number of properties. This is repeated at the re-registration stage, with the inspections generally carried out by local authority employees. Between 36 and 48 months appears to be the standard duration for each registration period. One exception to this we discovered is the De Montfort University accreditation scheme whereby membership lasts for five years.

Within the East Midlands local authorities follow the ANUK policy of not requiring landlords to register all their properties on becoming a member of an accreditation scheme and actively encourage landlords to include other properties at a later date.

Each local authority in the East Midlands area actively promotes accreditation schemes and utilizes a variety of methods to raise awareness. These include mailshots to new landlords, advertizing in council offices and the local press, leaflets, and one authority supplies all first-year students moving into halls of residence with information packs on accreditation schemes.

The East Midlands area currently demonstrates a strong commitment to both accreditation schemes and the raising of standards within the PRS. This is illustrated by the DASH initiative – Decent and Safe Homes in the East Midlands, a project funded by the Government Office East Midlands.[34] Three authorities – Derby, Leicester and Nottingham – are at the forefront of this venture which was established less than a year ago. This initiative works in collaboration with ANUK and it is believed that a successful collaboration regionally may lead to others on a national basis.

The purpose of the project is to assist in the establishment and development of accreditation schemes, self-regulation and the encouragement of landlords to raise their standards through advice and training. The project further aims to harmonize accreditation schemes throughout the East Midlands by developing a regional model accreditation scheme. Once this has been established (and it will be similar to ANUK's models) a review mechanism will be necessary to ensure landlords are meeting required standards. It is anticipated that the scheme will become self-funded through revenue generated from training course fees.

DASH is further active in generating awareness of accreditation schemes by, for example, establishing the Accreditation Network East Midlands (ANEM).

Current Legislative Policy and Its Possible Impact on Accreditation

The Housing Act 2004 embodied Government initiatives aimed at improving the conditions of privately rented accommodation with the intention of creating a healthy and thriving rental sector.[35] The Act focuses primarily on the housing conditions in the PRS and, to a lesser extent, housing management. Tenants residing in PRS are more

34 www.eastmidlandsdash.org.uk.

35 Carr, H., Cottle, S., Baldwin, T. and King, M., *The Housing Act 2004: A Practical Guide* (Bristol, Jordan Publishing Ltd, 2005).

likely to find themselves living in sub-standard housing.[36] Particular concerns apply to multiple occupied dwellings (HMOs) as residents in this type of accommodation suffer due to '... poor safety standards, overcrowding, inadequate facilities and poor and unscrupulous management'.[37] Acknowledging the difficulties faced by tenants residing in HMOs the Act seeks to improve the standards of HMOs through mandatory licensing provisions contained in Part 2 and specific sections of Part 7 of the Housing Act 2004. University and commercially provided student accommodation technically falls within the definition of a HMO under section 254 of the Housing Act 2004. However, Schedule 4 paragraph 4 exempts accommodation provided by educational establishments who are complying with an accreditation scheme from the definition of a HMO, and section 233 of the Act further permits approval of codes of practice for university or commercially provided accommodation.

The PRS currently accounts for 11 per cent of all households and provides homes for 2.2 million people,[38] 40 per cent of whom are young people under the age of 30.[39] The significant concentration of young people in the PRS and, in particular, the increasing student population, have arguably played an important role in the revival of this sector.[40] Currently some two-thirds of the student population resides in the PRS; about one-third of these students inhabit either university or commercially provided student accommodation.[41] Hypothetically some 400,000 students are currently residing in accommodation that could, in theory, be classified as HMOs.[42]

The Housing Act 2004 recognizes that students living in shared accommodation do attract multiple occupation status, but due to the specialist nature of this niche market the Act makes specific provision for it. During the consultation phase on HMO licensing, it was proposed that student accommodation provided by establishments listed as recognized bodies in The Education (Recognized Bodies) (England) Order

36 ODPM (Office of the Deputy Prime Minister), *English Housing Condition Survey 2001 Private Landlords Survey* (London, ODPM, 2003) p. 21.

37 Carr *et al.*, *The Housing Act 2004: A Practical Guide*, 2006, para 3.6.

38 ODPM, *Housing in England 2003/04, Part 1: Trends in Tenure and Cross Tenure Topics* (London, ODPM, 2005) p. 7.

39 ODPM, *Licensing in the Private Rented Sector – Consultation on the Implementation of HMO Licensing: Regulatory Impact Assessment, Housing Bill Part 2: HMO Licensing* (London, ODPM, 2004).

40 Lowe, p. 219; Lister, D., 'Young people's strategies for managing tenancy relationships in the private rented sector', *Journal of Youth Studies*, 7, 3 (2004) pp. 315–30; Hughes, D., Davis, M., Houghton, R. and Ball, J., 'The Housing of Students: Legal and Structural Implication of Changing Patterns of Housing Provision in England, and a comparison with experience in France' (Unpublished Conference Paper 2005).

41 ODPM, *Codes of Practice for Students Accommodation: Approved Codes under Section 233 of the Housing Act 2004 – Consultation*, para. 6.

42 ODPM, *Codes of Practice for Students Accommodation: Approved Codes under Section 233 of the Housing Act 2004 – Consultation*, para. 33.

2003[43] should not be subject to HMO licensing.[44] Subjecting university-run student housing to mandatory licensing was not thought necessary as such accommodation was considered to be '… responsibly managed by semi-public bodies'.[45] As a consequence the specified educational establishments whose properties are occupied by persons pursuing full-time courses of education[46] were listed on 6 April 2006. The regulations list 155 educational establishments complying with either Universities UK or ANUK's codes of conduct.[47] These codes were approved under section 233 of the Housing Act 2004 by the then ODPM under regulations which came into effect on 6 April 2006.[48] They include the ANUK Code in respect of Larger Developments of student accommodation *not* managed and controlled by Educational Establishments, even though HMO licensing will apply to such commercially managed property.

Recent years have seen dramatic changes within this niche market. Commercial companies have identified changing trends in student housing requirements and have developed purpose built residences comprising cluster flats with communal living areas and en-suite bedrooms. Some of the newer developments provide bed spaces for 800 students. With such large concentrations of students within developments mechanisms are needed to protect residents' interests. Accreditation schemes have the potential to ensure this type of housing is of a high standard and the student housing market demonstrates that schemes can be successful in improving the standards of private rented housing. Furthermore there is the potential for such schemes to infiltrate other sectors of the PRS as our evidence from the East Midlands demonstrates.

Notes of Caution

Though there is evidence that landlords, particularly large commercial providers of student accommodation, remain keen to embrace accreditation for the advantages it confers, questions still remain in connection with this form of governance within the PRS:

---

43 HMSO, The Education (Recognised Bodies) (England) (Amendment) Order 2005 (SI 2005 No. 2957) (London, The Stationery Office Limited, 2005).

44 ODPM, *Licensing in the PRS – Consultation on the Implementation of HMO Licensing: Regulatory Impact Assessment, Housing Bill Part 2: HMO Licensing*, Part 3, Section 3, para 4.

45 ODPM, *Codes of Practice for Student Accommodation: Approved Codes under Section 233 of the Housing Act 2004 – Consultation*, para 11.

46 HMSO, The Houses in Multiple Occupation (Specified Educational Establishments) (England) (No. 2) Regulations, 2006 (SI 2006 No. 2280) (London, The Stationery Office Limited, 2006).

47 The Universities UK/Standing Conference of Principals Code of Practice for the Management of Student Housing dated 20 February 2006, and the Accreditation Networks UK/Unipol Code of Standards for Larger Developments for Student Accommodation Managed and Controlled by Educational Establishments dated 20 February 2006.

48 HMSO, The Housing (Approvals of Codes of Management Practice) (Student Accommodation) England Order 2006 (SI 2006 No. 646) (London, The Stationery Office Limited, 2006).

- How will schemes develop with regard to ongoing monitoring of the condition and management of properties included within schemes?
- Should there be concern about the development of different types of scheme with varying requirements within particular regions and local authority areas, or is such diversity to be welcomed as reflecting the existence of various sub-sectors within the rental market?
- Will landlords, whether traditional 'small' operators or large commercial concerns, be willing long-term to embrace accreditation given that they may, in the case of multiple occupied properties at least, be subject to HMO controls and licensing: where is the further advantage that accreditation must provide if it is to be attractive?

Chapter 9

Regulating a Deregulated Market

David Hughes and Stuart Lowe

This collection began by asking a number of questions about why the private rented sector (PRS) in Britain has grown so rapidly in recent decades, after nearly a century of persistent decline. It was made clear that the twenty-first century PRS was a new market very different from 'traditional' private renting. Rather than offering long-term settled family accommodation, it became a rapid turnover tenure comprised very largely of young single people and containing a number of niche markets serving a variety of purposes. Where the traditional picture persisted was in the type of landlords that provide the bulk of this housing: small-scale, amateur investors.

The 'new PRS' was the creation of the 'assured shorthold tenancy' (following the Housing Act 1988, and even more accelerated following the Housing Act 1996, which made this tenure the normal mode of tenancy, as opposed to an option for private landlords), bringing in its wake a liberalized market able to respond to existing pent-up demand for easy-access accommodation, mainly from young people leaving home for the first time, and from hundreds of thousands of students in a rapidly expanding higher education system. In addition, the sector was significantly boosted between 1988 and 1995 by the unintended consequences of an unreformed housing benefit system, allowing about 300,000 council tenants per annum to move into the PRS, in effect an exit strategy from the so-called worst estates. Finally the property industry itself created the basis for a phenomenal investment boom through the vehicle of buy-to-let mortgages, which currently account for over one in ten property transactions. All this together amounts to a new, vibrant and expanding PRS, attracting a wave of new investment anticipated in earlier legislation but not achieved until after the 1988 Act, when a window of opportunity opened due to this confluence of social, economic and political streams.

This story demonstrates the complexities of policy change, how new social trends and new markets have interacted in shaping this sector of British housing, and indeed how the sector relates and interacts with the wider housing system. Who could have foreseen the impact that deregulation of the PRS and the unreformed housing benefit system would have in depressing demand for council housing on such a large scale? We argue that it is important to appreciate the bigger picture, because it is only by seeing how institutional structures (such as the markets, law, new policy and policy implementation agencies and bodies) mediate and filter wider social and economic change that we can make sense of the critical moment of delivery and implementation, when, as some policy analysts argue, policy is 're-made'. This is one of the reasons why this text has been written by law specialists, policy analysts and specialist housing researchers. The chapters, we hope, draw together different sorts of knowledge, respectfully crossing disciplinary boundaries that sometimes inhibited a clearer view of what is going on, and more importantly producing a more informed picture of what might or should happen in the future.

As part of this response, it is also clear to us that we need to take seriously the claims of 'new governance' scholars who have shown how radically the policy process has changed in recent decades. Without time to explore it, we simply urge readers to take on board some key ideas about how policy delivery happens. The theme for this purpose is the increasing separation of policy making and delivery. Although the instinct and reality of central government is to draw power to itself, one of the main legacies of the Blair era will be that the implementation and delivery of policy have become much 'looser'. Gone are the days of command and control (from the top down, largely through local government); instead delivery takes place through deregulated agencies, quasi-private bodies, the outright privatization of major public services and the use of the device of contractualization even within public service agencies, so that (for example) the delivery of the homelessness service now depends to a considerable extent on arrangements made between local housing authorities and private landlords. In short, we see a much more fragmented and 'networked' policy, with important implications for accountability and the distribution of political power. One important theme here has been the monitoring of delivery agencies through a variety of 'new public management' methods, league tables, performance targets and, our special concern, new forms of market regulation.

The particular focus of this collection has been to assess evidence on the impact of the new regulatory framework, following on from the deregulation and expansion of the PRS. Will regulation dampen or distort this thriving market? How will landlords and investors respond either to voluntary opportunities (such as accreditation schemes) or more hard-nosed regulation? Almost all the chapters address this question, either implicitly or explicitly. Beginning at the beginning, one fundamental issue we needed to raise about any system of legal control, and especially the relationship between landlord and tenant – whether it be the traditional style of command and control, or the more recent styles based on voluntary compliance – is, why do people obey it? Indeed, do they consciously obey at all, or is their behaviour motivated by other factors?

Diane Lister's chapter raises this in the context of the Law Commission's proposed reforms of the landlord–tenant regime. She argues that there is a very deep-seated psychological issue at the heart of the landlord and tenant relationship, one that is hardly affected by legal forms and niceties. In law, a let dwelling is the tenant's possession, and the landlord's freehold rights are, pro tem, subordinated to that. But is that how landlords behave in practice? Furthermore, is that how landlords and tenants can be expected to behave without a most intensive and expensive package of training, and – some might say – indoctrination? Ignorance of the law may be no excuse, but its prevalence in practice leads to actions far at odds with what legal requirements might suggest.

Certainly, so far as 'small' or 'hobby' landlords – those who for many years have made up the core of the PRS – are concerned, the answer appears to be 'no'. Such landlords maintain a highly proprietorial and controlling attitude to 'their' houses, and a considerable desire to regulate the lives of their tenants. Such attitudes are not confined to the PRS, of course; the public sector can furnish many historic examples of the paternalism of council landlords towards their tenants, and a failure to appreciate the distinction that must be implicit in the divide between a property being a landlord's house and also a tenant's home. However, the evidence on which Lister bases her arguments is very strong with regard to the PRS, and can be traced back to the seminal work of David Nelken,[1] which demonstrated the very weak effect the law has on the actual conduct of relationships within the sector.

It may be, of course, that with the diversification of the PRS away from the traditional small landlord towards the growth of those who pursue letting as a career, and the emergence of large commercial concerns who have letting, particularly student letting, as a core activity, that the law could play a rather more effective role. Certainly such landlords are quite likely to be image conscious, and aware of competition issues, and are therefore, arguably, more likely to be observant of legal requirements. However, again it must be asked whether their desire to comply or conform to expectations is derived from a respect for the law, or from more commercial motives. In this respect the chapter on accreditation indicates that the latter may be the explanation. Indeed in recently published regulations the cost benefit to HEIs of signing up to accreditation schemes compared to formal HMO licensing of student accommodation by a local authority are shown to be very considerable.

The Houses in Multiple Occupation (Specified Educational Establishments) (England) Regulations (SI 2007/708) were made on 6 April 2007 and revoke the previous regulations referred to by Hughes and Houghton in their chapter on Accreditation Schemes. Though these new regulations only add certain specified educational establishments to the list of those that existed already under the scheme of exemption from HMO control, and make no change to the standards that are imposed by the relevant codes of practice that are referred to in the scheme, it is of interest to note the comments made in the explanatory memorandum which has been issued by the Department of Communities and Local Government in connection with the new regulations.

It is accepted that the control and supervision of student accommodation was an issue of some controversy during the passage of the Housing Act 2004 through Parliament, and the normal complexity of HMO regulation is considerably increased with regard to the student sub-sector of accommodation that is multiple occupied. For that reason there was a desire to introduce higher standards of management for the student sub-sector which would lay down requirements specifically designed to meet the needs of both students and those of their institutional accommodation providers. The government considered that the best way forward here was to provide the Codes of Management to which Hughes and Houghton refer in their chapter, and that such codes would enable the exemption of relevant Higher Education Institutions from the requirements of otherwise having to undergo HMO licensing by their local authorities. In this latter connection it should be remembered that some

1 Nelken, D., *The Limits of the Legal Process: A Study of Landlords, Law and Crime* (London, Academic Press, 1983).

such institutions may have relevant properties in more than one local authority area, and applications for licensing would then have to be made on a plural basis.

The Codes of Management that have been provided and to which Hughes and Houghton refer cover many more issues than those of property maintenance and safety, and lay down considerable requirements for the general good management of relevant properties by HEIs. However, while compliance with the codes exempts the listed HEIs from the need to obtain HMO licences, it must be remembered that such an exemption is not entirely uncontroversial, and that the Codes themselves, and compliance therewith, are to be kept under regular review. On the other hand the explanatory memorandum points out that compliance by the relevant HEIs with the codes ensures that they obtain considerable cost benefits. In any year, the memorandum states, the number of students in university-maintained property is some 300,000 people. There are a further 100,000 students currently in privately maintained residences. The indicative maximum licensing fee per bed space under the HMO regime would be £180 for a five-year period, some £36 per annum. This would be a considerable burden for HEIs to bear, and would be well in excess of £10 million. However, the costs of complying with the Codes of Practice are, according to the Explanatory Memorandum, only some £0.70 per bed space, producing a figure for 300,000 spaces of some £210,000.

It might also be noted that the costs of obtaining a HMO license varies from place to place and this might be a further complicating factor for HEIs if they operated outside the codes. *Business Moneyfacts* found that some administrative charges levied on landlords were as high as £1,750, while others were as little as £150, depending on the local authority concerned (the average being £515).[2] Across the PRS as a whole and, notwithstanding the question why there is such variation between the authorities, it seems probable that responsible landlords will pay up, but profit-mongers may balk at these fees, especially in places where they are at the upper end of the scale. Given, for example, the considerable variation in the size of the 'housing benefit market' in different local authority areas, as pointed out in Julie Rugg's chapter, differential fees will further complicate matters, adding to the uneven pattern of response round the country. As is so often the case, mundane administrative detail is the source of problems in achieving beneficial patterns of compliance.

In respect of HEIs it can be seen that there is a strong incentive to sign up to the system of accreditation that has been developed for the residences they provide. The wider body of landlords who sign up for accreditation schemes do so for reasons of market advantage, and because they are likely to be able to meet accreditation requirements anyway; in other words they are likely to be those who would be regarded as 'good' in any case. If this argument is correct then we can draw two conclusions. First, no matter how the law is altered, its function is likely to remain limited to its historic role: that of being the final resort, the sanctioning deterrent for those who simply will not comply, and who have done their utmost to evade control for as long as possible. Under that view, the ghost of Rachman still haunts us. Secondly, the

2 Cited in Hawkins, P., 'The Licence Shakeout', *The Times (Bricks and Mortar section)*, 12 January 2007, p. 27.

interaction between commercial interest and the new regulatory framework is likely to be complicated and with uneven impacts round the country reflecting the different patterns of sub-markets that have been identified in this collection. One beneficial result may be that some of the landlords at whom deterrence is properly aimed will either drop out of the market (which early evidence on the costs involved in HMO licensing seems to support), although the most evasive no doubt will continue to flout the law but in time may be more easily exposed.

The geographical unevenness of the modern PRS market is most clearly exposed in the more 'technical' chapter by Peter Bibby and his colleagues. This provides very useful 'hard' research on variance in rents in different locations, down almost to the level of individual houses. GIS (geographical information system) mapping brings new advances in helping policy makers through evidence from spatial modelling. The use of direct indices and proxy indicators (especially those measuring the all-important context of the neighbourhood in which a property is located) may become key information in setting levels of housing benefit support. Such a high level of detail that builds from the bottom up would enable much more sensitive and better targeted policy design, and even at this stage helps to provide perspective on the diverse nature of the modern PRS to which other contributors, particularly Julie Rugg, refer.

Arising from the great diversity of the sector, Rugg's chapter reinforces the point that the PRS is exceptionally difficult to regulate, and represents an economic and social activity in respect of which policy making is difficult at best, and often ineffective at worst. We have seen in the chapter from Hughes and Houghton how the student market has developed with the intervention of large commercial providers, and Rugg's work further complements this by pointing out that 'traditional' small landlords in university towns may find themselves trying to let in a glut situation, and thus being forced into other sectors of the market; she demonstrates that the PRS is in reality a fragmented series of sub-sectors or niches, and thus we must reiterate the question whether a unified policy stance in relation to such a varied market can hope to be successful. One size does not fit all!

If policy cannot be unified, there are also implications for law and regulatory activity. One unifying strand throughout the diverse PRS is the fact that it depends on the existence of leasehold tenure. The law thus imposes a surface unity on what is in reality a highly diversified activity, but this strand of unity is not enough of itself to ensure that a one-stop shop approach to the regulation and governance of the sector can work, either via traditional command-and-control approaches such as those typified by fitness standards, or by more recent innovations such as 'fair trade' requirements and accreditation schemes. Rather more we see the need for a 'horses for courses' approach, and that may call in question the attempt to impose a simplified legal structure with regard to tenancy types as referred to in Diane Lister's chapter. Julie Rugg demonstrates the emergence in particular of a type of renting that is highly dependent on, indeed almost synergistic with, the provision of state assistance to tenants in the form of housing benefit, and shows furthermore how landlords become adept at modifying their activity and economic expectations to meet the confines that the benefit system imposes on them. Yet she also makes the telling point that many of those who are housed by such landlords, who in effect have a guaranteed income stream, would be much better off in social housing. This is particularly apparent for those tenants who are 'sponsored' into private letting by voluntary and statutory agencies.

The dilemma may be even worse for tenants at the bottom end of this part of the market – those who are in severe difficulties but are not from the sponsored categories. There is already some evidence of landlords planning to withdraw from the benefit sector, following the roll-out of the Local Housing Allowance (LHA) in 2008. This major change to the housing benefit system, giving payments to tenants and not directly to landlords, might become a disincentive for landlords to enter or stay in this sector. If evidence from *Mortgages for Business* is to be believed, well before LHA comes on stream, a quarter of landlords say they will withdraw from the housing benefit market, citing probable difficulties in collecting rent from people in severe financial circumstances and/or suffering alcohol or drug abuse problems.[3] We also know that about a third of the housing benefit market comprises single parents, many of whom struggle to survive on meagre incomes. Previously, as Rugg points out in her chapter, the benefit to landlords of direct payments was their regularity, even if they were lower than market value. In the eventuality that some landlords do pull out, however, it still leaves the majority in the market, and perhaps those that are more socially responsible. A great deal remains to be seen, but if the LHA roll-out does create such an effect, it could damage the interests of some of the most vulnerable tenants by further limiting their choices.

The diversity, indeed the myriad aspect, of the PRS is brought out in the chapter by David Rhodes. It is clear that much of the revival of the sector since the major legislative changes of the period 1988 to 1996 has been brought about by the re-entry of 'small' landlords into the market, especially under the influence of buy-to-let finance. However, it is clear from this study that these landlords are themselves a very diverse group of people, with a wide range of motivations for coming into this form of business activity. Their properties are likewise diverse, as are their target tenant constituencies, though it is not surprising to find that students figure quite prominently in these groupings. There is undoubtedly a degree of competition between large commercial providers of accommodation for students, as studied by Houghton and Davis, and the smaller providers, who form a clear sub-sector of the landlord group studied by Rhodes. Indeed the existence of competition, both to gain and retain tenants, within the 'small landlord' group emerges as a considerable force in relation to a whole range of issues affecting the maintenance and management of their properties, and this affects rent setting as well, with clear divisions of practice and attitude between landlords in relation to all of these matters. Such a strong competitive motivation does not appear to affect, as yet at least, the attitudes of the larger commercial student accommodation providers, many of whom can rely on a supply of students as a result of arrangements made with universities.

It would also appear that, again as yet, the practices and attitudes of the group of landlords studied by Rhodes are little affected by regulatory issues such as the law relating to multiple occupation and the enforcement of housing standards (at the 'hard' end of the regulatory spectrum), or by the law of fair trading (to take

3 Ibid.

a 'softer' regulatory form) – or even by the voluntary form of accreditation, even though the study by Hughes and Houghton indicates that some local authorities, for example those in the East Midlands, are keen to see this form of control extend throughout the PRS in their areas. However, as accreditation does offer advantages with regard to competition, there may over time be an increasing willingness for buy-to-let landlords to embrace membership of accreditation schemes, as maintaining a competitive edge is so important for so many of them.

Yet again, the message of Rhodes's work echoes those coming from our other contributors: formal 'hard' legal regulation is rarely used with regard to the control of the PRS – and that has been a constant feature of the sector for many years, but especially since the ending, in 1988, of the old Rent Control regime of the Rent Act 1977. It is only the unscrupulous fringe of 'rogue' landlords who are likely to attract the attention of regulatory bodies such as local councils in the guise of Environmental Health Authorities. 'Soft' regulation and voluntary regulation may be beginning to assume a greater role, but it would appear to be economic issues, especially in the form of competition with other landlords, which will serve to ensure that standards of management and maintenance are upheld. As we have seen in cases already discussed, it is very difficult to predict how the spectrum of regulatory mechanisms, whether voluntary, 'soft' or 'hard', will interact with the commercial imperative that in reality drives this market. It is almost a law of policy analysis that outcomes rarely follow what was intended or foreseen by the framers of legislation and their executive officers, who write the all-important regulations that precede delivery on the ground.

The chapter from Davis and Houghton on fair trading laws and their application to lettings in the PRS demonstrates yet another strand in the emerging 'new pattern' of regulation for that sector, and should be considered alongside Hughes and Houghton on accreditation systems. Whereas the latter are in essence a completely voluntary form of self regulation, which depends on attracting landlords into membership by offering them some competitive edge for their service, the former may be considered to be a 'soft' form of regulation which keeps the traditional pattern of an external body with supervisory powers in the form of the Office of Fair Trading (OFT), but which is nevertheless much less intrusive and consensual in its operation than, for example, a licensing system. The consensual approach appears to result in a system that is essentially 'closed' and private in operation, and which lacks the open and revealing qualities which attach to more traditional means of regulation dependent on action in court. The latter may also be accompanied by reported decisions which are themselves legally binding and hence, in theory at least, normative in effect. It has to be asked whether the OFT's bulletins can achieve the same degree of influence in moulding behaviour. True, as Davis and Houghton point out, they are published and do contain details of what the OFT does and does not consider 'fair', but they are not mainstream legal literature, and lack the traditional profile of case law.

As Davis and Houghton point out, even in those cases where the OFT has investigated contracts of letting, and especially with regard to the use of 'legal jargon', the fact that adverse findings have been made in relation to such documents gives cause for concern that those who are responsible for drawing up the documents in the first place have little conception that the rules of 'fair trading' apply to their work. It may be assumed that documentation of this sort is produced by those with training in either the law or the cognate profession of property management, but how aware are they of the OFT's potential impact on their work, and what does that say about the public profile of that institution? As with the chapter on accreditation, a particular issue arises here: the need for much greater education of all those involved in property management in the various aspects of the regulatory matrix within which they operate.

Yet it must be asked whether this matrix can ever be as effective as might be hoped, given the essentially migratory nature of much of the PRS, especially outside London, and most particularly in relation to the student lettings market. It is simply too easy for those who are unhappy with the properties they rent to resort to the mechanism of 'exit' in order to express their unhappiness. Most lettings are for no more than a year; many are for the shorter period of six months, thus inviting a 'grin and bear it' response. Complaint in a vocal form is much less likely in such situations, and even less so the taking of the complaint to a formal outside regulatory body. Furthermore, the landlord is cushioned by the knowledge that, as with buses, so far as an exiting tenant is concerned, 'there will be another along in a short while' – maybe even one provided by a university which has an agreement with an accommodation provider. In such circumstances, it has to be asked whether any system of regulation, be it 'hard', 'soft' or voluntary, can ever achieve what its framers hope for it, and why there has always been such a gap between the theory and practice of the law – no matter what its form. The Unfair Terms in Consumer Contracts Regulations (UTCCR) 1999 were a significant legal and policy step towards the creation of fairer tenancy agreements, or at least agreements that would dilute somewhat the market advantages enjoyed by landlords against the needs of tenants to live freely in their home unmolested by unfair and restrictive practices, but in practice their impact is less than might have been hoped for.

Once again, the issues of governance enter the debate, for this is not only a question of the one-sidedness of the landlord–tenant relationship and the general ignorance of the law, as described by Lister in her contribution, but also of enforcement. As Davis and Houghton tellingly point out, a tenancy agreement is not like a normal commodity which a young person (or any consumer) might object to because it is faulty or overpriced. But the consumerist ethic and language are increasingly utilized with regard to housing agreements, and this may lead many into false assumptions about how tenancy agreements are made, and, once made, how they operate in practice.

The question of enforcement is highlighted by Ormandy and Davis in their chapter on the new Housing Health and Safety Rating System (HHSRS), which has replaced the older 'fitness standard'. They make the point that the new 'prohibition orders' and 'hazard awareness notices', which replaced existing 'repair and closure' notices, are still highly dependent on the same enforcement mechanisms as before, meaning essentially the willingness of local authorities to proactively intervene, and, crucially, that they have the personnel and resources to chase recalcitrant landlords. Controlling HHSRS hazards is exercised through the means of Part 1 of the Housing Act 2004, not through licence conditions. Detailed guidance has been drawn up, together with a comprehensive method for measuring conditions, but this is crucially dependent on local authorities for enforcement of the improved system. Ormandy and Davis can but urge that local authorities become more proactive, and as we have seen in other chapters, our authors are sceptical about the ability of public authorities to do this in the absence of new resources, and/or following the long history of neglect in this area and of postcode lottery. The new HHSRS standards are a major achievement, because they codify what has been the reality since the 'year dot': that at the bottom end of the market (and even higher up), failures in a dwelling's structures and fitness have major implications for residents' health, welfare and safety. The opportunity, particularly for health services and local authorities, to collaborate around a housing agenda is potentially an exciting and innovative step forward – but delivery is everything.

Our final observation is to note that the Law Commission itself, through its work on the nature of the rental tenure[4] and the associated Renting Homes Bill, means that this area of public policy is unlikely to remain dormant. Ideas for a wider package of reform include that of the cumbersome and over-legalistic court possession proceedings by their removal to the Residential Property Tribunal (which already exists for other purposes under the Housing Act 2004). This would be a step towards the creation of a specialist Housing Court, an idea long since canvassed by some housing lawyers. The aim would be to resolve disputes through mediation, rather than costly and confrontational formal court proceedings. A simplified and more flexible procedure for landlords to gain possession when tenants abscond and abandon their homes is part of this new package, aiming at less complex and more transparent proceedings. One major question, however, hangs over these potentially exciting and certainly much needed reforms: the matter of parliamentary time and ministerial commitment. The former Office of the Deputy Prime Minister (ODPM), together with other departments of state, took up much time in the Parliament that ended in 2005 with housing regulation and other housing-related bills, such as measures on anti-social behaviour. Now that the ODPM has been turned into the Department for Communities and Local Government, with a new Secretary of State at its head, policy emphases may change; it may also become hard to find time in the parliamentary timetable for new legislation that is not on a 'sexy' political issue affecting the majority of people, and what could be seen very much as an exercise in 'lawyers' law', even though that would be a misconception.

However, if we may still hope for legislative time to be found, the Law Commission, as its draft bill makes clear, also proposes that the balance between the rights of landlords and tenants must be retained by the use of standard form contracts, following guidance from the OFT (see Chapter Seven). This would encourage some of the issues outlined in this book to be addressed head on, particularly the blind eye that is turned by many landlords to the fact that, once let, the property is no longer 'theirs' in legal terms, and the claimed ignorance of the law by all parties – a phenomenon which generally operates to underpin the market power enjoyed by landlords. Ignorance of the law should be no defence, and the Rented Homes Bill – should it ever be enacted (perhaps under a Cameron government) – would certainly

4 Law Commission, *Renting Homes: The Final Report,* Law Com. no. 297 (London, Law Commission, 5 May 2006).

bring the issues of non-compliance, lack of knowledge and the imbalance in the relationship between landlords and tenants (especially younger and less experienced tenants) into much sharper focus. Or so we might hope! The changes that the Law Commission's bill would introduce would also affect the implementation of the new health and safety system, for, as the Commission envisages, it would be unlawful for a landlord to rent out accommodation affected by a category 1 hazard.

Meanwhile, the 'new regulatory framework' will begin to bed down. It is a complex matrix of measures, mostly (but not entirely) arising from the Housing Act 2004. The main features of the system are as follows:

- Three new forms of licensing:
  - mandatory licensing of the largest HMOs;
  - discretionary licensing of smaller HMOs;
  - selective licensing of landlords in areas of 'low demand'.
- Voluntary accreditation schemes (originating in the 2000 Green Paper).
- The HHSRS standards regime.

This, of course, with the exception of accreditation schemes, is quite 'traditional' command-and-control regulation, and that indicates that, while such a form of control may only be (as we have previously argued) a 'last resort' to deal with those who will not otherwise comply with standards of acceptable housing provision, nevertheless there continues to be a need for a final 'hardline' mode of control.

It is universally acknowledged, from the Law Commission down, that the modern PRS is a very diverse entity; indeed, some of our contributors incline to a view that it should not be treated as a single entity at all. Moreover, the point is made loud and clear that this is indeed the *private* rented sector, which in contemporary parlance means that the legal restraints of the 'old PRS' enshrined in the Rent Act 1977 have been confined very largely to the dustbin of history. Over-rigid control of the modern PRS would drive many of the new wave of small investors back to safer and easier investment options, of which there are many. This would certainly damage the improving quality of the housing stock, because it is through the new market that standards have improved, as the buy-to-let stock is generally in better condition (and newer) than the longer-standing properties in the sector. Moreover, the modern PRS is not only market based, but is also a more 'networked' market, supported by an extensive industry of insurance providers, management advisers, letting agencies, specialist legal firms and so on, and the implementation of the new regulatory framework is partly dependent on them. It should never be forgotten that properly functioning markets, and generally those that work best, have a strong regulatory periphery and institutional supports. In this situation, ideally the heavy-handed sanctioning approach should be needed only in limited circumstances, such as possessory or other 'hard' regulatory action where mediation or other forms of voluntary or 'soft' regulation are exhausted. Because the new PRS is characteristically one of rapid turnover, in which the 'exit' option is the mostly likely response to a breakdown in landlord–tenant relationships and other associated problems, it may be that an increasing part of the investment market will come to see the benefit of accreditation schemes, giving them, as Hughes and Houghton point out in their chapter, a competitive edge and at the same time laying down a baseline of acceptable standards. One thing is sure. Old fashioned top-down methodologies can never succeed in this mostly new institutional environment, and a return to the old days enshrined in the Rent Act 1977 would very likely bring the whole new economy of private renting crashing down.

Bibliography

Adair, A.S., McGreal, W.S., Smyth, A., Cooper, J. and Ryley, T., 'House prices and accessibility: the testing of relationships within the Belfast urban area', *Housing Studies*, 15/5 (2000) pp. 699–716.

Alder, J. and Handy, C., *Housing Associations, Law and Practice,* 4th edition (London, Sweet and Maxwell, 2002).

Allen, C. and Blandy, S., *The Future of City Centre Living: Implications for Urban Policy* (London, Office of the Deputy Prime Minister, 2004).

Allen, J. and McDowell, L., *Landlords and Property: Social Relations in the Private Rented Sector* (Cambridge, Cambridge University Press, 1989).

Atiyah, P. S., *The Rise and Fall of Freedom of Contract* (Oxford, Oxford University Press, 1979).

Awan, K., Odling-Smee, J. and Whitehead, C.M.E., 'Household attributes and the demand for rental housing', *Economica*, 49 (1982) pp. 183–200.

Balchin, P. and Rhoden M. (eds), *Housing: The Essential Foundations* (London, Routledge, 1998).

Bates, B., *et al.*, *Housing in England 2000/1* (London, Department for Transport, Local Government and the Regions, 2002).

Bates, B., Joy, S., Roden, R., Swales, K., Grove, J. and Oliver R., *Housing in England 1999/00* (London, Department of the Environment, Transport and Regions, 2001).

Bates, B., Joy, S., Kitchen, S., Perry, J., Swales, K., Thornby, M., Kafka, E., Oliver, R. and Wellington, S., *Housing in England 2000/1: A Report of the 2000/1 Survey of English Housing* (London, Department of Transport, Local Government and the Regions, 2002).

BBC News (22 July 2002), 'Van Hoogstraten: How the net closed in', http://www.bbc.co.uk/2/low/uk_news/england/2123150.stm [accessed 10 February 2005]. BBC News (9 September 2003) 'Van Hoogstraten's life of controversy.' http://newsvote.bbc.co.uk/mpapps/pagetools/print/news.bbc.co.uk/1/hi/uk/3301361.stm [accessed 16 March 2006].

Bevan, M., Kemp, P.A. and Rhodes, D., *Private Landlords & Housing Benefit* (York, Centre for Housing Policy, University of York, 1995).

Blandy, S. and Goodchild, B., 'Tenure to Rights: Conceptualising the Changing Focus of Housing Law in England', *Housing, Theory and Society*, 16/1 (1999) pp. 31–42.

Blau, P., *Exchange and Power in Social Life* (London, John Wiley and Sons Inc, 1964).

Bone, M. and Walker, E., *Private Renting in Five Localities* (London, HMSO, 1994).

Bourassa, S.C., Hamelink, F., Hoesli, M. and MacGregor, B.D., 'Defining housing sub-markets', *Journal of Housing Economics*, 8 (1999) pp. 160–83.

Bourdieu, P., 'Social space and symbolic space', *Sociological Theory*, 7, 1 (1989) pp. 14–25.

Bourdieu, P. and Wacquant, L., *An Invitation to Reflexive Sociology* (Cambridge, Polity Press, 1992).

Bovaird, A., Harloe, M. and Whitehead, C. M. E., 'Private rented housing: its current role', *Journal of Social Policy*, 14, 1 (1985) pp. 1–23.

Bramley, G., Satsangi, M. and Pryce, G., *The Supply Responsiveness of the Private Rented Sector: An International Comparison* (London, Department of the Environment, Transport and the Regions, 1999).

Bretherton, J., Rhodes, D. and Rugg, J., *Accommodation Preferences, A Study for the Accommodation Office, University of York*, unpublished report to the University of York Student Accommodation Office (2005).

Bright, S. and Gilbert, G., *Landlord and Tenant Law: The Nature of Tenancies* (Oxford, Clarendon Press, 1995) p. 69.

British Medical Association, *Housing and Health: Building for the Future* (London, BMA, 2003).

Buchel, S. and Hoesli, M., 'A hedonic analysis of rent and rental revenue in the subsidised and unsubsidised housing sectors in Geneva', *Urban Studies*, 32, 7 (1995) pp. 1199–213.

Burridge, R. and Ormandy, D., *Unhealthy Housing: Research, Remedies and Reform* (London, E & FN Spon, 1993).

Burridge, R., Ormandy, D. and Battersby, S., *Monitoring the New Fitness Standard* (London, HMSO, 1993).

Burrows, L. and Hunter, N., *Forced Out!* (London, Shelter Publications, 1990).

Carr, H., Cottle, S., Baldwin, T. and King, M., *The Housing Act 2004: A Practical Guide* (Bristol, Jordan Publishing Ltd, 2005).

Chambers, D., 'The racial housing price differential and racially transitional neighbourhoods', *Journal of Urban Economics*, 32, 2 (1992) pp. 214–32.

CML press release, *Buy-to-let sets new records*, www.cmlorg.uk (16 August 2006).

CML, Press Release 14 February 2007 (London, Council of Mortgage Lenders, 2007).

CML, *Statistics, Table MM6*, (London, Council of Mortgage Lenders, 2007).

Collins, H., *Regulating Contracts* (Oxford, Oxford University Press, 2002).

Conley, J. M. and O'Barr, W. M., *Rules versus Relationships – The Ethnography of Legal Discourse* (Chicago and London, The University of Chicago Press, 1990).

Cooperative Research Centre (CRC), *Building Regulation and Health* (London, Cooperative Research Centre, 1995).

Cotterrell, R., *The Sociology of Law: An Introduction* (London, Butterworths, 1992).

Cowan, D. and Marsh, A., 'There's Regulatory Crime and then there's Landlord Crime: From Rachmanites to Partners', *The Modern Law Review*, 64, 6 (2001) pp. 831–54.

Crook, A.D.H., 'Housing Conditions in the Private Rented Sector within a Market Framework', in Lowe, S. and Hughes, D. (eds), *The Privately Rented Sector in a New Century* (Bristol, The Policy Press, 2002).

Crook, A.D.H. and Hughes, J.E.T., 'Market signals and disrepair in privately rented housing', *Journal of Property Research*, 18, 1 (2001) pp. 21–50.

Crook, A. D. H. and Kemp, P. A., *Private Landlords in England* (London, HMSO, 1996).

Crook, A.D.H. and Kemp, P.A., 'The Revival of Private Rented Housing in Britain', *Housing Studies*, 11, 1, pp. 51–68.

Crook, A.D.H. and Kemp, P.A., *Financial Institutions and Private Rented Housing* (York, York Publishing Services, 1999).

Crook, A.D.H., Hughes, J. and Kemp, P.A., *The Supply of Privately Rented Homes: Today and Tomorrow* (York, Joseph Rowntree Foundation, 1995).

Crook A.D.H., Henneberry, J.M. and Hughes, J.E.T., *Repairs and Improvements to Privately Rented Dwellings in the 1990s* (London, Department of the Environment Transport and the Regions, 1998).

Crook, A.D.H., Henneberry, J.M., Hughes, J.E.T. and Kemp P.A., *Repair and Maintenance by Private Landlords* (London, Department of the Environment Transport and the Regions, 2000).

Dale, M., *Successful Recruitment and Selection – A Practical Guide for Managers* (London, Kogan Page Limited, 1995).

Damer, S. (1980), 'State, Class and Housing: Glasgow 1885–1919' in J. Melling (ed.), *Housing, Social Policy and the State* (London, Croom Helm, 1980) pp. 73–112.

Daunton, M. J., *House and Home in the Victorian City – Working Class Housing 1850–1914* (London, Edward Arnold Ltd, 1983).

Davies, H., 'The crying game' (*The Sunday Times*, 6 August 2006).

Davis, M. and Hughes, D., 'Changing Rooms: the legal and policy implications of a burgeoning student housing market in Leicester' in Lowe, S. and Hughes, D. (eds), *The Private Rented Sector in a New Century: Revival or False Dawn?* (Bristol, The Policy Press, 2002).

Deleuze, G., 'Postscript to Societies of Control', *October*, 59 (1992) pp. 3–7.

DETR (Department of the Environment, Transport and the Regions), *English House Conditions Survey 1996,* (London, The Stationery Office, 1998).

DETR, *Houses in Multiple Occupation in the Private Rented Sector* (London, Department of the Environment, Transport and the Regions, 1999).

DETR, *Housing Health and Safety Rating System – The Guidance (Version 1)* (London, Department of the Environment, Transport and the Regions, 2000).

DETR, *Housing Health and Safety Rating System – Report on Development* (London, Department of the Environment, Transport and the Regions, 2000).

DETR, *Quality and Choice: A Decent Home for All. The Housing Green Paper* (London, HMSO, 2000).

DETR, *Voluntary Accreditation for Private Landlords,* Housing Research Summary No. 144 (London, Department of the Environment, Transport and the Regions, 2001).

Din, A., Hoesli, M. and Bender, A., 'Environmental values and real estate prices', *Urban Studies*, 38, 100 (2001) pp. 1989–2000.

DoE (Department of the Environment) *Housing Policy: A Consultative Document* (Cmnd 6851) (London, HMSO, 1977).

DoE, *Housing: The Government Proposals* (Cm 214) (London, HMSO, 1987).

Englander, D., *Landlord and Tenant in Urban Britain 1838–1918* (Oxford, Clarendon Press, 1983).

Finer, S. E., *The Life and Times of Sir Edwin Chadwick* (London, Methuen, 1952).

Foucault, M., 'Technologies of the Self: A seminar with Michel Foucault', in Martin, L. H., Gutman, H. and Hutton, P. H. (eds), *Technologies of the Self*, (Amherst, The University of Massachusetts Press, 1988).

Garvie, D., *Housing Asylum Seekers in Privately Rented Accommodation* (London, Shelter, 2001).

Gilbertson. J., Green, G. and Ormandy, D. on behalf of Sheffield City Council, Sheffield Homes, and the Sheffield (NHS) Primary Care Trusts.

Gillen, K., Thibodeau, T. and Wachter, S., 'Anisotropic autocorrelation in house prices', *Journal of Real Estate Finance and Economics*, 23, 1 (2001) pp. 5–30.

GLA (Greater London Authority) 'Homelessness in London' (Greater London Authority, Homelessness Bulletin 65, June 2005).

Gray, P. and McAnulty U., 'The increased role of the private rented sector in catering for social housing in Northern Ireland', unpublished paper given to the Housing Studies Association Conference, York, 2006.

Gray, P., Hillyard, P., McAnulty, U. and Cowan, D., *The Private Rented Sector in Northern Ireland* (Londonderry, University of Ulster, 2000).

Green, H., Deacon, K. and Down, D., 'Factors which affect rent', in *Housing in England 1996/97* (London, Department of the Environment, Transport and the Regions, 1998).

Green, S., *Rachman* (London, Hamlyn, 1981).

Hardwick, G., *Social Security Committee Sixth Report Housing Benefit* (London, The Stationery Office. 2000) p. 131–2.

Harloe, M., 'Landlord/Tenant Relations in Europe and America – The Limits and Functions of the Legal Framework', *Urban Law and Policy*, 7 (1985) pp. 359–83.

Harloe, M., *Private Rented Housing in the United States and Europe* (Beckenham, Croom Helm, 1985).

Hawke, J.N. and Taylor, G.A., 'The Compulsory Repair of Individual and Physically Substandard Housing: The Law in Practice', *Journal of Social Welfare Law* (1984) p. 129.

Hawkins, P., 'The Licence Shakeout', *The Times (Bricks and Mortar section)*, 12 January 2007, p. 27.

Heath, S. and Kenyon, L., 'Single Young Professionals and Shared Household Living', *Journal of Youth Studies*, 4, 1 (2001) pp. 83–100.

Hillier, J. and Rooksby, E. (eds), *Habitus: A Sense of Place* (Aldershot, Ashgate, 2005).

Hirschman, A. O., *Exit Voice and Loyalty: Responses to Decline in Firms* (Cambridge, Massachusetts, 1970).

HMSO, The Unfair Terms in Consumer Contracts Regulations 1999 (SI 1999 No. 2083) (London, The Stationery Office Limited, 1999).

HMSO, The Education (Recognised Bodies) (England) (Amendment) Order 2005 (SI 2005 No. 2957) (London, The Stationery Office Limited, 2005).

HMSO, The Houses in Multiple Occupation (Specified Educational Establishments) (England) (No2) Regulations, 2006 (SI 2006/2280) (London, The Stationery Office Limited, 2006).

HMSO, The Housing (Approvals of Codes of Management Practice) (Student Accommodation) England Order 2006 (SI 2006 No. 646) (London, The Stationery Office Limited, 2006).

Hoesli, M., Thion, B. and Watkins, C., 'A hedonic investigation of the rental value of apartments in central Bordeaux', *Journal of Property Research,* 14, 1 (1997) pp. 15–26.

Hollowell, P., (ed.), *Property and Social Relations* (London, Heinemann Educational Books Ltd, 1982) p. 12.

Holmans, A. E., *Housing Policy in Britain* (London, Croom Helm, 1987).

Houghton, R., *The provision and governance of student accommodation with reference to the impact of fair trading and consumer protection* – a forthcoming PhD thesis.

Housing Quality Network Services, *Local Authority Homelessness Strategies: Evaluation and Good Practice* (London, Office of the Deputy Prime Minister, 2004).

Howden-Chapman, P. and Carroll, P., *Housing & Health: Research, Policy and Innovation* (New Zealand, Steele Roberts, 2004).

Hughes, D. and Davis, M., 'Student Housing: a cautionary tale of one city', *Journal of Social Welfare and Family Law*, 24, 2 (2002) pp. 135–55.

Hughes, D., Davis, M., Houghton. R. and Ball, J., 'The Housing of Students: Legal and Structural Implication of Changing Patterns of Housing Provision in England, and a comparison with experience in France' (Unpublished Conference Paper 2005).

Hughes, D., Davis, M., Jones, A. and Matthew, V., *Text and Materials on Housing Law* (Oxford, Oxford University Press, 2005).

Harvey, J. and Houston, D., *Research into the Single Room Rent Regulations*, Department for Work and Pensions Research Report No. 243 (2005).

Jew, P., *Law and Order in Private Rented Housing: Tackling Harassment and Illegal Eviction* (London, Campaign for Bedsit Rights, 1994).

Karn, V., Lickiss, R. and Hughes, D., *Tenants' Complaints and the Reform of Housing Management* (Aldershot, Dartmouth, 1997).

Keenan, P., 'Residential mobility and low demand: a case history from Newcastle' in Lowe, S., Keenan, P. and Spencer, S. (eds), *Housing Abandonment in Britain: Studies in the Causes and Effects of Low Demand Housing* (York, Centre for Housing Policy, University of York, 1998).

Kemp, P., 'Some aspects of housing consumption in late nineteenth century England and Wales', *Housing Studies*, 2, 1 (1987) pp. 3–16.

Kemp, P.A. (ed.), *The Private Provision of Rented Housing* (Aldershot, Avebury, 1988).

Kemp, P.A., 'Private renting in England', *Netherlands Journal of Housing and the Built Environment,* 13, 3 (1998) pp. 233–53.

Kemp, P. A., *Private Renting in Transition* (Coventry, Chartered Institute of Housing, 2004).

Kemp, P. A. and Keoghan, M., 'Movement Into and Out of the Private Rented Sector in England', *Housing Studies*, 16, 1 (2001) pp. 21–7.

Kemp, P. A. and Rhodes, D., *The Lower End of the Private Rented Sector: A Glasgow Case Study* (Edinburgh, Scottish Homes, 1994).

Kemp, P.A. and Rhodes, D., *Private Landlords in Scotland* (Edinburgh, Scottish Homes, 1994).

Kemp, P.A. and Willington, S., 'Students and the Private Rented Sector in Scotland', *Housing Research Review*, No. 7, (Edinburgh, Scottish Homes, 1995).

Kemp, P. A., Crook, A.D.H. and Hughes, J.E.T., *Private Renting at the Cross-roads* (London, Coopers and Lybrand, 1995).

King Sturge, *The UK Student Accommodation Market in 2004/5*. Accessible at www.kingsturge.com

King Sturge Newsletter, *The UK Student Accommodation Market 2005/2006* (September, 2006) p. 2.

Lambert, R., *Social Security Committee Sixth Report Housing Benefit* (London, The Stationery Office, 2000).

Law Commission, *Scoping Paper* (London, Law Commission, March 2001).

Law Commission, *Renting Homes 1: Status and Security* (London, Law Commission, 2002).

Law Commission, *Consultation Paper No. 162, Renting Homes 1: Status and Security* (London, Law Commission, 2003).

Law Commission, *Renting Homes,* Law Com. no. 284 (London, Law Commission, 2003).

Law Commission, *Renting Homes: The Final Report*, Law Com. no. 297 (London, Law Commission, 5 May 2006).

Law Commission (website accessed 5 May 2006) *Press Release – A clean-sheet new start for renting homes*, www.lawcom.gov.uk/rentinghomes.htm (London, Law Commission).

Leather, P. and Morrison, T., 'The State of UK Housing: A Factfile on Dwelling Conditions, (York, Joseph Rowntree Foundation/The Policy Press, 1997).

Leather P., Revell, K. and Appleton N., *Developing a Voluntary Accreditation Scheme for Private Landlords: A Guide to Good Practice* (London, Department of the Environment, Transport and the Regions, 2001).

Lipsky, M., 'Street-level bureaucracy and the analysis of urban reform', *Urban Affairs Quarterly*, 6 (1971) pp. 391–409.

Lister, D., 'The nature of tenancy relationships – landlords and young people in the private rented sector' in Lowe, S. and Hughes, D. (eds), *The Privately Rented Sector in a New Century* (Bristol, The Policy Press, 2002).

Lister, D., *Negotiating the Impossible? The Pursuit of Fair and Equitable Relationships between Landlords and Under 25s in the PRS* – unpublished PhD thesis (2002).

Lister, D., 'Young people's strategies for managing tenancy relationships in the private rented sector', *Journal of Youth Studies*, 7, 3 (2004) pp. 315–30.

Lister, D., 'Controlling letting arrangements? Landlords and surveillance in the private rented sector', *Surveillance and Society*, 2, 4 (2005) pp. 513–28.

Lister, D., 'Tenancy agreements: a mechanism for governing anti-social behaviour', in Flint, J. (ed.), *Housing, Urban Governance and Anti-Social Behaviour* (Bristol, The Policy Press, 2006).

Lister, D., 'Unlawful or just awful? Young people's experiences of living in the private rented sector in England', *YOUNG – The Nordic Journal of Youth Studies*, 14, 2 (2006) pp. 141–55.

Lowe, S., *Housing Policy Analysis: British Housing in Cultural and Comparative Context* (Houndmills, Palgrave/Macmillan, 2004).

Lowe, S. and Hughes, D. (eds), *The Private Rented Sector in a New Century: Revival or False Dawn?* (Bristol, The Policy Press, 2002).

Lowe, S., Keenan, P. and Spencer, S., 'Housing Abandonment in Inner Cities: The Politics of Low Demand for Housing', *Housing Studies*, 14, 5 (1999) pp. 703–16.

Maclennan, D. and Tu, Y. 'Economic perspectives on the structure of local housing markets', *Housing Studies*, 11 (1996) pp. 387–406.

Malpezzi, S.,'Welfare analysis of rent control with side payments: A natural experiment in Cairo, Egypt', *Regional Science and Urban Economics*, 28, 6 (1998) pp. 773–96.

Malpezzi, S., 'Hedonic pricing models: A selective and applied review', in O'Sullivan, T. and Gibb. K. (eds), *Housing economics and public policy* (2003).

Marsh, A., 'Private renting: the regulatory challenge', paper given to the Housing Studies Association Conference, York, 2006.

Marsh, A. and Mullins, D. (eds), *Housing and Public Policy, Citizenship, Choice and Control* (Buckingham, Open University Press, 1998).

McCrone, D. and Elliott, B., *Property and Power in a City – The Sociological Significance of Landlordism* (London, The Macmillan Press Ltd, 1989).

Molm, L. D., *Coercive Power in Social Exchange* (Cambridge, Cambridge University Press, 1997).

Mumford, K. and Power A., *The Slow Death of Great Cities: Urban Abandonment or Urban Renaissance?* (York, York Publishing Services, 1999).

Murie, A. 'Moving with the times: changing frameworks for housing research and policy', in Malpass, P. and Cairncross, L. (eds), *Building on the Past: Visions of Housing Futures* (Bristol, The Policy Press, 2006).

Nelken, D., *The Limits of the Legal Process: A Study of Landlords, Law and Crime* (London, Academic Press, 1983).

ODPM (Office of the Deputy Prime Minister) *Quality & Choice: A Decent Home for All – Housing Policy in England* (London, ODPM, 2000).

ODPM, *English Housing Condition Survey 2001 Private Landlords Survey* (London, ODPM, 2003).

ODPM, *English Housing Conditions Survey 2001, Building the Picture*, (London, ODPM, 2003).

ODPM, *Statistical Evidence to Support the Housing Health and Safety Rating System, Vols I, II and III* (London, ODPM, 2003).

ODPM, *Licensing in the Private Rented Sector – Consultation on the Implementation of HMO Licensing: Regulatory Impact Assessment, Housing Bill Part 2: HMO Licensing* (London, ODPM, 2004).

ODPM, *Codes of Practice for Student Accommodation, Consultation Paper* (London, ODPM, 2005).

ODPM, *Codes of Practice for Student Accommodation: Approved Codes under Section 233 of the Housing Act 2004 – Consultation* (London, ODPM, September 2005).

ODPM, *Housing in England 2003/04, Part 1: Trends in Tenure and Cross Tenure Topics* (London, ODPM, 2005).

ODPM, *Survey of English Local Authorities About Homelessness*, Office of the Deputy Prime Minister Policy Briefing 13 (2005).

ODPM, *Sustainable Communities: Settled Homes; Changing Lives* (ODPM, London, 2005).

ODPM, *Codes of Practice for Student Accommodation: Responses to Consultation on Approved Codes under Section 233 of the Housing Act 2004* (London, ODPM, March 2006).

Osborne, D. and Gaebler, T., *Reinventing Government* (Reading, MA., Addison-Wesley Publ. Co., 1992).

Pannell, B. and Heron J.,'Goodbye to Buy-to Let?', *Housing Finance*, No. 52 (2001) pp. 18–25.

Partington, M., *Landlord and Tenant*, 2nd edition (London, Weidenfeld and Nicholson Ltd, 1980).

Phillips, R.S., 'Unravelling the rent–value puzzle: An empirical investigation', *Urban Studies*, 25 (1998) pp. 487–96.

Quinn, T. M. and Phillips, E., 'The law of Landlord–Tenant: A critical evaluation of the past with guidelines for the future', 38 *Fordham L Rev* 225 (1969) p. 228.

Ranson, R., *Healthy Housing: A Practical Guide* (London, E & FN Spon, 1991).

Raw, G.J., Aizlewood, C.E. and Hamilton, R.M. (eds), *Building Regulation, Health and Safety* (Watford, Building Research Establishment, 2001).

Reviews on Environmental Health, 19, 3–4 (Tel Aviv, Freund Publishing House, 2004).

Rhodes, D., *The Modern Private Rented Sector* (Coventry, Chartered Institute of Housing/Joseph Rowntree Foundation, 2006).

Rhodes, D. and Bevan, M., *Private Landlords and Buy to Let* (York, Centre for Housing Policy, University of York, 2003).

Rhodes, D. and Kemp, P.A., *The Joseph Rowntree Index of Private Rents and Yields: Technical Specification* (York, Centre for Housing Policy, University of York, 1996).

Rhodes, D. and Kemp, P.A., 'Rents and returns in the residential lettings market', in Lowe, S. and Hughes, D. (eds), *The Private Rented Sector in a New Century: Revival or False Dawn?* (Bristol, The Policy Press, 2002).

Rhodes, D. and Rugg, J., *Landlords and Agents in the Private Rented Sector* (London, Department for Work and Pensions, 2005).

Rhodes, R.A.W., 'The New Governance: Governing without Government', *Political Studies* 44 (1996) pp. 652–67.

Rhodes, R.A.W., *Understanding Governance: Policy Networks, Governance, Reflexivity and Accountability* (Buckingham, Open University Press, 1996).

Roberts, S., Beckhelling, J., Phung, V., Boreham, R., Anderson, T. and Lie, N., *Living with the LHA: Claimants Experiences after Fifteen Months of the LHA in the Nine Pathfinder Areas* (London, Department for Work and Pensions, 2006).

Robinson, C., Humphrey, A., Kafka, E., Oliver, R. and Bose, S. *Housing in England 2002/03: A Report from the 2002/03 Survey of English Housing* (London, Office of the Deputy Prime Minster, 2004).

Rose, N., *Powers of Freedom: Reframing Political Thought* (Cambridge, Cambridge University Press, 1999).

Rugg, J. *Opening Doors: Helping People on Low Income Secure Private Rented Accommodation* (York, Centre for Housing Policy, University of York, 1996).

Rugg, J., 'The use and "abuse" of private renting and help with housing costs', in Rugg, J. (ed.), *Young People, Housing and Social Security* (London, Routledge, 1999).

Rugg, J., *Local Housing Allowance Final Evaluation: The Qualitative Evidence of Landlords and Agents Experience in the Nine Pathfinder Areas* (London, Department for Work and Pensions, 2006).

Rugg, J. and Bevan, M., *An Evaluation of the Pilot Tenancy Deposit Scheme* (London, Office of the Deputy Prime Minister, 2002).

Rugg, J., Rhodes, D. and Jones, A., *The Nature and Impact of Student Demand on Housing Markets* (York, York Publishing Services, 2000).

Scottish Executive, *Scottish House Conditions Survey 2002* (Edinburgh, Communities Scotland, 2003).

Sharp, C., *Problems Assured! Private Renting after the 1988 Housing Act* (London, SHAC Publications, 1991).

Sheppard, S., 'Hedonic analysis of housing markets', in Cheshire, P.C. and Mills, E.S. (eds), *Handbook of Regional and Urban Economics,* (1999) vol. 3.

Smith, S.J., Munro, M. and Christie, H., 'Performing (housing) markets', *Urban Studies*, 43, 1, (2006) p. 82.

Stewart, A., *Rethinking Housing Law* (London, Sweet and Maxwell, 1996).

Stewart, J., 'A Step in the Right Direction', *Environmental Health Journal,* (April 2002) pp. 104–07.

Thomas, A.D. with Hedges, B., *The 1985 Physical and Social Survey of HMOs in England and Wales*, (London, HMSO, 1987).

Thomas, A., Snape, D., Duldig, W., Keegan, J. and Ward, K., *In from the Cold – Working with the Private Landlord* (London, Department of the Environment, 1995).

Todd, J.E., Bone, M.R. and Noble, I., *The Privately Rented Sector in 1978* (London, HMSO, 1982).

Treitel, G.H., *Law of Contract*, 10th edition (London, Sweet and Maxwell, 1999).

Unipol, *Code of Standards Members 2006/2007* (Leeds, Unipol Student Homes, 2006).

Walker, B., *Local Housing Allowance Final Evaluation: Implementation and Delivery in the Nine Pathfinder Areas* (London, Department for Work and Pensions, 2006).

Wilcox, S., 'Housing benefit and social security' in Lowe, S. and Hughes, D. (eds), *The Private Rented Sector in a New Century: Revival or False Dawn?*, (Bristol, The Policy Press, 2002).

Index

Printed in the United States
by Baker & Taylor Publisher Services